Legalizing Identities

THE UNIVERSITY OF NORTH CAROLINA PRESS   Chapel Hill

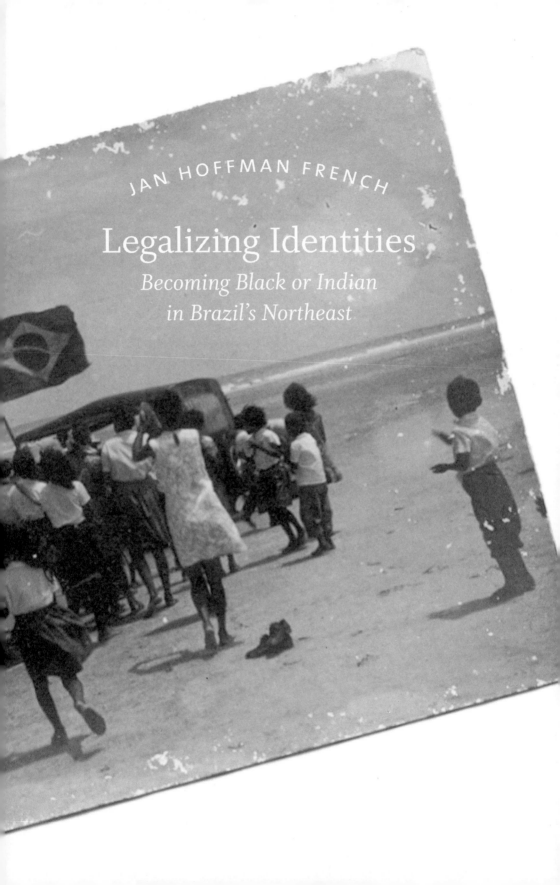

JAN HOFFMAN FRENCH

Legalizing Identities

Becoming Black or Indian
in Brazil's Northeast

*Portions of this work appeared
earlier, in somewhat different
form, in "Dancing for Land: Law
Making and Cultural Performance
in Northeastern Brazil,"* POLITICAL
AND LEGAL ANTHROPOLOGY
REVIEW *25, no. 2 (May 2002);
"Mestizaje and Law Making in
Indigenous Identity Formation
in Northeastern Brazil: 'After
the Conflict Came the History,'"*
AMERICAN ANTHROPOLOGIST
*106, no. 4 (December 2004);
and "Buried Alive: Imagining
Africa in the Brazilian Northeast,"*
AMERICAN ETHNOLOGIST
33, no. 3 (August 2006).

Designed by Rebecca Evans
Set in Whitman and The Sans
by Tseng Information Systems, Inc.
Manufactured in the United States of America

The paper in this book meets the guidelines for
permanence and durability of the Committee
on Production Guidelines for Book Longevity
of the Council on Library Resources.

The University of North Carolina Press has been a
member of the Green Press Initiative since 2003.

Library of Congress Cataloging-in-Publication Data
French, Jan Hoffman, 1953–
Legalizing identities : becoming Black or Indian in
Brazil's northeast / Jan Hoffman French.
p. cm.
Includes bibliographical references and index.
ISBN 978-0-8078-3292-9 (cloth : alk. paper) —
ISBN 978-0-8078-5951-3 (pbk. : alk. paper)
1. Ethnicity—Brazil—Sergipe. 2. Ethnology—
Brazil—Sergipe. 3. Group identity—Brazil—
Sergipe. 4. Blacks—Legal status, laws, etc.—
Brazil—Sergipe. 5. Shocó Indians—Legal status,
laws, etc.—Brazil—Sergipe. 6. Blacks—Brazil—
Sergipe—Ethnic identity. 7. Shocó Indians—
Brazil—Sergipe—Ethnic identity. 8. Blacks—Land
tenure—Brazil—Sergipe. 9. Shocó Indians—Land
tenure—Brazil—Sergipe. 10. Sergipe (Brazil)—
Social conditions. I. Title.
F2636.F74 2009
305.800981'41—dc22
2008050472

cloth   13 12 11 10 09   5 4 3 2 1
paper   13 12 11 10 09   5 4 3 2 1

To CLÉIA BEZERRA DOS SANTOS ROCHA
and RACHEL MARIE DIPIETRO JAMES,
two inspiring young women — gone too soon

CONTENTS

MAPS AND ILLUSTRATIONS

Maps

Illustrations

PREFACE

In the poverty-stricken backlands of northeastern Brazil, since the late 1970s, groups of peasants have been recognized by the government as either indigenous tribes or descendants of fugitive slave communities. In this book, I explain how two such groups, who are neighbors and kin, came to self-identify as ethnoracially separate, calling upon different federal laws for recognition and land. I was introduced to the area that would become my field site through the Centro Dom José Brandão de Castro, a nongovernmental organization, which only a few years earlier had been linked to the Catholic Church. Knowing of my interest in Native Americans with African ancestry in the United States, a Brazilian friend had mentioned to me that he knew of a group of "black people" in the northeastern state of Sergipe who had been issued cards by FUNAI, the national indigenous protection agency, identifying them as members of the Xocó Indian tribe.[1] When he put me in touch with the Centro staff and I expressed interest in learning more about the Xocó, they explained that the crux of their work at that time was with the neighboring village of Mocambo. The majority of Mocambo residents, most of whom had kin among the Xocó, were rural workers who, the year before, in 1997, had been recognized by the Brazilian government as a community of descendants of fugitive slaves (*quilombo*) under a one-sentence provision (the "quilombo clause") of the 1988 Constitution, the first democratic constitution since the military regime took power in 1964. This set the stage for an unimaginable situation, by U.S. standards: two neighboring, related communities whose fates had, for generations, been completely intertwined, were now separated by ethnicity, race, politics, and land. Each community was recognized by a different federal government agency. One is considered Indian and the other black, although all are descended from Africans, Indians, and Europeans.

Intrigued by such an ethnoracial and demographic configuration, I traveled to Sergipe in May 1998 for the first time.[2] When I arrived at the single-runway airport in Sergipe's capital, Aracaju, the first thing I noticed was a mural on yellow tiles in the baggage claim area. It portrayed a group of dancing Indians with shafts, feather skirts, long hair, and geometrical designs on

Sergipe and Alagoas with the São Francisco River. Adapted from Clarice Novaes da Mota, *Jurema's Children in the Forest of Spirits: Healing and Ritual among Two Brazilian Indigenous Groups* (London: Intermediate Technology Publications, 1997).

their skin.[3] I already knew from preliminary research that the mural was not representative of the inhabitants of the area. It was, however, a powerful part of the discourse about Sergipe's heritage and history. I was whisked away by the Centro staff to a meeting of Mocambo residents, members of other rural black communities, a Brazilian anthropologist, and staff members of a local black consciousness organization. My introduction to the first recognized quilombo in Sergipe occurred as I sat on the floor with leaders of the community, young and old, women and men. I watched them draw pictures of the spatial arrangement of their village and learned about the jobs, land, and services they lacked. A few days later I boarded a bus and traveled over rutted roads into the interior of the state where I would begin my acquaintance with the two villages located on the banks of the São Francisco River: Mocambo, the recognized quilombo, and São Pedro Island, where the Xocó live. During that first four-hour bus ride, all the images I had seen, music I had heard, and stories I had read about the Northeast and its rustic, semiarid backland known as the *sertão* crowded my mind. I watched the landscape change from green fields to dusty expanses dotted with cows, from palm trees to cactus.

Over the years since my first visit, I have conducted extensive ethnographic, historical, and legal research focusing on these two communities. I learned about law, race, ethnicity, politics, and socioeconomic relations in Brazil. In addition to participant observation, I conducted more than a hundred interviews (fifty of them recorded and transcribed) with residents, former landowners, lawyers, anthropologists, activists, politicians, and government officials; analyzed historical and current legal cases; and carried out documentary research in court, government, Catholic Church, newspaper, and personal archives. Methodology, however, is more than just how data is collected. It involves constant analysis and revision of understanding about the people and places experienced. In this case, my analytical approach allowed me to build on each interaction and bit of knowledge obtained to develop a theoretical model, which I call "legalizing identity," that explains how cultural practices, legal provisions, and identity formation are interrelated.

As I researched, I learned that in the early 1970s a group of rural workers of mixed African, Native, Portuguese, and Dutch descent living along the São Francisco River had sought to obtain rights to land and protection from local landowners whose violence was legendary. This claim for rights was facilitated by the arrival of a Franciscan priest, who, with the encouragement of his bishop, spoke to the people about the potential significance of the indigenous strand of their ancestry. Their newly articulated claim of indigenous identity was facilitated in 1973 by the enactment of a new national law governing indigenous peoples and their rights. In this book, I explain how that law inadvertently opened the door to government recognition for many groups in the Northeast previously considered to be fully assimilated into the dominant society. Despite local skepticism in the early years of their struggle, these people, who had come to be called the Xocó, achieved official tribal recognition in 1979 and won full land rights in 1991. The Xocó is the only recognized indigenous group in Sergipe and the only community to claim Indian identity. Recognition was the culmination of encounters with landowners, police, judges, and lawyers, including the illegal occupation of São Pedro Island. Their story is told in this book.

More than two decades after the Xocó struggle for recognition began, people in the neighboring, riverside village of Mocambo, sometimes referred to as the "blacks (*negros*) of Mocambo," won government recognition as a community descended from a quilombo. With recognition came a change in attitude about their identity as a black community, as well as title to the land on which they had labored for generations. This was accomplished through the quilombo clause, adopted in the 1988 Constitution in response to pressure from black movement representatives and as a desire to address the issue of pluralism in Brazilian society at a moment when the national ideology of racial democracy was increasingly being challenged. This book explains and analyzes the twisting path the Mocambo residents traversed to their revised identity.

Before the advent of the first of the struggles, the individuals in the area identified themselves as sharecroppers of the landowners for whom they worked and whose interests they served under a traditional patronage system. The two struggles, assisted by successive generations of Catholic liberation theologians (priests, bishops, nuns, and lay clergy), resulted in a drastic revision in each community's collective ethnoracial and political identification and in the political power dynamics in the region. The parallels between the two generations of pastoral agents inspired by liberation theology will become apparent as the histories of the Xocó and Mocambo struggles are told. The stories are different, in part because the Xocó struggle took place under a military dictatorship with a strong liberationist Church, while the Mocambo community waged its struggle in a democratic environment with a Church hierarchy that was attempting to move away from its progressive legacy. As the country was democratizing, people of color around the world were reshaping and asserting their respective identities to gain land, resources, and power. In Brazil itself, a national conversation about race and color had begun in earnest. Those changes are reflected in the lives of these people who chose a mode of struggle and survival that has changed their ethnoracial identities and led to reconfigurations of their cultural practices.

Members of the Xocó and Mocambo communities share kin relations and a common history as *sertanejos* (backlanders) and *vaqueiros* (cowboys). They have always been deeply involved in each others' lives, and this connection has continued despite their new distinct, legally defined ethnoracial identities. However, since the 1970s, they have also come to distinguish themselves from each other through the revising and retelling of old and new histories of struggle. In other words, people who were no different from other sertanejo peasants were successful at claiming an Indian or quilombo identity, winning government recognition and land rights, and displacing elite landowners. This was accomplished even though the anthropologists called upon to assess the validity of their claims recognized that their asserted ethnoracial identities were "constructed," thus demonstrating that "authenticity" is not a definitional requisite of identity. In an unusual turning of the tables, the notion that race and ethnicity are social constructions *enhanced* rather than *undermined* Xocó and Mocambo claims of difference (see Clifford 1988).

Through governmental efforts on behalf of indigenous and rural black communities, the state's role has inadvertently become one of instigator, if not creator, of new indigenous and quilombo identities. Acknowledgment of this has not stopped the forward motion of recognitions and redistribution of land. Self-identification as an Indian or *quilombola* (member of a quilombo community) draws upon historical narratives intertwined with social solidarity forged in recent recognition and land struggles. However, the success of these struggles is contingent upon laws that were enacted to recognize, but have succeeded in creating, ethnoracial minorities with rights. The boundaries of this process were shaped by growing political divisions and cultural differences between the Xocó Indians and Mocambo quilombolas as each group sought to affirm internal unity. Although family relations and a common history link the two communities, the specificities of each group's struggle for land and the expectations associated with being Indian or black led them to distinguish themselves from each other. The people in these two communities now see each other as different yet related. The differentiation is maintained primarily through different bodies of law, different government institutions, political differences, competition for resources, and the shifting side taking in family disagreements.

The successive struggles of the Xocó and Mocambo communities are ideal for considering how such differentiation operates, both on the ground and in the discursive and cultural practices of the people assuming and living these new identities—in other words, how the legalization of identities works to alter their lived experience. In Brazil, where slavery was not abolished until 1888, peasants of African and indigenous descent have related closely to each other for centuries. Only with the enactment and enforcement of legal provisions have these strands begun to be disentangled, with sometimes tangled consequences. As I demonstrate in this book, seeking social justice involves interpersonal conflict, shifting enmities and alliances, inventions and reinterpretations, and historical contingencies.

The stories told and analyzed here bring to light how the people living in a relatively isolated place have been actors in, and creators of, these stories. However, this book is not only about stories that reveal the logic of identity transformation in a local setting. More important, this book examines a series of phenomena that are transforming Brazil and the hemisphere. Movements for ethnoracial recognition and redistributive justice, many of which were initiated in the early 1970s, have swept the Americas. The examples and explanations presented in this book elucidate the processes under way in many parts of the world in terms of relationships among law, race/ethnicity, economic inequality, and cultural practices. This book, therefore, is not only about law, identity, land rights, and social movements but is also about the transformation of peoples' lives and the effects, over the course of generations, of changes in ideological perspectives and engagement with new laws. As recognition of asserted cultural difference and redistribution of land and resources move up on the agenda of many nations in the Western Hemisphere as the result of pressure from below and above, the logic of property rights is also being transformed. Through a new conceptualization of "legalizing identity," we can begin to understand the processes set into motion as part of the worldwide reaction to the Vietnam War, the defeat of the United States in that war, assertion of civil rights in the First World, military regimes in Latin America and subsequent redemocratization, the successful anticolonial struggles in the Third World, and the globalization of rights. As demands for equitable distribution of land and resources gained strength, they began to be refracted through the prism of Indian and black identity recognition, providing a new way to be and become people empowered to have a say in their lives. Understanding the sources and effects of those struggles, their successes and failures, is the aim of this book.

ACKNOWLEDGMENTS

The research for this book was funded by fellowships from the Social Science Research Council, the J. William Fulbright Scholarship Board, and the National Science Foundation, as well as travel grants from the Duke University Latin American and Caribbean Studies Center and the Tinker Foundation. The opportunity to work through issues that would be clarified in the writing of this book was provided by postdoctoral fellowships from Northwestern University's Latin American Studies Rockefeller program, the Kellogg Institute for International Studies at the University of Notre Dame, and the Latin American Studies Center of the University of Maryland at College Park. Summer stipends and travel funds from the University of Richmond gave me the time to complete the manuscript and to research the status of the communities and the current Brazilian government's actions and attitudes toward quilombos and Indians.

There are three people who were key to the launching of this project. Alexandre Fortes suggested the region that would become my field site and introduced me to those who would become my companions and friends during my fieldwork in Sergipe. Before leaving for my first visit, I was introduced to Clarice Novaes da Mota, an anthropologist who had done her doctoral fieldwork with the Xocó and Kariri-Xocó in the early 1980s, and who was, miraculously enough, living nearby. An early reading of her newly published book as well as our personal discussions prepared me for what I would find when I first arrived in that distant place. We also overlapped in Sergipe during my year of field research, where she introduced me to the people living on São Pedro Island. During that early visit to Sergipe, I met José Maurício Andion Arruti, an anthropologist who was also conducting research in Mocambo. From the beginning, Maurício was generous in sharing his perspectives on events in Mocambo, and our friendship has given me a window onto the practice of anthropology in Brazil.

In Brasília, David Fleischer and Edyr Resende provided helpful advice and access to sources about the Constituent Assembly of 1987. While there during an early visit, I also met José Jorge de Carvalho at the University of Brasília, who had worked on the anthropological analysis of one of the first quilombos, Rio das Rãs, and immediately saw the value of my research. In the years that followed, Jorge and his wife and colleague, Rita Segato, as well as their wonderful family, proved lovely hosts, important friends, and intellectual mentors. During my visits to São Paulo, Sonia de Avelar and Salvador Sandoval kept a place set aside for me, and we spent hours telling stories, discussing my work and theirs, and keeping warm in a display of quintessential Brazilian hospitality. Tânia and Rosemiro Magno da Silva of the Federal University of Sergipe helped me find a place to live and introduced me to the least-known but surely the best capital of the Northeast—Aracaju. I will never forget our discussions about local politics, land reform, the history of radical movements in Sergipe, and their wonderful food.

I am forever grateful to my friends in Sergipe who walked with me down many paths. The first person I laid eyes on in Sergipe was Margarette Lisboa Rocha, from whom I learned so much in our first encounter that in retrospect she must have been clairvoyant. From day one, Margarette's probing questions and intense intellect have been priceless, while her unmitigated friendship makes my tie to Sergipe lifelong. Inês dos Santos Souza, the first person who took me to Mocambo, opened her heart to me without hesitation. Her political acumen and ability to read people were more important than any sources I could have found in an archive. I would also like to thank the rest who have helped to make the Centro Dom José Brandão de Castro a vibrant organization in the struggle for a better life in rural Sergipe, including Cléia Bezerra dos Santos Rocha, who died in 2005 in childbirth and in the prime of her active commitment to a better life for rural women, Adelmo Pires dos Reis, Anailza de Sá Lisboa, Emanuel Souza Rocha, Manoel Cícero de Souza, Deildes dos Santos, Carlos Alberto Santos, Anna Maria Gomes Torres, and the rural workers who served on the Centro's council.

I owe everything to the people of Mocambo and São Pedro Island. I especially thank Dona Maria das Virgens Santos, who made her home my home in Mocambo, as well as Sr. Antônio Lino dos Santos, Dona Neuza de Souza Melo, Maria da Glória da Silva, Dona Marieta das Dores de Souza, and Antônio Marques de Souza, the last two no longer living but alive in this book. Special thanks go to Dona Maria's activist children, Maripaulo Acácio dos Santos and Paulameire dos Santos Melo—for the hours of conversation, Paulomary Acácio dos Santos, and Lourdes dos Santos Melo. Lourdes's daughters Daniela and Poliana accompanied me and answered many questions. On São Pedro Island, I would like to thank then-chief Heleno Bezerra Lima; Maria José and Magnolia Faustino Bezerra for housing and feeding me and for helping me understand how everyone was related; José "Zuza" Acácio and Rosalia Machado Freitas; and José Valmir Rosa, who explained where people stood.

Almost immediately after my arrival to conduct fieldwork, people began talking to me about two key actors in Mocambo's story, the nun and lawyer Mariza Rios and the radical priest Isaías Nascimento. Mariza invited me to visit over the years in Colatina, Espirito Santo, where we talked for two days straight, then in Rio de Janeiro and Belo Horizonte, where we continued to talk without taking a breath. Her contribution to my knowledge of the early years of the Mocambo struggle and to my understanding of the structure and politics of the Catholic Church in Brazil, as well as the legal issues surrounding land rights and quilombos were priceless. Padre Isaías's ongoing dedication to improving the lives of the rural poor of Sergipe brought him to Mocambo, but his presence is felt in all parts of the diocese and he is renowned for his political action. A native *sergipano* (a resident of Sergipe), Padre Isaías's personal story allowed me to better understand his world.

Although I may no longer be a practicing lawyer, I did not leave lawyers behind when I went to Sergipe. Peoples' lawyers Márcia Menezes Nascimento and Demóstenes Ramos de Melo never tired of explaining the underlying legal issues, as well as their moral commitment to popular struggle. We shared and compared notes on lawyering in our respective countries, and they were always there when I needed them. They introduced me to lawyers who had participated in the struggles and helped me gain access to documents and case files. Crucial to this book was Paulo Vasconcelos Jacobina, the federal attorney stationed in Aracaju who began working on the Mocambo/São Pedro Island situation in 1999 and became deeply involved with the quilombo movement in Mocambo just as I was beginning my fieldwork. I watched as he wrote letters and filed lawsuits to assure that the Mocambo land title would survive legal challenges and that the people there would be safe. He was always available to talk with me, whether about law, the role of government lawyers, the legal issues involved in Mocambo, or the blues, of which he is an aficionado.

At the federal land reform agency, INCRA, I would like to thank Antônio Vieira dos Santos in the Sergipe office and Claudio Rodrigues Braga in Brasília, both of whom provided me with key sources on Mocambo. In Brasília, the Palmares Cultural Foundation and FUNAI and their staff members deserve my gratitude for helping with sources and interviews. Also in Brasília, Angela Baptista and the other anthropologists and lawyers at the federal attorney's office helped me whenever I needed it and whetted my appetite to learn more about their unusual institution. In Aracaju, for their help when I often needed it most, I want to thank Paulo and Dominique Neves. Fernando Araújo Sá, historian of the sertão, shared sources with me and became a friend. Also in Aracaju, I was fortunate to get to know and interview Apolônio Xokó, Luiz Antônio Barreto, Cesar and Carlos Britto Aragão, Carlos Ayres Britto (who has since become a federal Supreme Court justice), Beatriz Dantas, Frei Enoque Salvador de Melo, and the former governor of Sergipe, João de Seixas Dória. Although Helena Weiss Gonçalves, of Campinas, São Paulo, was at the other end of Brazil from Sergipe, she offered insightful reflections as she transcribed my interviews.

The first people to engage with my thoughts and concerns about the subject matter of this book deserve special thanks. William O'Barr, my supervisor, pushed me to rethink my assumptions about law and its relationship to society. His uncanny ability to pinpoint strategic issues at decisive moments proved invaluable. Katherine Pratt Ewing supported my early yearnings for a graduate education after the years I had spent dreaming about writing in my own voice. Kathy's work prepared me for going into the field and set a standard of sensitivity to, and insight into, individuals and their relationships that helped me immensely during this entire process. John Conley, anthropologist and law professor, challenged me to think like more than a lawyer about legal and philosophical issues. Irene Silverblatt's incisive comments, as well as her warmth and support, always came just when I needed them. Orin Starn was gracious in sharing his knowledge of Latin America and peasant movements, North American Indians, and the political issues surrounding the construction of cultural identity. Always enthusiastic, his helpful comments taught me much about critical thinking and how to work through tough issues. When I first read Barbara Yngvesson's work in the mid-1980s, I had no idea I would meet her on an elevator at a Law and Society meeting over a decade later. Barbara shaped my view of law as a cultural and psychological phenomenon that never stands alone.

I would also like to thank the scholars who took the time to discuss issues that shaped this book, including Joan Bak, Merle Bowen, John Burdick, Janet Chernela, Susan Coutin, Katherine Pratt Ewing, Brodwyn Fischer, Susan Fitzpatrick-Behrens, John French, Seth Garfield, Tracy Devine Guzmán, Mark Healey, Susan Hirsch, Daniel James, Scott Mainwaring, Bill Maurer, David McCreery, Jody Pavilack, Timothy Power, Thomas Rogers, Kenneth Serbin, Alejandro Velasco, Jonathan Warren, Barbara Weinstein, Mary Weismantel, and Wendy Wolford. I would also like to thank Elaine Maisner, my editor at the University of North Carolina Press.

Over the years since graduating from law school, I have had the great fortune to have the continuing advice and encouragement of Mark Janis of the University of Connecticut School of Law. His direction and wise counsel, beginning with my first publication on Brazilian tax law in 1982, continues to this day. Assistance with the research for that article and friendship over the last twenty-five years has been given to me by José Luiz Cabello Campos, the Brazilian attorney who gave me the opportunity to see international business from a South American perspective. At Duke, I would like to thank Natalie Hartman, associate director of the Duke Center for Latin American and Caribbean Studies, for her willingness to share her insights, good judgment, and emotional strength. Leslie Damasceno deserves special thanks for teaching me Portuguese and for engaging me with her passion for modern Brazilian literature and theater. Maryse Bacellar opened her home to me for six weeks in Rio while I studied Portuguese and roamed that marvelous city. My department at the University of Richmond, since I arrived in 2006, has provided an encouraging environment, protecting me from extra duties, so that this book could come to fruition. The importance of the emotional support and intellectual stimulation provided by my friends cannot be emphasized enough. My warm thanks to Daniel James and Lynn DiPietro, Leon Fink and Sue Levine, Roger French and Barbara Brown French, Thomas DiPrete and Katherine Ewing, Barbara Armentrout, Terence and Julie Connor, Barbara Weinstein, Edith and Justin Wolfe, Michael Hanchard, Joyce Dalsheim, and Styliane Philippou. Karen Willis helped me understand the unbreakable chain, and so gave me the freedom to write. I would like to acknowledge the effervescent presence in my life for too short a time of Rachel James — she is missed everyday.

Finally, I thank my father, Edward Hoffman, who bequeathed me his insatiable intellectual curiosity, and my mother, Phyllis Hoffman, who has always amazed me with her ability to get at the feelings behind the words. My children, Paul Joseph and Elizabeth Nora, share intellectual curiosity, a love of words and argument, and a commitment to peace and justice, all of which are a source of my hope for a future without war and misery. My greatest debt is to my *companheiro*, John David French, with whom I have shared everything from the very beginning. If I could, I would joyfully relive every minute of our ongoing conversation — from the streets of New York and Philadelphia during the bicentennial year, to walks on the beach in Chincoteague, runs around the reservoir in Pittsburgh, pinecone walks in New Haven, drives through the pass in Utah, strategizing sessions and tax dates in Miami, and ambles around the golf course in Durham and the Hollywood Cemetery in Richmond, to our *Treze de Julho* riverside strolls in Aracaju. May there be at least as many more in the years to come.

ABBREVIATIONS

ABA Brazilian Anthropological Association (Associação Brasileira de Antropologia)

CEB Base Ecclesial Community (Comunidade Eclesial de Base)

CIMI Indigenist Missionary Council (Conselho Indigenista Missionário), founded by the CNBB in 1972 to be in charge of indigenous rights policies of the Brazilian Catholic Church

CNBB National Conference of Brazilian Bishops (Conferência Nacional dos Bispos do Brasil), founded in 1952

CODEVASF Development Company of the São Francisco Valley (Companhia de Desenvolvimento do Vale do São Francisco)

CPT Pastoral Land Commission (Comissão Pastoral da Terra), founded by the CNBB in 1975 to advance the cause of land reform

FUNAI National Indigenous Foundation (Fundação Nacional do Índio), the federal agency governing indigenous peoples. FUNAI replaced the SPI in 1967 as the result of corruption, land sales, and inhumane practices.

INCRA National Institute of Colonization and Agrarian Reform (Instituto Nacional de Colonização e Reforma Agrária)

MEB Base Education Movement (Movimento de Educação de Base)

MNU Unified Black Movement against Racial Discrimination (Movimento Negro Unificado Contra a Discriminação Racial), founded in 1978

MST Landless Rural Workers' Movement (Movimento dos Trabalhadores Rurais Sem Terra), founded in 1984

NGO nongovernmental organization

PT   Workers' Party (Partido dos Trabalhadores), founded in 1980; its candidate (Luiz Inácio Lula da Silva) won the presidency twice, in 2002 and 2006.

SPI   Indigenous Protection Service (Serviço de Proteção aos Índios), the first federal agency dedicated to the protection of indigenous peoples, founded in 1910. It was replaced by FUNAI in 1967.

Introduction

Over forty new tribes, including the Xocó, have been recognized in the Brazilian Northeast since the late 1970s.[1] These new Indians are composed primarily of African-descended individuals who possess few of the "traditional cultural diacritics," who speak only Portuguese, and whose Indianness is "not always evident from their physical appearance" (A. C. Ramos 2003:370), but who nonetheless self-identify as indigenous. Although the Brazilian government has legally recognized them as Indians, members of the press, the public, and academics have questioned their "authenticity," in light of the popular representations of Indians derived from the Amazonian experience featured in films and classic ethnographies as isolated communities of naked natives. This is exemplified by the following set of questions raised by anthropologist Beatriz Dantas two decades after Xocó recognition:

> When they meet the Xocó on São Pedro Island, people often ask: Where is the village and where are the Indians? When they see the same kinds of houses, a church, children playing under the trees, everyone wearing the same simple clothes that all people who till the land wear; when they see some people with copper-colored skin and straight, dark hair and others with black skin with kinky hair, brown skinned people with wavy hair and others who are blonde with blue eyes, they ask, are these real Indians?[2]

Just as some rural black communities have self-identified as Indians, others have asserted a quilombo identity as descendants of fugitive slaves, related to an increase in black activism in both urban and rural settings around Brazil. New laws and policies requiring affirmative action in higher education and federal agencies have been enacted, with quotas for black Brazilians already in place. Both controversial, the issue of quotas and the claims of rural black communities for recognition and land under the 1988 quilombo clause of the Constitution are often linked in discussions about the new prominence of ethnoracial mobilization in Brazil.[3]

Rural folk organizing themselves as Indians or quilombolas rather than as peasants or rural workers may be considered a form of "identity politics."[4] Academics and activists have been debating, since the early 1990s, whether class-based mobilization would be more effective than identity-based organization, since each "identity" has its own demands and potentially exclusionary practices. Some scholars have accused Latin American governments of co-opting identity politics to implement a form of "neoliberal multiculturalism," essential to neoliberal governance, that appears to accommodate the needs of the subaltern classes but in reality does very little to provide them with a better life (Hale 2002, 2006). Others insist that popular mobilization has been the catalyst for multiculturalism, which has the potential to provide a voice and economic power to the previously powerless indigenous and black people of Latin America (Van Cott 2000, 2005). An alternative approach has been asserted in which the "current context of globalization" provides "resistance" with the "potential, through the constitutive power of social struggle, to challenge sovereign power by utilizing the tools at hand and asserting alternative logics" (Speed 2008:37). In my view, international support for state-sponsored multiculturalism, reflected in International Labor Organization Convention 169 on Indigenous and Tribal Peoples (1989), the Durban World Conference against Racism (2001), and the United Nations Declaration on the Rights of Indigenous Peoples (2007), has created an opening to consider the benefits and drawbacks of ethnoracial mobilization in a world of globalizing rights. In this book, I propose that debates over modes of organizing are best addressed within a broad conceptual framework of social and redistributive justice (Fraser 1998). When recognition and resources come together, the opportunity for people to fully participate in the life of the nation is enhanced.

In many parts of the world, including Latin America, the right to land is integral to the conception of social justice, yet what it means to acquire, hold, and work land is often taken for granted (see Moore 1986). However, as will become clear, there are multiple meanings of land. It can signify the ability to feed one's family or represent the possession of political or economic power. The meaning of land can also vary by region and locale. It can change over time for collectivities, as well as for individuals, as the context of their lives change. This is what happened for the Xocó Indians and the Mocambo villagers. As will be seen, even the form of land title granted, whether individual or collective, can affect both land-use patterns and the sentiments associated with historical ties to a given place. Although such issues are presented in all forms of land struggle, the two movements I examine in this book and others like them throughout Brazil, because of their ethnoracial character, are sometimes represented as distinct from previous and parallel struggles for land reform, including the northeastern peasant leagues of the 1950s, Church-sponsored land reform movements, and the Landless Rural Workers' Movement (MST), one of the largest social movements in Brazil.

Rather than presenting movements for land and identity as being in conflict with each other, an either-or proposition, I suggest that ethnoracially based movements are an alternative (although not the only one) to other forms of political mobilization. In this book, I argue that the creation of land-based ethnoracial groups in the Brazilian Northeast constitute "new geographies" (Harvey 2000:557). This does not exclude other forms of organization but rather incorporates a certain richness in modes of struggle and cultural practices associated with all forms of mobilization. I argue that understanding how social justice is conceived and embodied in Brazil's Northeast requires an appreciation of the impact its pursuit can have on the cultural lives of the people who pursue it.

Therefore, rather than being another book about race relations, indigenous struggles, or the black consciousness movement in Brazil, this book is fundamentally concerned with how each of those issues intersect with, and may even reshape, the law and its effects on the lives of people like those living on the banks of the São Francisco River in Mocambo and on São Pedro Island. In this book, I explain how the invocation of laws can inspire ethnoracial identity formation along with revisions of cultural practices—revising physical boundaries is not enough (Sahlins 1999; Vlastos 1998). In this book, I also show how such local transformations of social and cultural practices can, in turn, reshape the meanings of the laws themselves. Since law operates as a powerful social force once it is invoked by people with a purpose, it not only imposes categories and orders social relations, but it also provides structures for self-identification, mobilization, and social justice (Thompson 1975:266–67).

The effects of new tribal and quilombo recognitions are often seen through the prism of racial discourse. However, it is important to understand that racial discourse in Brazil operates differently from the United States, with its historical rule of hypo-descent ("one-drop rule") and years of legal definitions based on blood and genealogy (Domínguez 1986). In Brazil, there are people who may appear to be white but who self-identify as black and people who appear to be black but who self-identify as indigenous. This is because, in Brazil, political commitment often precedes racial designation; in the United States racial designation most often precedes political commitment.[5]

Therefore, for example, Mocambo residents who self-identify as quilombolas consider themselves to be black, although with a definition that is up for grabs. As illustrated in this book, interpretations of phenotype and descent are not necessarily the key to self- and other-identification for quilombolas and Indians. Commitment to struggle and "performance" (Gross 2007:470; Jackson 2001) of ethnoracial identity are deciding factors in Brazil, although constant discussion of skin color and facial features serves as the everyday social backdrop, reflecting effects of the continuing glaring racial inequalities in Brazil. This contradiction is one of the puzzles scholars of race in Brazil confront (Guimarães 1999; Sansone 2003; Sheriff 2001; Telles 2004; Racusen forthcoming 2009).

Prior to the 1980s, academics often avoided the issues of race and ethnicity, dealing with undifferentiated "peasants" as a category (Cândido 1964; Johnson 1971; Queiroz 1976). This was largely because nation and class were considered the essential organizing principles of both the state itself and activists interested in lessening inequality (Pereira 1997). With the spread and consolidation of constitutional multiculturalism in Latin America, scholarship on ethnoracial identity politics has viewed indigenous and African-descended communities and struggles as separate entities and endeavors. Published scholarship that encompasses and analyzes both is scarce (Hale 2004:20), although with increased interest by the World Bank and other international funding agencies in "indigenous and Afro-descendant" peoples, some scholars have begun to explore similarities and differences between the two (Greene 2007; Hooker 2005; Safa 2005). These are tentative moves toward viewing the struggles of rural indigenous and black communities in tandem, although there has not been much, if any, theorization of the issue; nor has there been an attempt to build a model to encompass both. To a certain extent, the division in scholarship derives from the view that "black" is a racial identity while "Indian" is an ethnic one (Wade 1997:25, 37). Such a divide "generates a conceptual system of serious scholarship wherein historical and ethnographic treatises on native peoples, *or* black peoples, hermetically seal off the data of the alternative people from analytical salience" (Whitten and Corr 1999:213). This is common in Brazil, where there has been a preference for categorization based on "ethnic" over "racial," derived from the long-held view that race is less analytically useful than class.

Disagreeing with that perspective, Jonathan Warren (2001) has argued that there are political benefits to be had from shifting the emphasis to a discourse of race for Indians in Brazil, because, in his view, Indians' anti-racist discourse is more developed than that of black Brazilians (a category

left underdeveloped). As such, he argues, Indians have more cohesive political organizations. In my view, Warren's position does not consider how a
particularly Brazilian perspective on ethnoracial identity actually *enhances*
political mobilization. In fact, discourses of mixture in Brazil allow people
to choose to be Indian and/or black, while discourses of race in the United
States force people into a single category—African American (Brooks 2002;
French 2004).[6] In Brazil, there has never been legal segregation, and racial
categories have not been defined by law (Goldberg 2002:215), reflecting
and reinforcing a national ideology that has historically held that mixture
vitiates any such endeavor. The Indian Statute of 1973 and the 1988 quilombo
clause are *implicitly* race-based laws that have opened up opportunities for
new ethnoracial identities based on legal rights. However, because they are
not *explicitly* race based, they result in political identities connected to, but
not solely defined by, race. Another problematic assumption runs throughout discussions of these newly salient categories, primarily by non-Brazilian
scholars (Hooker 2005; Safa 2005) (compare with Arruti 2006; Oliveira
Filho 1999a). It is generally assumed that even if the residents of a particular
area have a common background or have lived in the same or contiguous
physical space(s), their posited differences and separateness are intrinsic to
their efforts to obtain land and resources. Those differences are represented
as preexisting the enactment of the law.

In this book, I take a different tack. While observing, researching, and
participating in the unfolding of revised ethnoracial self-identifications in
Mocambo and on São Pedro Island, I developed a theoretical model I call
"legalizing identity." This model is demonstrated in this book through the
examples of the Xocó and Mocambo, but it is intended to be broadly applicable wherever such changes are taking place. As an analytical tool for
understanding the process by which national legal and political institutions
interact with local identity transformation, the concept of "legalizing identity" provides a framework that encompasses both black and Indian struggles
for recognition and resources, while retaining the ability to understand their
specific differences based in history and struggle.

Later in this introduction I will enumerate the elements of legalizing
identity and indicate how it organizes my analysis of the events that took
place in these backland villages. At this point, however, I argue that for the
process I am theorizing as legalizing identity to be visible, there must first
be a particular law that has come into existence with the purpose of protecting or regulating the rights of specific groups to maintain ethnoracial and
cultural difference.[7] The law may originate with lawmakers or government

officials or as the result of mass mobilization. Also, rather than follow the tacit order of things in which the law is mechanically applied to preexisting identities in the form of groups known to be either "Indian tribes" or "quilombos," we must understand that an unanticipated consequence of the application of a law can be the production of new categories of personhood. To further explain how these prerequisites come into being, I propose we use an alternative logic to assess the legislative process.

POSTLEGISLATIVE NEGOTIATION AND GOVERNMENTALITY

Just as identity does not necessarily preexist law, one should not assume that law fully preexists its application. In a process I call "postlegislative negotiation," the examples I explore in this book shed light on a popular Brazilian expression. People often ask whether the law will stick ("A lei vai pegar?"). As was the case with the laws regarding Indians and quilombos, laws are often not the result of mass public demand. This is in contradistinction to civil rights legislation in the United States, which is certainly the model used when scholars presume the healthy character of American democracy in comparison to Latin America (Armony and Schamis 2005). The popularity in Brazil of the assertion that a law will not stick or take hold ("a lei não vai pegar"), often expressed in the public sphere, provides a clue as to why prelegislative motivations, such as response to public concern, receive more attention from the populace than the actual passage of laws by the legislature. In the process of open-ended postlegislative negotiation, the impact, consequences, interpretations, and even the meanings of any given law are often determined only *after* it is enacted. That determination is made at the levels of the populace, police, judges, lawyers, government officials, and the press.[8] Each of the laws analyzed in this book are examples of the process of postlegislative negotiation. The Indian Law of 1973 came to be used for purposes far from the original intentions of the military government to colonize the far reaches of Brazilian territory; the quilombo clause of 1988 was thought to be a purely symbolic gesture to appease black consciousness movement activists but became the basis for the expansion of land rights for rural black communities.

Crucial to my conceptualization of postlegislative negotiation is the notion of governmentality, which provides a further underpinning for the workings of such negotiation. As with the multiplex forms of negotiation surrounding legal provisions, "governmentality" is a process that engages more than the government itself (Foucault 1991; Rose, O'Malley, Valverde 2006).

It is about how governing takes place, specifically as it "chang[es] the shape of the thinkable" through the strategies that produce social order involving public and private, the state and civil society (C. Gordon 1991:8). It is the "ensemble formed by the institutions, procedures, analyses and reflections, the calculations and tactics that allow the exercise of this . . . form of power . . . a whole series of specific governmental apparatuses" and "the development of a complex of knowledge" (Foucault 1991:102–3). Therefore, governmentality also involves a series of other actors and institutions as disciplinary agents—international, national, and local, associated or not associated with the government—who originate, and participate in, the dissemination of information about new categories available to be claimed for the rights associated with them. These new categories are available as tools of subjection as well. The example often given is the professional nongovernmental organization (NGO) (Hale 2002; Li 2001), of which there are many involved in the stories told in this book: the Catholic Church (acting locally through priests, nuns, missionary organizations, and lay clergy), rural trade unions, black movement activists, land reform organizations, anthropologists, and many local, state, and national government agencies, which tend to act independently of the central Brazilian government.

With the blurring of the lines between state and civil society, especially in a relatively weak state such as Brazil, governmentality provides a nonbinary view of the process by which potential rights bearers are identified and rendered recognizable by the state. This new "modality of government works by creating mechanisms that work 'all by themselves' to bring about governmental results . . . through the 'responsibilization' of subjects who are increasingly 'empowered' to discipline themselves" (Ferguson and Gupta 2002:989). Chapters 2, 3, and 4 show how governmentality operated in the Xocó story and in the path that Mocambo took to quilombo recognition. In both cases, nongovernmental entities and individuals were key agents of change. Their efforts reinforced the dispersal of state power just as they encouraged people to appeal for recognition to the very government they feared or despised. This irony is at the core of governmentality.

In addition to the Catholic Church and NGOs, there were at least two other crucial agents of governmentality in the continuing dramas of the Xocó and Mocambo: lawyers and anthropologists. Individual government lawyers who worked with the federal attorney's office (ministério público federal) were important allies of both groups in their bids for recognition; anthropologists were called upon to write the expert reports that provided evidence for tribal and quilombo recognition. One of the first visitors from outside the area to each village was an anthropologist. In the case of the Xocó, by the time an anthropologist was sent to consider their claim in 1978, Brazil was on the verge of redemocratization. Anthropologists, many of whom had faced repression under the dictatorship, were finally in a position to support new opportunities for dispossessed people. Chapter 2 charts the legal, historical, and social changes, as well as the shifts in anthropological thinking, that led to a revised perspective on who is considered an Indian in Brazil. Chapter 3 traces the importance of anthropological work to the easing of historical requirements associated with quilombo recognitions in the years immediately following the enactment of the quilombo clause.

As key agents of governmentality in the process of recognition and land demarcation and therefore directly involved with the production of knowledge used by state agencies to provide resources and as tools of surveillance and discipline, Brazilian anthropologists are on the front lines of ethical issues that face all anthropologists. An ethnographer may be involved in a legal recognition process, but in the anthropological work itself knowledge "is achieved through exchanges that have startling, upsetting, sometimes profoundly disturbing consequences for all participants" (Fabian 1999:66), including the "unsettling of identities" (Li 2001:652). Reviewing the ethics of anthropological engagement, Peter Brosius (1999:181) has noted that anthropologists are participants

> in the production of identities, or in the legitimation of identities produced by others. To the degree that these movements represent an attempt to create new meanings and identities—which in turn have the potential to produce new configurations of power—such a role cannot remain unacknowledged.

Brazilian anthropologists, in addition to debating their direct role in the lives of the people about whom they write reports, are also concerned with the tension between advocacy and scholarly detachment (Arruti 2002; Sampaio Silva, Luz, and Helm 1994) and the impact that legal categories may have on their ethnographic work (Dallari 1994). Latin American anthropologists, more generally, are required by their activities to address the themes of "the relationship between activism and anthropology, and issues surrounding the notion of authenticity," particularly when confronted with direct requests from indigenous people who are "using essentialism as a key political tool in their fight to preserve their cultural identity and their access and control of land and other resources" (Vargas-Cetina 2003:50).

Each time they are called upon to produce an expert report for recognition, Brazilian anthropologists are faced with the tensions inherent in anthropology's dual task: "to produce empirical knowledge of others *and* to address the question of the possibility and validity of such knowledge" (Fabian 1999:65). To address this epistemological problem that faces all anthropologists, I suggest that we consider Gadamer's "fusion of horizons," which "operates through our developing new vocabularies of comparison . . . [so that we may reach judgments] partly through transforming our own standards" (Taylor 1992:67). Gadamer (1975) saw the ties to individuals' horizons (their knowledge and experience) as the grounds of their understanding. A new intermediary creation can be constructed through the transcendence of one's own horizons. I propose that this can occur through exposure to others' cultural traditions because such views place one's own horizons into relief. Many Brazilian anthropologists are striving for such communication with the people they are helping and studying at the same time (Oliveira Filho 2005). Because they are so directly entrenched in the governmentality of their knowledge production, in this book I examine with some care the contributions made and difficulties faced by Brazilian anthropologists on the front lines of that knowledge production.

In considering the legitimating role of anthropologists in Brazil, I should also address my own role as an anthropologist and lawyer from the United States. At certain moments during my fieldwork, my presence facilitated the government attorney's intervention on behalf of the Mocambo residents. It was no secret that many people in the community considered my interest in their fate a positive force that was putting pressure on the government to act more swiftly. Each time a representative of the community came to the capital, he or she would request my presence at the lawyer's office. I was also invited to every meeting held to resolve land title issues and disputes with community members. When visiting the Xocó and Mocambo communities, I was treated as an anthropologist who, like the others (all Brazilians) who had been there before, could advance their respective causes. For the Xocó, who were suspicious of outsiders and who were already ensconced in the federal system of services and resources to recognized tribes, I was often treated as a go-between and a source of information about what was happening in Mocambo. With the help of a U.S.-trained Brazilian anthropologist, Clarice Novaes da Mota (1997), who had done her dissertation fieldwork with the Xocó in 1983, I was able to make important connections with individuals, including leaders of the community, who were related to people in Mocambo.

They provided me with insights about the intertwined histories of the two communities.

In Mocambo, I was welcomed by the quilombo supporters who were gaining land through government recognition, which they attributed to the work of another Brazilian anthropologist, José Maurício Arruti. Because I was identified with him and the NGO responsible for shepherding Mocambo through the recognition process, I was viewed with suspicion by residents who opposed the quilombo movement. Although I had access to their perspective on occasion, there was no doubt that the landscape of the many Brazilian anthropologists who share a clear commitment to the cause of new quilombo recognitions informed my experience and affected my relationships. However, I find solace in the observation that "participant observers need not be fully accepted or trusted in order to learn many things" (Duneier 2000:220). I was often reminded, through interactions that highlighted my foreigner status and my whiteness, that there are "no pristine spaces" where researchers can "operate freely, unconstrained by the conditions and circumstances which created the relationship between first-world research and third-world informant in the first place" (Hanchard 2000:178).

Being a white woman from the United States with a family that included adolescents who occasionally accompanied me to Mocambo, my relationships were shaped by both the distance of relative wealth, privilege, and education and the closeness of family relations and problems. Although I attempted to perform a balancing act, I could not avoid the perception that I was a favorite of certain families, so I determined to use the proximity they permitted to help me understand their motivations and feelings about what was important to them. I viewed my "political task not as 'sharing' knowledge with those who lack[ed] it but as forging links between different knowledges that are possible from different locations." My interlocutors included not only the indigenous or quilombo activists and residents but also "the constituencies, organizations, and people with which we, and they, engage and interact" (Hodgson 2002:1045).

LEGALIZING IDENTITY: BEYOND THE MUTUALITY HYPOTHESIS

Sociolegal scholars have explored law's constitutive powers, positing that law plays an indispensable role as a shaper of social and economic relations (Bourdieu 1987; Hunt 1985; Merry 1990; Silbey 1985). They have also identified law as a cultural system, a way of "imagining the real," whose symbols and meanings order communication and determine which events become "legal facts" (Conley and O'Barr 1990; Geertz 1983). Laws, in this view, constitute new "relations," "meanings," and "self-understandings" (Sarat and Kearns 1993:27). Legal systems are seen as contested sites of meaning where not only rights and obligations, but also identities, are constantly under negotiation, always within the context of historical processes (Starr and Collier 1989). In the course of that negotiation, law exercises transformative effects on culture and identity (Bower, Goldberg, and Musheno 2001; Collier, Maurer, and Suárez-Navaz 1995; Darian-Smith 1999; Greenhouse, Yngvesson, and Engel 1994; Merry 2000; Pavlich 1996; Sarat 1990). Some of the scholars who introduced the constitutive perspective have also proposed that the relationship between law and society is mutually embedded (Engel and Munger 1996; Yngvesson 1993). Subject to some subsequent critiques (Fitzpatrick 1997; Valverde 2003; Weston 1997), the constitutive theory has continued to prevail in sociolegal studies (Coutin 2000; Maurer 1995; Rivera Ramos 2001).

In developing the concept of legalizing identity, I have picked up one strand of the constitutive trend—the view that law and its social context mutually shape one another. An expansion and deepening of what I call this "mutuality hypothesis" provides a tool useful for analyzing identity politics and multiculturalism, the positive and negative effects of the intertwining of law and identity, and historical phenomena. Proponents of the mutuality hypothesis "postulate a two-way process in which interchanges between the legal system and particular cultural settings 'mutually shape' both the law and the social context within which it operates" (Engel and Munger 1996: 14). Law can be resignified as people and courts interact. "The 'double reality' of neighborhood struggles at the courthouse is constituted in a play with rights that both enmeshes people in the power of law and reinterprets the law" (Yngvesson 1993:14).

For example, identity transformation of individuals with "disabilities" is apparent in the years since the passage of the Americans with Disabilities Act (ADA) in 1991. In analyzing that transformation, Engel and Munger (2003:253) propose a "recursive theory of rights" in which identity is a "precursor as well as a consequence of rights" and rights are "a result as well as a cause of change." However, a crucial difference between their reflections and my explication of legalizing identity has to do with the meaning of "rights." When I refer to "law," I include positive law (statutory, regulatory, judicial) as well as the rights and obligations that emanate from it. Engel and Munger are most concerned with how rights are active in peoples' lives, but it is not their project to investigate where those rights come from or how the laws have changed in relation to their usage. In fact, none of the subjects of their book had ever asserted a claim under the law. They specify that they do not want to "limit" their inquiry to the latest decisions handed down by appellate courts (2003:250).

My inquiry, on the other hand, includes how court interpretation of law changes in light of the way a particular law is being used or avoided. The model of legalizing identity helps explain how the law itself and its interpretations change over time as people who are touched by it use it in a variety of ways and, in the process, experience identity transformation. Significantly, what we learn by applying the legalizing identity framework is how that process influences officials responsible for the law and its interpretation, as well as those who disseminate it through political practice and organization. Unlike those who are primarily concerned with a penumbra of rights that seem to derive from, but are separate from, positive law, I do not see those elements as separable. In this book, I show how the use of Brazilian laws that provide rights to people based on presumed ethnoracial difference becomes integral to the reshaping of the laws themselves. This process operates through interpretation and revision by legal experts, lawmakers, and anthropologists in dialogue with the laws' intended beneficiaries and their allies. Because I developed the theory of legalizing identity through a study of struggles for rights and resources in the context of redemocratization, the use of the concept of legalizing identity is also intended to deepen, broaden, and clarify elements of political participation in a democracy.

By examining local examples in Brazil as they are constituted through the intertwining of strands that law, social movements, and anthropology provide, I also assess the fit between the values and interests of a political regime, as concretized in a constitution, administrative practices, and laws and policies that are enunciated through legislative enactment. As such, this book contributes to the ongoing debate about how to conceptualize the meanings of "rights," "difference," and "multiculturalism" in a democratizing polity and shows that rights are not just what the law provides, but are created through the process of governmentality as well as in the process of their pursuit. As "an ethnographic project at the heart of democratic change" (Greenhouse and Greenwood 1998:1), this book contributes to an understanding of how the meaning of law is molded and remolded and illuminates the tensions, both historical and current, that accompany policy decisions concerning issues of pluralism, democracy, and the nature of citizenship.

LEGALIZING IDENTITY DEFINED

Derived from my research on the lived experience of newly denominated Indian tribes and quilombos and the governmental and nongovernmental intermediaries that are integral to the process, I theorize that "legalizing identity" as a framework for analyzing ethnoracial identity transformation consists of five components, which, although presented as a numbered list for the sake of convenience, are not sequential but are played out simultaneously—a mutuality that highlights the flexibility of both law and identity and reveals the fissures in each that allow for change.

First, there is the experience of new or revised ethnoracial identities in the lives of the people who invoke rights based on newly codified legal identities. As the new laws are invoked and the rights associated with or extrapolated from them are put into practice, people begin to revise their self-identifications, to some extent as their designation by the larger society is also revised. In the cases examined in this book, the people in both communities have been identified and have self-identified over the years in a variety of ways: as *camponeses* (peasants), *trabalhadores rurais* (rural workers), *caboclos* (mixed race with indigenous ancestry), *negros* (blacks), *católicos* (Catholics), *pobres* (poor folk), *sertanejos* (backlanders), *sergipanos* (residents of Sergipe), *nordestinos* (northeasterners), *meeiros* (sharecroppers), *posseiros* (squatters), *índios* (Indians), *remanescentes* (descendants of fugitive slaves), and quilombolas, sometimes simultaneously and other times sequentially, as the state, its agents, the people themselves, and their advisers took up or ignored one or another of these sociolegal identities. Chapter 3 will trace the significance of these denominations and their relationship to stages of identity revision over time and in connection with laws.

Second, the meanings of the laws themselves are shaped and reshaped through the assertion of the new identities. As will be explained in chapter 3, for example, since the promulgation of the quilombo clause the requirements for recognition as a quilombo have narrowed (requiring historical proof of nineteenth-century enslavement and escape), broadened (in 1994 under the influence of anthropologists who had been working with rural black communities), narrowed (in 2001 to justify nonpayment to landowners whose land was being awarded to quilombos), and, although recently broadened substantially, qualifications have again been introduced. The meaning of the law is permanently in flux, with its regulation changing as quilombolas make new demands, anthropologists realize the difficulty of finding historical proof, international pressure increases for Brazil (as the country with the largest number of African-descended people outside of Africa) to make some provisions for its Afro-descendant communities, the black movement's influence in political life grows, and land reform takes on increased importance. By viewing the process of law making as an ongoing negotiation, conducted beyond the legislature and the courts, one can begin to see how the meaning of the quilombo clause, enacted as a form of symbolic politics, can change and be shaped through the participation of multiple parties. With regard to the Xocó Indians, chapter 2 explains how a statute designed to encourage integration could become the legal basis for recognition of African-descended peasants as Indians beginning in the late 1970s.

Third, local cultural practices are reconfigured. As interpretations of the laws have changed through their use over time, so too have the meanings of the cultural practices of both the Xocó and Mocambo. In each place, as described in chapter 5, a dance has been reconfigured for the legal recognition process. These dances have become vehicles for both expressing identity in relation to the law and addressing deeper yearnings for recognition as delineated communities with ties to the land. My conception of legalizing identity considers cultural change to be integral to the state's role in the formation and transformation of ethnic and racial identification, so long as it is "seen as something dynamic, something that people use to adapt to changing social conditions—and something that is adapted in turn . . . particularly in situations demanding rapid change" (J. Jackson 1995:18). Cultural practices, in such contexts, take "different forms, intensities, salience, and substance as individuals reinvent themselves and respond to wider politics and economics" (K. Warren 1992:201). At the same time, retaining this openness in the context of a recognition process requires acknowledgment that a group's self-identification is not inevitable, nor is it "simply invented, adopted, or imposed. It is, rather, a positioning which draws upon historically sedimented practices, landscapes, and repertoires of meaning, and emerges through particular patterns of engagement and struggle" (Li 2000:151). As described and analyzed in chapters 5 and 6, the effects of legalizing identity can also be seen in reconfigurations of local culture and in the lived experience of the people who, by their mobilization for legal rights, find their self-conceptions and relationships changing. They also find that their rights claims and cultural practices are intertwined. These two communities, the Xocó and Mocambo, differentiated and positioned themselves in particular ways, and that positioning was sometimes tactically tied to mobilization for resources, but it has also remained provisional. As chapter 6 demonstrates, through a process of constrained refashioning, the new generation of quilombolas are participating in quilombo cultural production. In that chapter, I analyze how new identities can be literally "enacted" through a play created and performed by Mocambo's teenagers.

Fourth, in the process of legalizing identity, accepted and assumed meanings of community are called into question, as best illustrated in chapter 4. Legalizing identity is as much about those who choose *not* to participate as it is about those who do. As such, the self-conceptions of the people living in Mocambo who opposed the quilombo movement (the *contras*, as they were referred to in Mocambo, an appellation used for opponents in other quilombos as well [Véran 2003]) were also altered by recognition, as were those of the landowners. Depending on the positioning of those opposed—whether they could technically be counted as quilombolas or were considered outsiders—self-identification varied and was changed in different ways. As emphasized throughout this book, embarking on a path bears no guarantee that the results will be as imagined. Decisions made by leaders of each community and the factions within them many times transcended both tactical elements and limitations imposed by law and its power of recognition. Such circumstances often lead to a reconsideration of the various uses of "community," whether as a religious affiliation (as in Base Ecclesial Communities (CEB) associated with liberation theology, as described in chapter 1), or as a political entity, as assumed in the quilombo clause. Community is often constituted through conflict (Creed 2004), an observation that is exemplified by the stories told in this book. Contesting the standard narratives of struggle for land and resources, often considered necessary to support a fledgling social movement, is also imperative for understanding the successes and failures of social movements. Assuming solidarity, community cohesion, agreement, and common cause are useful for the initial stages of a concerted effort for change or may even be necessary for the official moment when rights are recognized. However, once government officials go back to their offices, everyday life yields the tactical and strategic information needed to sustain the victories, confront the challenges posed by local authorities, landowners, family, and neighbors, and survive the defeats.

Fifth, and finally, even though the opportunity to take up an identity may originally emanate from, be extrapolated from, or be read into, the law, self-identification is experienced as the product of struggle. At the same time, once an ethnoracial identification is adhered to, it may be expressed as having essentialized characteristics. To illustrate this element of legalizing identity, I would like to quote leaders of the Xocó and Mocambo communities as they recalled the early days of their struggles. Apolônio, the forty-year-old former leader of the Xocó, told me when I first met him in 1998: "[When I learned I was an Indian] the emotional impact was very powerful, because I was born and raised on that land. Being a day laborer without education working the land, when suddenly I came to know that I was a person belonging to a community that had a past and that now we have a history. History that I never knew. I had no idea."

During that same field trip, I also met Maripaulo, a thirty-seven-year-old agricultural laborer and cousin of Apolônio from the neighboring village of Mocambo. "People from Mocambo are afraid of talking to whites, to people from the outside," said Maripaulo. "It's a legacy of slavery," he explained to me. As a leader of his community, this son of a Xocó man and a self-identified black woman had been instrumental in the quilombo struggle. The results were striking both for Mocambo and for individuals like Maripaulo. As he told me, "Before the struggle, I used to be [silent] like that too. Now I can talk to anyone—even the Pope."

1

Situating Identities in the Religious Landscape of the Sertão

The people who would become the Xocó Indians and the quilombolas of Mocambo share a common backland history, culture, and politics, all of which came to be mobilized and revised by them in the years since the first discussions of possible indigenous identity in the early 1970s. In addition to describing that common heritage, this chapter identifies the contradictory character of the place and culture of the rural hinterland that is known as the sertão.[1] My aim is to show how these historical contradictions informed and enabled the differentiation and legalization of Indian and black identities in a place where ethnoracial mixture has been, and continues to be, the operative assumption. The paradox of differentiation in a landscape of similarity is a primary theme of this chapter, in which I describe the physical and the imaginary characteristics of the sertão — its draw and its repulsion.

The Xocó village on São Pedro Island was built in the 1980s, while Quilombo Mocambo is a typical backland hamlet established in the 1930s. Although their layouts differ, neither stands out as distinguishable from other such places in the sertão, even though the inhabitants' relationship to each place has changed dramatically. Perhaps most important, the two communities and a vast majority of the people in the sertão share a religious commitment to the Roman Catholic faith. Church celebrations, processions, and visits by priests are central to their lives. The deep roots of folk Catholicism in the Northeast predate liberation theology, which developed a new and different approach to the rural poor and indigenous people than that of the traditional Church. Paradoxically, the very Church that for almost 500 years strove to convert and assimilate Indians, owned slaves, and punished runaways, in the 1970s became the driving force behind the legalizing of Indian and black identities in the sertão.

THE NORTHEAST AND THE SERTÃO IN THE BRAZILIAN IMAGINARY

The Brazilian Northeast is a nine-state region with a fertile coast and a large, semiarid interior. Vast stretches of the Northeast, which contains nearly 30 percent of Brazil's 190 million people, are chronically subject to drought, including the northern part of Sergipe where the Mocambo and Xocó communities are located. When I first arrived in 1998, the area had gone for nine months without rain. The misery, poverty, hunger, and disease of sertanejo populations inland from the river is so much greater than those who live along the river, even with exploitative economic relations, that only constant government assistance can alleviate the suffering. This was as true in 2000 as it was in 1971 and as it had been in the nineteenth century (Castro 1966, 1977). Therefore, these two communities were counted as lucky because their residents could carry water, albeit bacteria-ridden, from the river and so did not have to count on the trucked-in water that was often tainted with chemicals. Even so, life was quite difficult during these long droughts. The few cows were scrawny, gave no milk, and were rapidly dying. No crops could be grown, and there was virtually no work. People sat in front of their houses in the heat, gossiped, made trips to the river to bathe, wash dishes and clothes, and carry back pails of water on their heads. Once a month the elderly residents went to the county seat to collect their small pension checks, which they shared with their families and friends.

Until the 1920s, the nine states that now constitute the Northeast were considered part of the North.[2] At that time, for economic and political reasons involving a shift of power from the North (sugar and cotton plantations) to the South (coffee), the Northeast was first recognized and categorized as a geographically and culturally distinct region (Albuquerque 1999:69–70). The interior or backland of this poorest region of Brazil, the sertão, is often cited as the seat of messianic movements, banditry, paternalistic politics, peasant uprisings, unremitting poverty, drought, and an eerie countryside with little vegetation except thorn scrub (caatinga) and large expanses of savanna (cerrado). An economy developed in the interior of the Northeast based on cattle, rice and cotton cash crops, and subsistence farming.

Cattle raising is the activity most identified with the sertão, growing out of early needs to feed plantation slaves on the coast the dried, salted meat that rapidly became, and remains, a staple of the northeastern diet. In the sertão, there were no densely settled areas. Extended families would move from the backlands to the cities and back again with the drought cycles. Many died of thirst or hunger along the way. Often men would pursue work in the Amazon or move to southeastern Brazil, which was becoming the industrial center of the country, always with the intention of returning (Reesink 1981:43). Owners of the large swaths of cattle land in the sertão often lived in a county seat or state capital and hired local men to oversee their property, on which

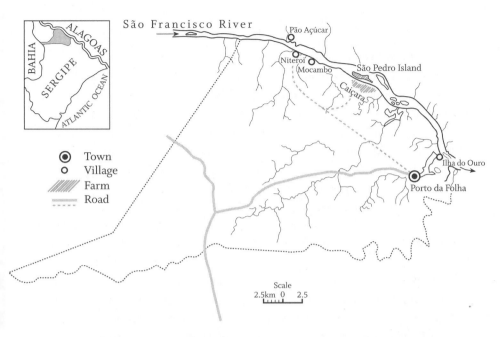

São Pedro Island and Mocambo. Adapted from Clarice Novaes da Mota, *Jurema's Children in the Forest of Spirits: Healing and Ritual among Two Brazilian Indigenous Groups* (London: Intermediate Technology Publications, 1997).

the sharecroppers lived. With cattle raising came rustlers, vendettas, and private forms of justice. In fact, some believe that the constitution of the Northeast as a separate region was an attempt to isolate an area felt to be out of control (Albuquerque 1999:71).

More common, however, is the belief that the Northeast as a region predates its designation as such. The invention of a regional history is often attributed to Gilberto Freyre, who popularized the view that the Northeast was born before the nation itself was constituted in 1822, when Brazil became independent from Portugal. The Northeast was portrayed by Freyre as the "cradle of Brazilian nationality and . . . the refuge of the country's soul and memories—under threat from the Europeanized modernism" of the South (Tribe 2001:23). Freyre and many others date the differentiation of the Northeast to the Dutch occupation of parts of it, including Sergipe (1637 to 1645), calling them "New Holland" (1630 to 1654). It is argued that this led to a regional consciousness that remained stronger than the eventual national one (Albuquerque 1999:75). Dutch influence continues to be part of the local mythology, with almost everyone claiming Dutch ancestry as a means of downplaying their southern European Portuguese and African descent.

The Northeast, and particularly the sertão, has held a special place in the Brazilian imaginary, with most people associating it with the universally renowned account by Euclides da Cunha of the state's destruction of Canudos in 1897, a messianic community in the sertão of Bahia, only 150 miles from the village of Mocambo.[3] Led by itinerant preacher Antônio Conselheiro, the town of Canudos resisted federal government troops for over a year before being wiped out by a large contingent of soldiers. Today, a monument nearby commemorates the community (itself inundated by a 1970s dam project) but not the federal troops. Films are made and festivals are held in honor of Canudos. Fascination with the Northeast continued through a body of twentieth-century literature and film, best represented by Graciliano Ramos, the author of *Vidas Secas* (Barren Lives).[4] It was reinforced by excitement and fear over the success of revolutionary peasant leagues in the late 1950s and early 1960s (Leeds 1964; Page 1972; Julião 1972). In addition to being synonymous with drought, the sertão has come to be seen as a place of dichotomies and contradictions: "God and Devil, tradition and modernity, sea and sertão, a hell of misery, hunger, drought, and prophecy of salvation" (Albuquerque 1999:121). In Ariano Suassuna's work, representative of popular visions of the sertão, it is portrayed as

> a sacred, mystical space that is reminiscent of a courteous and chivalrous society. Sertão of the prophets, pilgrims, horsemen, defenders of the honor of virgins, mortal duels. Sertão of flags, insignias, coats of arms, lances and masts, poor suits of armor made of leather. Sertão in which all are equal before God . . . [a place where there is both] hope and resignation to the most adverse conditions . . . a space and a people in search of mercy . . . a space that oscillates between God and the Devil. It is a card game whose rules have not been revealed to anyone. A world that exists in opposition to modern society, where all is mask, interest; all is bereft of eternal truths; all is artifice, lies, absurdity. Only religion and the Church . . . can ordain this world, give it meaning. (Albuquerque 1999:201)[5]

Inhabitants of the sertão, referred to as *sertanejos*, of mixed descent (indigenous, African, Portuguese, and Dutch), are noted for their individualism and skill on horseback. Some have even proposed that sertanejos are distinct ethnoracially because of their mixed heritage, their adaptation to drought conditions, their rustic lifestyle, and their practice of folk Catholic rituals (Cunha 1902; Souto Maior 1985). The vast majority of people living in the sertão are Catholic (the area under consideration in this book is over 95 percent Catholic). Their folk Catholicism embraces archaic beliefs based on Iberian practices dating to the fifteenth century, expressed through an apocalyptic outlook and an intense belief in saints. These features are distinct from the syncretic, African religious influence on the coast (F. M. S. Fernandes 1997), although some Afro-Brazilian cultural manifestations are incorporated into sertanejo life without explicit acknowledgment as such. For example, certain shamanistic and magical household practices, such as treating illness through enunciations by faith healers, have been associated with the African-descended religion Xangô (Brasileiro 1999).

Long penitential journeys to pilgrimage sites are still commonplace and when taken together with the periodic migration of families to cities to escape drought give a sense that sertanejos are constantly in motion. At the same time, most sertanejos feel they have an unbreakable connection to their hometowns and villages and return whenever they can from the farthest reaches of Brazil. When they cannot, they yearn to return—singing, writing, and telling stories about the sertão. This reinforces the commonly held view that sertanejos feel strong ties to their place of birth and hardscrabble existence. Literature about the sertão emphasizes its frontier character, providing a romantic sense of unremitting loyalty to place. It emphasizes that sertanejos have been living in these godforsaken areas for hundreds of years with practically no in-migration and out-migration only when absolutely necessary, always with the intention of returning to their rugged lives. The sertanejo ethos is most often associated with the yearning to return to the sertão, with its cactus, caatinga, and barren, rocky terrain. It is no wonder that land reform and rural unionization were the particular forms of social change embraced by revolutionaries, reformers, and the progressive wing of the Catholic Church beginning in the 1950s.

Often commented upon is the lack of planning by sertanejos, attributed to the generations of unpredictable onsets of drought, the timing and length of which are never known in advance (G. Ramos 1947). Long droughts are interspersed with just as unpredictable rainy seasons that wash away roads and make the desertlike environment appear green briefly—so ephemeral it is almost an optical illusion. As in Japan or Italy where people farm on the slopes of live volcanoes, sertanejos share a refusal to be too concerned with the possibility of disaster (Hirschman 1963:16). Drought and politics are inseparable, with each drought jerking the government into action, giving too little too late or instituting massive public works projects that benefit politicians and the oligarchical families who own the majority of the land.[6] This reinforces the "live in the moment" characterization of generations of sertanejos. True to the contradictory nature of life in the sertão, they are also considered a "subtle but stubbornly conservative" people (Pang 1974:347). Despite the cynicism of the press and politicians, who discuss the "industry of drought," romantic notions of independent, stubborn, sertanejos remain alive throughout Brazil and in its literature, films, music, and poetry (Arons 2004).[7]

The sertão is reserved in the Brazilian imagination as a space of nostalgia and yearning (*saudades*), as portrayed in films from the New Cinema years (1960s) through more recent internationally distributed films, such as *Central Station*. The regional music in the Northeast, different from the samba and bossa nova of Rio de Janeiro, has rhythms and accordion accompaniment reminiscent of Cajun music, and no event is complete without dancing *forró*. In addition to the belief in miracles performed by charismatic saintly priests, there is a strong history of banditry in the sertão. Bandits dating back at least to the early nineteenth century roamed the sertão until the 1940s. They were dangerous and arbitrary—tied to, yet preying upon, landowners and their cowhands simultaneously. Bandits avenged wrongs committed by police against their families. They escaped police and militias by crossing state lines, traveling over large expanses of the sertão and winning protection from, and instilling fear in, the powerful and powerless alike.

Mocambo and the surrounding area fully participated in the history of banditry. One of Latin America's most famous bandits, Lampião, spent much time there, befriended by some and terrorizing others. Lampião is often referred to as the Robin Hood of Brazil and is considered by many to have been a "social bandit" (Hobsbawm 1969; Joseph 1990). The oligarchical family, the Brittos, whose land was expropriated for the Xocó, aided Lampião (Chandler 1978:186). Most of the elderly people in Mocambo and on São Pedro Island have stories to tell about the "law" meted out by Lampião. The tenor of the telling depends on whether the teller was loyal or was suspected of revealing the bandit's whereabouts to the authorities. At least one marriage was saved under the threat that the husband had better be living with his young wife each time Lampião returned or he would be killed. I was told that the daughter of Lampião and Maria Bonita (female bandits were part of Lampião's band) was raised by a family from Mocambo. Lampião, Maria Bonita, and most of their band were captured and decapitated by police not far from Mocambo in 1938, an act of unmitigated violence both celebrated and mourned.

Their granddaughter, who has called for a reexamination of sertanejo banditry geared toward a sympathetic history, arranged to have the state government sponsor a memorial at the site where her grandparents were killed (Ferreira and Amaury 1999). The monument is a tourist attraction at which services are conducted on each anniversary of the capture. The lives of Lampião, Maria Bonita, and their band are celebrated by children in Sergipe and around the Northeast, who, during June saints' days festivities, dress up in their distinctive costumes with pride and affection.[8] Museum exhibits, even at shopping malls in the capital, trace the lives and histories of the bandits, and personal accounts have been published by both bandits and the police who pursued them (Gueiros 1956; Lira 1990; Souza 1997). Celebration and memories of terror reflect the ambivalent relationship that sertanejos have with law, police, and lawlessness.

The sertão is frontier land, vast and easy to disappear into, traditionally the preferred hideout for bandits. As such, it was also a refuge for slaves, free people of color, and city dwellers who wanted to gain some manner of independence from the structure and authorities of the cities and plantations, even if they had to achieve freedom while living in poverty. Alagoas, the state across the river from Sergipe, was the home of the largest and most famous quilombo in Brazilian history, termed by one historian an "African State in Brazil" (Kent 1965). The Palmares quilombo was celebrated by nineteenth-century writers and intellectuals and appropriated and publicized by Brazilian black movement activists in the 1970s and today occupies a place in the official history of Brazil. Since 1988, November 20 of each year is celebrated as Black Consciousness Day in honor of Zumbi, the last king of Palmares.

As the need for meat and leather increased in the eighteenth and early nineteenth centuries, there was a concerted effort to rid the region of the indigenous peoples who had populated the entire inland area of the Northeast since before the arrival of the Portuguese in 1500. Some indigenous people had been enslaved over the centuries, and Indian slavery was abolished in the 1830s. Portuguese and African people from the coast moved inland and mixed with the indigenous people who were being thrown off their land and incorporated into the general sertanejo population. As a place of refuge and freedom, as well as poverty and hardship, the sertão has even come to symbolize Brazil itself (N. T. Lima 1999).

It is important, however, to balance the romantic images of the sertão with the painful realities created by the concentration of land in the hands of a small number of oligarchical families.[9] Shortly after the colonization of Brazil in the sixteenth century, the Portuguese crown, exporting its own legal doctrine, granted *sesmarías* (the right to use large strips of land that stretched from the coast deep into the interior) to individuals who could make the land productive. They had only to contribute one-sixth of their produce to the crown. Sesmarías coexisted with larger political units, hereditary captaincies, granted to and governed by Portuguese noblemen. This was done so that the Portuguese crown could transfer the task and costs of colonization to private hands.[10] Following Brazilian independence in 1822 and the abolition of the sesmaría system, there ensued a period of violent conflict over land between those who claimed possession through the crown and *grileiros* (landgrabbers who used false documentation to obtain legal title) or squatters backed by armed bands. In 1850, the imperial government (Brazil was a monarchy from 1822 to 1889, when it became a republic) enacted the first land law, an attempt to regain control of land that had been distributed by the Portuguese crown before independence. It also declared that all land had to be purchased with money but left the demarcation of land in the hands of the owners and did not alter the system of adverse possession, which allowed those who physically possessed land for a legally determined period to claim ownership.

The 1850 land law, which on its surface was intended to regularize a confused situation, actually operated to allow large landowners to declare the titles asserted by small producers illegal. They then purchased the land redefined as public (Silva 1996). It also included all the land occupied by Indians, finishing off whatever claims northeastern indigenous peoples may have had to their lands. This forced some of the (by that time) largely assimilated Indians to gather around missions owned by the Church, such as the mission church on the island of São Pedro that became the Xocó community (B. G. Dantas 1991). As a result of the 1850 land law, *latifúndios* (large landed estates) that had been merely possessed or simply claimed were transformed into legally owned property, increasing the power of the oligarchical families over life in the rural interior.[11]

Over a hundred years later, and in a move eerily reminiscent of the nineteenth-century land law, the military regime (1964–1985), at its height of power, enacted the Indian Statute of 1973. The statute was intended to regulate a provision revising indigenous land rights that had been included in a 1969 constitutional amendment,[12] put into place by the military president in connection with the most repressive legislation of the regime, Institutional Act Number 5 (AI-5) (Gomes 2000:83), to be discussed later. From the perspective of Amazonian tribes, the most significant provisions were those requiring delimitation of indigenous lands and permitting relocation if national development required it.[13]

Why did the military government at the height of its most repressive period take an interest in issuing laws and policies that gave indigenous people *more* rights than they had previously enjoyed? In fact, indigenous land rights took shape only after the military began a concerted expansion into the interior Amazon region. As the government was creating administrative means for defining indigenous areas, nonindigenous settlers were invading their territory (Schwartzman, Araújo, and Pankararú 1996). The military was, therefore, motivated by a perceived need to occupy the Amazon with Brazilians for fear that it would be overrun by foreigners (Albó 1994). The best way to rationally order Amazon development, they felt, was to remove Indians from the "path of progress" and to place them in specified, legally demarcated territories. Since property relations in that region were murky, the demarcation of indigenous land would also serve the purpose of creating marketable title (Schwartzman, Araújo, and Pankararú 1996:37, 38).[14]

As pointed out by historian Seth Garfield, the implementation of the new law operated as a double-edged sword. At the same time that economic development and private investors were destroying indigenous communities in the Amazon, streamlined demarcation, as championed by the military, "broke political ground for the Indians to stake their claims" (Garfield 2000:546). Perhaps more important is that the military's policy was an attempt to consolidate and centralize federal power vis-à-vis regional and state elites in traditionally indigenous regions, such as Amazônia Legal (nine states in the Amazon River Basin making up over 60 percent of Brazilian national territory), historically considered "vulnerable to foreign invasion and communist infiltration" (Garfield 2000:542).

Although the Northeast does not fall within Garfield's analysis, since it is not particularly vulnerable to foreign invasion and has a stable population with very little immigration and a declining economy, the 1969 Constitution and the 1973 Indian Statute inadvertently and paradoxically created opportunities for indigenous identity expansion. The law operated to increase indigenous lands in the Northeast, but in a very different manner and using different provisions from those used in the Amazon.[15] The next chapter analyzes how the Indian Statute, over time and in the period of redemocratization, came to be used to justify the recognition of newly (re)constituted tribes in the Northeast. Whereas the military was interested in consolidating federal power in the Amazon, paradoxically, in the Northeast the government found itself supporting a nationalist project of rooting Brazilian heritage in its indigenous history. To quote Brazilian anthropologist Alcida Ramos (1998:166):

> In this rather subliminal fashion, reminiscent of Proust's involuntary memories, the Indian question works as a magnifying glass under which the nation's fabric shows its knots, broken lines, and convoluted texture, the result of the uneven warp and weft of the historical process of trying to weave odd threads together in a single social design.

Discovering and reconstituting tribes in the Northeast has contributed to consolidating Brazil as an indigenous nation, continuing the tradition of indigenism in a new form.

PLACING MOCAMBO AND SÃO PEDRO ISLAND
IN THE SERTANEJO LANDSCAPE

Keeping in mind the contradictions inherent in the history and perception of the sertão, I would like to place the two communities that are the subject of this book into the context of the sertanejo historical and geographical landscape. Both Mocambo and São Pedro Island are located in the largest county (*município*) in the heart of the Sergipe sertão, Porto da Folha.[16] The two villages sit on the banks of the São Francisco, the longest river in Brazil, sometimes called the Brazilian Nile because of its 1,800-mile length and its placement in the midst of a desertlike environment. There are approximately 300 people who are counted as Xocó, almost all of whom live on São Pedro Island or have a home there. Since 1991, the Xocó have controlled a large piece of land on the mainland as well, known as Caiçara, much of which had been the property of the Brittos before being expropriated for the Xocó. Mocambo is home to about 500 people, half of whom are children.

If a visitor has informed one of the Xocó, there might be a boat waiting at a dock near Mocambo. If not, a flat-bottomed boat with a covered passenger compartment containing two facing rows of benches leaves a few times every day from this dock to a small city in Alagoas on the other side of the river, Pão de Açucar. Once on the other side, again there is a wait for the boat that transports teachers and students back across the river. The river trip can take most of an afternoon. Another way to reach the Xocó on São Pedro Island is to drive along a narrow pathway through the brush for almost an hour,

Mocambo houses (photograph by the author)

park the car, and then ford a small river, which may be low enough to wade through or may be higher, then requiring donkey or canoe transportation.

Mocambo itself is composed of two unpaved, dusty (or muddy) streets that run parallel to the river, each flanked by two rows of attached houses with small, pastel facades facing the street and long, narrow interiors with backyards where women wash dishes and chickens peck at the ground. Many of these backyard areas are also used to grow a few vegetables when the weather cooperates. For many of the hundred Mocambo families, until late 2000, houses did not have bathroom facilities, so the far area of the backyard would be used as a toilet. For those with bathroom fixtures, because there was no running water, each day family members would carry vessels on their heads from the river up the steep embankment to the village. The river water would also be used for drinking, which led to stomach disorders. Having only received electricity in mid-1997, some of Mocambo's houses had only recently acquired televisions when I first visited.[17] By 2004, a few houses had small pumps that forced water up from the river over a bathroom wall to serve as a shower, and by 2008, the government had installed running water in all the houses as a result of its new dedication to improving conditions for quilombos.

At the end of the lower street, closer to the river, lies the church and a

Houses on São Pedro Island (photograph by the author)

nearby gathering spot that served as a bar until the federal government bulldozed it in 2004 as part of the dispute over the quilombo movement (see chapters 3 and 4).[18] The daily routine I became familiar with included women sweeping the dirt in front of their houses each morning. Many of them would then spend the day tending the collective garden on the riverbank, caring for children, feeding their families, and cleaning dishes and clothes in the river. The men who could find work on local farms would leave in the early morning for the fields. Before leaving for the day, however, a number of men would go to the village corral to milk the half dozen cows owned by individuals in Mocambo. Those who did not have work and the elderly would spend their days sharing stories and gossiping. Once the quilombo association was granted land in 2000, many of the men would spend most mornings clearing brush and then planting and harvesting beans a few kilometers from the village.

The Xocó community on São Pedro Island is smaller and laid out a bit differently from Mocambo. The fifty houses, unattached to each other, are organized around a large central space, with grass when there is no drought, which serves as a meeting area and soccer field. At one end of this plaza is the large mission church and the ruins of a monastery, behind which lies the cemetery. The Xocó families also grow vegetables on the riverfront, but because of services they receive from the federal government as Indians, they sometimes have some basic forms of irrigation. When the island received electricity, after Mocambo, the government installed a large water pump and tower in the center of the plaza, which, when it functioned, provided running water to some of the houses (by 2008 all the homes had running water). The houses themselves varied, from ones that were relatively well-appointed with bathroom facilities to mud and stick two-room houses, as poor as can be imagined.

The background of the Mocambo and Xocó villagers is much the same as for the majority of sertanejos. They survived for generations as cowhands, sharecroppers, and day laborers, planting and harvesting cotton and rice, both of which are no longer produced in the area. Sertanejos generally live in small settlements (no more than 50 to 100 two-to-four-room houses) or in scattered outlying dwellings, sometimes miles apart. The people in the sertão are overwhelmingly Catholic, and these villages are no exception. Local sertanejo culture is entwined with folk Catholic practices, such as praying over people who are ill, using local plants to treat ailments, predawn processions dedicated to patron saints, passion plays, festivals, and a complex system of god-parentage. Villages, including Mocambo, throughout the sertão have saints days, with their own processions going up and down the one or two dirt streets carrying a statue of the village's patron saint, singing hymns, and stopping to kneel and pray. There are typical sertanejo houses, church designs are modeled on medieval Portuguese rural churches, and artisanal ceramics, rope, fishing net, and carved wood are produced.

At the center of each of these communities is a large church building. For the Xocó, the church is the seventeenth-century baroque structure of the original Capuchin Franciscan mission. The last time I visited in 2008, it still had a hole in the roof and was in sore need of restoration despite its status as a state historical monument.[19] The church in Mocambo was built in the 1950s—before then people in Mocambo buried their dead in the cemetery on São Pedro Island. Rural churches, including these two, are cared for by religious lay people who keep the keys, clean the church and altar, and lead the services in place of the priest who comes about once a month to perform baptisms, weddings, and the Mass to commemorate the seventh day after a death.

Far from the metropolitan areas of Brazil, where Afro-Brazilian identity is becoming an important mode of organizing against discrimination and where issues of race and color are being debated, which is related to recent changes in the law and the strengthening of the black movement (Telles 2004), people in the sertão have retained the ideology of mixture as their op-

Xocó Indian children (photograph by the author)

erative assumption about phenotype. The residents of Mocambo are mostly dark skinned, some with apparent traces of indigenous ancestry (what the inhabitants call "*traços*") and some lighter skinned, with typically sertanejo features (ruddy skin, light eyes, and straight hair streaked with blond). Skin color and facial features are discussed and used descriptively but do not serve as the basis of inclusion in or exclusion from social life. The Xocó who live on São Pedro Island are indistinguishable from Mocambo residents in appearance — although some say they are "blacker" in hue and facial features than their Mocambo neighbors and relatives. Comments such as these are made to emphasize the connections and similarities between the two communities but are also tinged with resentment and skepticism, hinting that the people now living on São Pedro Island were once "just blacks" like their cousins in Mocambo and had somehow pulled the wool over the eyes of the government.

Statements such as these reveal the contradictory nature of perceptions of race and color in Brazil, where there is often a denial of racial difference but at the same time a prevailing hegemonic assumption that blacks are inferior. On the part of the Xocó, from the earliest days of their struggle for recognition, many of them differentiated themselves from people in the surrounding area to improve their chances of success. Such discourse of difference, however, was always taken with a grain of salt. In the same conversation, members of the Xocó tribe might insist on their distinction as Indians and then go on to talk about their relatives in Mocambo. There are a few light-skinned Xocó who have the recognizably sertanejo wind-beaten faces with straight blond-streaked hair, although they are considered Indians and as such have held leadership roles and are not differentiated from the others.

LIBERATION THEOLOGY AND ITS WORK IN THE SERTÃO

The Brazilian Catholic Church and its engagement with liberation theology is a key component to understanding how knowledge of the laws on Indians and quilombos came to São Pedro Island and Mocambo over the course of two decades beginning in 1973. The development of liberation theology as a social movement in Latin America is generally attributed to a "convergence of changes within and without the Church in the late 1950s," a "complex evolution of links between religious and political cultures, in a context of modernization and intense social and political conflict" (Löwy 1996:40, 2). Internally, new theological currents inspired by European experiences during World War II culminated in the pontificate of John XXIII (1958–63) and the Second Vatican Council (1962–65), which began to systematize new concerns with inequalities and social justice that were already afoot.

These Church concerns coincided with events in Latin America that began with intensive industrialization and the concomitant dependency on the Northern Hemisphere during the 1950s (Frank 1967). Reaching a head with the Cuban Revolution in 1959, social struggles ignited in the rest of Latin America. These were some of the conditions that made possible the "*radicalization* of Latin American Catholic culture" (Löwy 1996:41) and that led to liberation theology, described by Phillip Berryman (1987:6) as "one manifestation of a worldwide movement for emancipation." Berryman defined liberation theology as "an interpretation of Christian faith out of the suffering, struggle, and hope of the poor"; "a critique of society and the ideologies sustaining it"; and "a critique of the activity of the church and of Christians from the angle of the poor" (1987:6).

Liberation theology teaches that "people do not simply happen to be poor; their poverty is largely a product of the way society is organized. . . . It is [therefore] a critique of economic structures that enable some Latin Americans to jet to Miami or London to shop, while most of their fellow citizens do not have safe drinking water" (Berryman 1987:5). Of all the countries in Latin America, including Peru, from which the first treatise on liberation theology emanated (Gutierrez 1971), Brazil is most associated with

the doctrine. Brazil's was "the only Church on the continent where liberation theology and its pastoral followers . . . won a decisive influence" (Löwy
1996:81). That influence grew rapidly in opposition to the military dictatorship, beginning in 1968 when the generals cracked down on the Church's
sympathetic stance toward the poor. As exemplified by the story of the Xocó,
liberation theology played a critical role in the Church's changing attitudes
toward land struggles and indigenous rights and served as the catalyzing
force behind the creative use of law to advance those goals.

The stories of identity transformation told in the chapters that follow began
in the early 1970s, as both religious and secular attitudes and policies toward
indigenous people in Latin America and elsewhere were changing. Until the
last quarter of the twentieth century, the primary goal of nation-states was to
facilitate the assimilation of their indigenous populations into the dominant
society, often under the guise of modernization. In Latin America, for centuries prior to the establishment of independent states, the Catholic Church
had devoted itself to missionizing and "cleansing" indigenous peoples of
their institutions, cultural practices, and identities (J. W. Warren 2001:146).
In Brazil, the process of assimilation through the taking of indigenous land
and incorporating Indians into the labor force transformed many of them
into *caboclos*, a term that "originally meant 'half-breed,' 'mestizo,' the child
of an Indian with a white or a black" (Gomes 2000:54).[20] Many indigenous
peoples have disappeared into the caboclo category through the constant
"process of invasion of their lands, economic coercion, epidemics, mixed
marriages, and forced migrations" (Gomes 2000:55).

In the early 1970s, indigenous people throughout the Western Hemisphere began forming organizations to insist on rights to land, religious freedom, and freedom from discrimination. Liberal democracy, with its focus on
procedural rights that guarantee "fairness" but fail to address social and economic inequality, was increasingly being criticized. Challenges came from
the U.S. civil rights, women's, and antiwar movements, and examples were
being set by successful national liberation movements in the Third World.[21]
One of these challenges came from people who began to emphasize indigenous ancestry and rights to land pursuant to treaties. Native American activist and scholar Vine Deloria published *Custer Died for Your Sins: An Indian
Manifesto* in 1969, and Dee Brown's *Bury My Heart at Wounded Knee* was first
published in 1970. The landmark event in North America was the seventy-
day occupation of the Pine Ridge Reservation town of Wounded Knee by
American Indian Movement activists. In addition to demands for recognition, land, and civil rights, these activists rediscovered indigenous religious

ceremonies and incorporated them into their political activities. Since the 1970s, "indigenous groups and their advocates have sought to challenge the continuing dominance in international legal discourse of the doctrine of discovery and its conception of diminished indigenous rights and status" (R. A. Williams 1990: 676). Therefore, the movement became internationalized very rapidly, leading to the establishment of a United Nations Working Group on Indigenous Populations in 1982 (culminating in 2007 with the adoption by the General Assembly of the Declaration on the Rights of Indigenous Peoples) and a redefinition of indigenous peoples by the International Labor Organization's Convention 169 in 1989. That definition, which focuses on self-identification, was designed to remove assimilationist assumptions prevalent in earlier documents (Hodgson 2002:1038).

In Latin America, the spark for the formation of indigenous rights movements came from a combination of the liberalizing Catholic Church, anthropologists, and the formation of grassroots associations among large, organized groups such as the Shuar in Ecuador in response to governmental development policies and private enterprise raids on their territories (Brysk 2000). Indigenous people began organizing to counter the external pressures on their small-scale agricultural ways of life. They called for self-determination, and their demands reached a culminating moment in 1975 in Canada with the first meeting of the World Council of Indigenous Peoples. In Australia, an "Aboriginal Embassy" was established in a tent in front of the parliament building for six months in 1972, and the following year the government established an Aboriginal Land Rights Commission (Bodley 1999:160).

The 1971 Barbados Symposium on Inter-Ethnic conflict in South America is often cited as an even earlier decisive moment when a group of "dissident anthropologists . . . pledged to promote indigenous self-determination and enter politics to save endangered culture" (Brysk 2000:18). Signatories of the declaration included anthropologists from Latin America (including Brazil), Switzerland, and the United States. Their document redefined the indigenous issue in Latin America by criticizing the policies of the governments and the missionary stance of the Catholic Church (Montero 1996:111; Bodley 1999:206–7). These trends contributed to the establishment of international indigenous rights advocacy organizations, such as Cultural Survival, which was founded in 1975 by an anthropologist of the Amazon, David Maybury-Lewis. Roots of "the indigenous peoples' movement are commonly located in the post–World War II elaboration of an international human-rights apparatus," in which revelations about the Holocaust sensitized "the world to issues of racial discrimination" (Sylvain 2005:356). Other factors include decolonization of Third World nations, newly educated indigenous leadership, and the expansion of a "global NGO community" (Niezen 2003). In Brazil, equivalent organizations came into existence, such as the Pro-Indian Commission. The primary demand of indigenous rights advocates in Brazil has been for the demarcation and protection of indigenous reserves. This has reinforced the ongoing connection between struggles for land reform and indigenous rights.

Most relevant to the stories in this book is the role of the Catholic Church in instigating, sustaining, and supporting these struggles. From the centuries-old mission church on São Pedro Island, which came to represent an indigenous past, to the reintroduction of an indigenous past to local residents by a priest and a bishop, the Catholic Church was the instigating force. The post–World War II Church found itself with a majority of its faithful outside Europe, from different cultural milieus and backgrounds. Beginning in the 1950s, the Church was also feeling the effects of decolonization on an international scale and found itself moving away from being a "European church" to becoming a "world church" (Montero 1996:108–109). This posed the problem of constructing a fruitful relationship between the universality of the Church and the diversity of the peoples it was evangelizing. In the immediate postwar period in Brazil, the Church was trying to consolidate a relationship with the state that had been problematic since the nineteenth century and in the 1950s endorsed the government's development strategy (Löwy 1996:61).[22]

In 1952, Dom Hélder Câmara, who was in later years the Catholic Church leader most associated with liberation theology in the Brazilian hierarchy, helped found the National Conference of Brazilian Bishops (CNBB), which came to occupy a central position in the Church.[23] Until the 1964 military coup, the CNBB was run by a group of mostly northeastern bishops dedicated to land reform and to moving the whole Church to a progressive sociopolitical position. It was helped along by a democratic government that was open to structural change in society, supporting new rural trade unions, and initiating basic education programs (Bruneau 1982:51–52). However, Church leadership was by no means monolithic, and even with progressive elements in positions of authority there were many men in its leadership who did not support those views and who looked for opportunities to reduce the influence of the Left in the Church.

A close friend and colleague of Dom Hélder Câmara in Rio de Janeiro, Dom José Vicente Távora, was assigned to the archbishopric of Aracaju,

Sergipe, in 1960. Dom Távora had founded the Young Catholic Workers movement in 1948 and devoted the rest of his life to promoting the cause of workers, the poor, and the dispossessed. Ironically, Dom Távora's left-leaning political activities were largely responsible for the decision to send him to the smallest state in the poorest region of the country, presumably hoping it would reduce his influence. However, in 1960 upon his arrival in Sergipe, Dom Távora immediately founded the Base Education Movement (MEB) with federal financial support and served as its national leader (Piletti and Praxedes 1997:275; see also De Kadt 1970). The MEB was designed to produce workers and peasants who were literate, both literally and politically.[24] In that same year, Dom José Brandão de Castro arrived in the riverside city of Propriá in Sergipe to become the first bishop of a newly created diocese. The jurisdiction of the Propriá diocese included the northern half of the state along the entire length of the lower São Francisco River extending from its mouth to the Paulo Afonso falls, the site of a massive hydroelectric dam and water flow control turbines that were put on line incrementally over two decades, displacing a number of villages.

Shortly after the arrival in Sergipe of these two bishops, the Second Vatican Council convened, laying the groundwork for what would become in the early 1970s the Church's commitment to social change—and particularly its interest in correcting the historical wrongs it had perpetrated against indigenous peoples. However, during the Vatican II meetings, which had the participation of 130 Brazilian bishops, led by Hélder Câmara, the Brazilian military overthrew the democratically elected government, and the rest of the CNBB jumped on the conservative bandwagon. After twelve years of progressive leadership, a conservative slate came to power in the CNBB a few months after the coup in 1964 and dismantled the Catholic youth movement and land reform organizations in the Northeast, sending progressive bishops and priests to hinterland posts away from the centers of power (Mainwaring 1986:82). Dom Hélder Câmara was replaced as secretary general of the CNBB and, like Dom Távora, was sent to a post in the Northeast. As late as 1968, after the Episcopal Conference at Medellín, Colombia (considered the official founding moment of liberation theology), which was attended by progressive Brazilian bishops and lay leaders, the CNBB was still pursuing a conservative path and refused to offer criticism of the military government.[25]

Around the time of the Medellín conference, events were unfolding in the Amazon region, where the majority of indigenous peoples lived. These events would begin to turn the Church toward the more antimilitary stance it would take in the 1970s. Church leaders in the Amazon began reacting to the government's policies supporting the expansion of agribusiness and expulsion of peasants and Indians from the land, essentially resettling the frontier. This led to violent conflict throughout the region. Important pastoral meetings in the Amazon region were held to discuss solutions to the expulsions of indigenous people from their land. At this critical moment, the government released the twenty-volume Figueiredo Report on corruption, landgrabs, and massacres committed by the Indigenous Protection Service (SPI), which led to that body's dissolution and the creation of the National Indigenous Foundation (FUNAI). In 1968, as well, twenty-six priests from the northern region of the CNBB called on the Church to defend the poor and serve the interests of the Indians rather than imposing the Church's values on them (Mainwaring 1986:86). This was the beginning of the Brazilian Church's shift toward liberation theology, with bishops of the Amazon region being the first to urge their brethren in the CNBB to criticize government policies. As these criticisms took hold and became public, the military government itself was instituting its most repressive period of rule, culminating in a full denunciation by the bishops of the government's development policies and a call for widespread land redistribution.

In 1970, the military's dedication to rooting out subversion, exemplified by the rise to power of the most radically right wing of Brazil's military presidents, reached the Catholic Church leadership. Conflict between the Church and the government began in earnest when security agents invaded Church houses in Rio de Janeiro. In addition to jailing and torturing militant priests and activists, security forces mistreated the provincial head of the Jesuit order and president of Rio de Janeiro's Catholic university. They also detained the secretary general of the CNBB. Brazil's cardinals and Pope Paul VI began openly to condemn and protest the violence of the regime (Serbin 2000:2). For the Church in Brazil, 1971 was a key year (Montero 1996:110). All four regional bishops' groups from the Amazon issued strong denunciations of the military regime's policies, including criticisms of torture, repression of peasants trying to protect their land, and the invasion and dispossession of indigenous groups. Following up on the first indigenist pastoral meeting in 1968 and research on the social conditions of Indians in 1969, bishops in the Amazon region issued a statement in November 1971: "We see in the entire country the invasion and violent dispossession of Indian lands. Their human rights are practically not recognized, bringing them to the brink of cultural and biological death, as has already happened to many Brazilian tribes."[26] This was the first time that a nonassimilationist approach was considered and asserted by the Brazilian Church.[27] Centralization of Church decisions in the CNBB was decisive in renovating missionary philosophy and pastoral work among the poor and indigenous peoples (Montero 1996:111). It is not coincidental that the Indigenist Missionary Council (CIMI) was created the following year.

Development policy, in the opinion of the bishops, had led to violence by entrepreneurs, terrible living conditions, and a widespread practice of debt peonage (Mainwaring 1986:87). The establishment of CIMI was the result of rapidly radicalizing bishops in the Amazon and the Northeast. The bishops were meeting on a regular basis and issuing ever-more militant episcopal statements, breaking with government development policies, calling for widespread land distribution, and even questioning capitalism itself—this during the moment often referred to as the "Brazilian economic miracle" (Mainwaring 1986:87). As mentioned earlier, in 1971, a group of well-respected anthropologists from around the world, including Darcy Ribeiro, the well-known Brazilian anthropologist and policymaker, met in Barbados and issued a declaration critical of Latin American states' indigenous policies, religious missions, and anthropological work among Indians. The Barbados Declaration called for a "suspension of all missionary activity."

This provoked a response from the Church through an ecumenical meeting in March 1972 with representatives of nine countries, in which those representatives promised to open space for a dialogue and for participation of Indians in the missions, with the goal of rethinking its long-standing "civilizing" mission. "Stung by the condemnation of severe old-style missionaries in the 1971 Barbados Declaration," the CNBB established CIMI in 1972 and at the same time, in an incipient discourse connecting anthropology and the Church, "issued revolutionary new guidelines for the missionaries dealing with Indians" (Hemming 2003:328). "Henceforth, such priests must receive anthropological training before going into the field. They must respect native cultures. Far from being ridiculed or suppressed, indigenous beliefs should be respected and every manifestation of spirituality should be encouraged" (Hemming 2003:328).[28] A month later, in April 1972, a group of twenty-five Brazilian missionaries gathered at the suggestion of Ivo Lorscheiter, secretary general of the CNBB, to discuss a new law that was to become the Indian Statute of 1973. This was the birth of CIMI, which is still active today.[29]

However, CIMI was not just a political expression of the bishops' interest in the subaltern classes. It can also be seen as the implementation of a longer-standing theological commitment of the Catholic Church to a precapitalist, communal sensibility. As elements in the leadership of the Church experienced intensifying state repression, they began to find solace in older ways of imagining property and attendant social relations. There was increasing interest in land reform, as well as a rapid deployment of resources in favor of restitution to indigenous peoples for the wrongs perpetrated by the Church since the "discovery" of Brazil in 1500. Moreover, increased valorization of a communal ethos in relation to land occupation had much to do with the traditional ways of life associated with the Church, many of whose leaders, themselves from rural or peasant families, were interested in recuperating the peasant tradition that had served as the basis of Church doctrine (Martins 1985:125).

The Church's commitment to advancing the cause of indigenous peoples, therefore, went beyond an intention to redeem the Church's behavior toward their ancestors. Key to obtaining agreement from conservative bishops to pursue the new indigenous support strategy must have been, in part, the Church's need and desire to missionize. Undoubtedly, the project of missionizing in the late twentieth century required even more flexibility than earlier. Although the Church had always been known for its willingness to accept popular and syncretic forms of folk Catholicism, it now became interested in reviving indigenous religious practices. Maintaining the flock, increasing its numbers worldwide, identifying new priests and nuns, and bringing into the fold new generations were all essential to the Church's survival. Even the name of the Church entity, CIMI, which includes the word "missionary," reflected one of the purposes of its dedication to indigenous communities and their rights. The character of that missionizing remains a topic of much discussion in Church literature, ranging from "the paradigm of inculturation" to "Indian Theology" and "religious pluralism."

Another consideration that may have led to Church leaders' consensus on the indigenous question was the intensified repression by the military government against bishops, priests, nuns, and religious lay workers, as mentioned earlier, beginning in 1970 and eventually leading to the most radical pronouncements made by a Church apparatus—statements issued by the Amazon and Northeast region bishops in 1973 (Löwy 1996; Mainwaring 1986; Martins 1985; Serbin 2000).[30] The crackdown on civil society occurred after the president, General Costa e Silva, issued the notorious repressive measure, AI-5, on December 13, 1968, which, as noted earlier, marked the beginning of the most repressive period of the regime. The Archdiocese of São Paulo, in its report on torture in Brazil, described AI-5 as "barefaced dictatorship." The national Congress, six state legislative assemblies, and dozens of city councils were disbanded. Sixty-nine members of Congress were removed from office (Dassin 1986:52). All of this taken together meant that "the Church lost its invulnerability and became subject to attack" (Mainwaring 1986:102).

Although government repression forced other organizations into retreat, ironically it acted as a catalyst for change within the Church. "Even conservative bishops perceived attempts to neutralize the progressive clergy as an illegitimate intrusion" (Mainwaring 1986:102). Conservative bishops may have disagreed with the political perspectives of their progressive brothers, but they banded together to resist interference with the Church's work, so that, in an unusual twist, repression served to strengthen the position of the progressive elements within the Church. In the scheme of things, supporting poor, dispossessed, and numerically limited Indians was not as radical a move as some of the other aspects of the progressive bishops' program, which were eventually reflected in the overtly anticapitalist statements issued in 1973 as liberation theology hit its stride.[31]

During the most repressive years of military rule, the Catholic Church became the primary and most effective proponent of the powerless on two fronts: the defense of indigenous populations and the struggle for land reform. As the Church's actions on behalf of indigenous peoples advanced, the progressive bishops were advocating for land reform more every year. This led to the establishment in 1975 of the Pastoral Land Commission (CPT), still active in the twenty-first century. In fact, the better-known one-million-member Landless Rural Workers' Movement (MST) originated with militants of the CPT in the early 1980s (B. M. Fernandes 2000:47). During the 1970s, land reform and indigenous struggles were often intertwined. In 1975, a thirty-nine-page mimeographed document was produced as the result of a series of meetings with indigenous leaders and trade union federations: "A Single Outcry of Indians and Peasants: The Land for Those Who Work It."

On the local Sergipe scene, when Dom Távora died in 1970, he was eulogized as "the pastor of the workers" (J. I. C. Dantas 1997:149). Within the next few years, Dom José Brandão picked up the gauntlet in the Propriá diocese and became a renowned champion for land reform in Sergipe and beyond. His testimony at inquests about rural violence gained national attention, and he obtained the mantel of "red bishop." Dom José Brandão decided to aid rural workers who had lived for generations on large land holdings of the local oligarchy under constant threat of expulsion. This threat came to a head in the 1970s when federal development policy became a reality in the São Francisco valley and particularly in his diocese. The development company of the São Francisco valley, CODEVASF, began instituting the irrigation phase of a development plan that was based on the need for hydroelectric power in the Northeast (Hirschman 1963). When the CODEVASF project was first put into practice, Dom José Brandão still had a cordial relationship with the leaders of the local landowners and political bosses, although throughout his life he had expressed a propensity for protecting his poor parishioners.[32]

At first it seemed that CODEVASF, with its talk of land reform and irrigation projects, was embarking on a path that would alleviate suffering. However, before long it became obvious to Dom José Brandão that not only was the government expelling peasants from the land, but that the reconfiguration of property rights would make the land more valuable to the companies who would become the ultimate owners. Proper delineation of boundaries would reduce legal ambiguity about property ownership and clarify who, in fact, were "mere squatters," albeit for generations. Dom José Brandão often told the story of his decision to stop supporting CODEVASF's expropriation and redistribution of land when he saw the dispossessed workers living in the most inhumane conditions. Dom José considered this a period of his own conversion to the defense of the *homem do campo* (man of the field) and his need for land (Bernardi 1984). The notion of the bishop being "converted" by rural workers is directly related to liberation theology, which describes itself, as outlined above, as "an interpretation of Christian faith out of the suffering, struggle, and hope of the poor" (Berryman 1987:6). An explanation for the development of liberation theology given by sociologists linked to the Christian Left was that the Church changed because the "people" took over the institution. Similar conversion stories can be found in other Latin American countries (Speed and Reyes 2001:71).

This was a bottom-up explanation that is not satisfactory in historical hindsight (Löwy 1996:40), but one to which Dom José Brandão would have been amenable. A more official acceptance within the Church of liberation theology was important to progressive bishops such as Dom José Brandão. He was hoping to achieve this acceptance through the discourse about his own "conversion" by his flock at the same time that he was reading the defining work on liberation theology, just published in Portuguese (Gutierrez 1975). However, it seems clear that when Dom José Brandão brought the priest who would be the catalyzing force behind the Xocó movement to Sergipe in 1970 from Dom Hélder Câmara's seminary, it revealed Dom José's sympathy for liberation theology practice well before his professed conversion to liberationist doctrine.

During this period, Dom José Brandão also began reading and taking notes from a three-volume study of the São Francisco valley, *O Homem no Vale do São Francisco*, by U.S. anthropologist Donald Pierson. In the 1940s Pierson had been commissioned by a development agency concerned with hydroelectric power projects to conduct a study of communities along the entire length of the river. Dozens of researchers collected data and conducted interviews during the 1950s. In 1959, Pierson submitted the manuscript to the Brazilian government, although it was not published until 1972, just in time for Dom José to use it as one of his reference works to learn about the history of his diocese. Dom José Brandão was particularly interested in the presence of indigenous people in the area of São Pedro Island, where he knew there was an old mission church. He took extensive verbatim notes from the Pierson volumes identifying every entry on the possible historical presence of indigenous groups along the banks of the São Francisco. This, together with the new Indian Statute of 1973, ironically enacted by the military regime, helped him mount a defense of the people who later occupied São Pedro Island and who were eventually recognized as Xocó Indians. Just as the "People's Church created an identity within the framework of liberation theology that also drew on [the] legal definition of rural worker" (Houtzager 2001:14), in the sertão of Sergipe in the early 1970s it helped create the identity of Xocó Indians that drew on the definition of "Indian" in the Indian Statute of 1973.

Implementing its decision to support indigenous struggles in the Amazon, the Church helped Indians organize cross-tribal federations and resist landgrabs and mistreatment. In the Northeast, the Church found itself encouraging the reconstitution of indigenous tribes that had been lost to history through Church practices once dedicated to suppressing expressions of indigenous culture and religion. Liberation theology doctrine held that the colonial Church had conspired with local elites to create a class of peasants to work on Church property associated with the missions. As further discussed in the next chapter, this perspective survived the Church's shift to the right in the 1980s. In Sergipe, Dom José Brandão was involved in the Church's pursuit, and the priest he brought, Frei Enoque Salvador de Melo, who began visiting the peasants in 1972, later recognized as the Xocó tribe, confirmed this stance. In an interview over twenty years later, Frei Enoque explained that the fault for the loss of indigenous identity lay with the Church. He explained that the "Italian Capuchin priests thought the dances of the Indians were expressions of the devil. . . . The Church was the most guilty for their loss of identity" (Melo interview 1998). With the help of anthropologists, Church activists and NGOs engaged in a veritable campaign to discover, reestablish, and lobby for recognition of Indian tribes in the Northeast, of which the Xocó recognition was the first.

2

We Are Indians Even If Our Faces Aren't Painted

An explosive conjunction of events led a small group of sharecroppers living on the land of their politically powerful patrons to take extreme action to declare themselves Indians. This action resulted in a radical change in their self-representation, self-experience, and cohesiveness. It also eventually provided them with land in the form of an indigenous reserve. The Xocó were the first of over forty new tribes in the Northeast to be recognized over the following two decades. In addition to the promise of land and government services, the Brazilian national myth of the Indian as pure, at one with nature and the land, survivors in the face of adversity (A. C. Ramos 1991) was a powerful draw and counterbalance to the negative stereotypes of Indians as dirty, lazy, and "uncivilized." For tribes recognized before the 1988 Constitution, such as the Xocó, there was also a loss of full citizenship rights, not unlike in the nineteenth-century United States, where Indians were "offered full civic rights" only if "they abandoned their self-governance and distanced themselves from people of African descent" (Gross 2007:470).[1] As the assimilationist model of Indian-Brazilian relations, known as "indigenism" (A. C. Ramos 1998), began to fade in the late 1960s, a new form of indigenism emerged that supported the protection of fragile, subsistence-based peoples while reinforcing the image of the Indian as an innocent-savant who lives an idyllic communal life and understands and protects the environment (Conklin 2002; Kuper 2005). This chapter addresses the puzzle of why a group of people would choose to trade full citizenship rights for the legal status of "Indian."

To see how the lives and self-image of the people who became the present-day Xocó Indians were transformed, this chapter tells an integrated history that includes all the actors, including landowners, church leaders, and activists. As such, it shows how the dramatic history of this community, far from the metropolis, emerged from a marriage of local activism and interaction with outsiders. Illustrating the operation of governmentality critical to the transformation of ethnoracial identity, this chapter also explains the role of anthropologists who proposed, and succeeded at, convincing government officials that social constructions of Indianness were sufficient for legal recognition. As such, it connects the production of knowledge by a priest fresh from a liberation theology seminary, his typically sertanejo flock, and scholars conducting historical research, to the early moments of realization that a struggle for land could become a search for identity. The priest, Frei Enoque, set into motion the revising and retelling of old stories of oppression and struggle, which, as this chapter reveals, lubricated the transition to Indian identity. Those stories drew upon historical narratives that quickly became intertwined with social solidarity. A goal of this chapter, therefore, is to tell those stories, both because we need to know them to be able to see how they have been revised and because they are now taught as history to new generations of Xocó Indians. I use my version of the history, based on archival research, legal documents, and interviews, to help us understand how these people chose the particular mode of struggle and survival they did.

Finally, through the Indian Statute of 1973, which provides an illustration of postlegislative negotiation as it serves the process of legalizing identity, this chapter analyzes how the law was used and interpreted so that the Xocó could win recognition even though they were not different from other sertanejo peasants. The chapter thus begins with the story of Raimundo, a man whose life is threaded throughout the chapter as his identity changes and he becomes the shaman of the Xocó Indians into the twenty-first century. I found this story in court records, but unlike many of the others in this chapter, it is never discussed publicly. It may not even be "remembered" and certainly represents an example of the revising and retelling of histories of struggle integral to the understanding of ethnoracial identity transformation.

A STORY NEVER TOLD: PREHISTORY FORGOTTEN

In August 1971, well before the dramatic occupation of São Pedro Island, Raimundo Bezerra Lima, a man with a wife and six children who possessed no land of his own, traveled for hours by boat and horseback to the local courthouse and filed a lawsuit against his employer. Raimundo and his wife, Maria dos Santos, had spent their entire lives working on the family property of the widow Elizabeth Guimarães Britto, an absentee landowner from a local oligarchical family. Raimundo brought his claim under the Rural Worker Statute of 1963, which guaranteed him payment for being dismissed and an annual extra month's salary for every year he had worked.[2] The case was brought without the aid of a lawyer or the local rural workers' union. Within one month, the court had ruled against Raimundo. The judge had determined that he was not a "rural worker," as defined by the statute, but was instead just an old-fashioned *agregado* (historically, a person who lived on another's property and was dependent on the landowner, sometimes a poor relation or servant who did not earn a wage).[3] In fact, Raimundo and Maria were not legally married, as came out in the brief filed by Antônio Britto on behalf of his mother, because they were married only in the church and had not had a civil ceremony.[4] This failure to legalize their marriage was key to the court's decision that Raimundo was not a statutory rural worker. Rather, it was Maria who was the sharecropper in the employment relationship with the Brittos, legally speaking, and she was not a party to the suit.

Written testimony in Raimundo's short-lived case[5] sheds light on the life of work at that time on the Brittos' ranches (*fazendas*), which, twenty years later, would be expropriated for the Xocó indigenous reserve. Raimundo and his family, like dozens of other sertanejo peasants in the area, worked and lived without electricity, running water, road access, motorized vehicles, or agricultural tools. They planted and harvested rice in lagoons that were created by the annual flooding of the São Francisco River. The women were the planters of the rice seed; their husbands helped with the harvest. Once the rice was harvested, the peasants were required to give some portion (usually half, *meia*) to the landowner and could keep the rest for themselves (hence the term by which they were known, *meeiro*, translated as "sharecropper"). The women also fashioned and fired clay pots under the sun that were sold at the market across the river. Their husbands collected firewood and carried mud from the river's edge for the pots.

Raimundo and the other men also fished but were required to share their catch with the landlord. Fishing always provided an important source of protein for these sertanejos who were fortunate enough to live on the banks of a large river. The other occupation for men was piloting boats owned by entrepreneurs from towns downriver. Travel up, down, and across the river was, and remains, intrinsic to the lives of Raimundo, Maria, and their neighbors. The boats provide transportation to sell and obtain goods and to socialize and have chance meetings with relatives—and for their children to attend school. From the court testimony in 1971, it is possible to discern a certain rhythm of life that persists even today in these riverine communities, which are constantly in motion—going to market and the bank, visiting relatives, selling and buying. One fundamental difference between then and now is that Raimundo, Maria, and their neighbors no longer share their harvests with the Brittos. Another difference is that there are no longer rice lagoons and fish are scarce.[6] Finally, their benefits come not from the county or landowners through the labor law, but from FUNAI, the federal indigenous protection agency.

OLIGARCHY, PATRONAGE, AND CHANGES AFOOT

Well into the twentieth century, oligarchical families, such as the Brittos, were powerful forces in the lower São Francisco valley. Such landowning, dynastic families became the representatives of national political parties at the local level. This "intermingling of private and public power" led to widespread "nepotistic control of public office by ruling elite families" (Lewin 1987:17). The party boss, referred to as *coronel*, "functioned locally as the broker between elite family interests and the national government" (Lewin 1987:18). "Coronel" is a title dating from the National Guard (founded in 1831), which issued honorary posts to wealthy landowners in each county. "Coronel" became the style of address used by the rural population for any political leader or man of influence (Leal 1977:xv). As a system of favor exchanges and control over the local populace, *coronelismo*, the rural Brazilian form of patronage, was "a compromise, an exchange of advantages between public power, progressively invigorated, and the decadent social influence of the local bosses, particularly the landowners" (Leal 1977:20). This system placed the coronel as a key broker who consolidated his position through loyalty from the peasants who lived on his land and through control over municipal revenues. Each coronel would compete for political power, leading to a warlike environment (Leal 1977; Faoro 1993; Forman and Riegelhaupt 1979; Reesink 1981:102).

The seemingly timeless patron-client system of coronelismo, with its powerful, absentee landowners and dependent peasants, was beginning to change in the 1960s (C. Barreira 1992:47). The relationship of dependency was founded on a stable if unequal exchange of loyalty for security. However, as the federal government pursued economic growth and independence, social and economic relations in the São Francisco valley began to change. This area was heavily affected by federal development policies aimed at hydroelectric power and modernization, which began before the 1964 military coup, accelerated in the mid-1960s, and continued into the 2000s.[7] The building of immense public water works upriver commenced in 1960, and as late as 1997 new turbines were going on line at the Paulo Afonso hydroelectric dam. Equally important for understanding the changes about to occur on the Sergipe side of the São Francisco River was the generational shift among traditional landowning families, such as the Brittos.

By 1971, the Britto family was exercising political power in the port city of Propriá, over fifty miles downriver from their ranches, known as Caiçara and Belém, which includes the island of São Pedro and which they had owned for four generations. Antônio Guimarães Britto, the widow's son, was about to become vice mayor of Propriá (in 1976, he became mayor for six years). Members of the family at that time were staunch supporters of the military government. Antônio's uncle, Judge João Fernandes de Britto (known to all as Dr. Britinho), was president of the local government party organization and a poet, amateur historian, and member of the Sergipe Academy of Letters. As the 1970s wore on and the Propriá diocese became committed to land reform and helping the poor, Dr. Britinho changed his position and supported those efforts, even though the targets of the indigenous struggle were his nieces and nephews.

Propriá, founded in 1801, became a vibrant port on the São Francisco River for the next 150 years, during which rail and roads were virtually nonexistent and the river was the sole form of transportation (Britto Aragão 1997). Reflecting the agricultural profile of the area, Propriá was home to textile-manufacturing and rice-processing plants. As early as 1859, Dom Pedro II, the last king of Brazil, voyaged up the river visiting towns and villages, writing that "Propriá is a town of 3,000 inhabitants with a rice husking factory that even has a steam engine" (Pedro II 1959:109). In 1972, while the city was still prospering, the federal government completed a bridge across the São Francisco River providing a north-south route for truck transportation. Although bridge construction employed people from across the state during a period of drought and in spite of Propriá's great expectations for increased commerce, the bridge was responsible for its demise. This has resulted in stagnation and population loss (Britto Aragão 1997:66). Nowadays, all that is left of the textile and rice plants are decaying buildings. There seems little doubt that the downturn in commerce in the Brittos' city of Propriá was a factor in the decreased need for rice production in the 1970s. The decline of trade in Propriá, together with the reduction in the annual flooding due to the upstream hydroelectric dam construction, contributed to the events that took a dramatic turn in 1978 on São Pedro Island. The Brittos considered the island to be part of the patrimony passed on to them by the family patriarch, Coronel João Fernandes de Britto (1855–1916).

Coronel João Fernandes de Britto was the grandfather of Dr. Britinho, whose brother had been Elizabeth Britto's husband, from whom she inherited Caiçara, Belém, and São Pedro Island. In the half century after his death, Coronel Britto was represented as a benevolent contributor to the prosperity and well-being of Propriá. He was a religious man who paid for nuns to come from Europe, founded schools and seminaries, was twice a state deputy, and established prosperous rice, textile, and newspaper businesses. His contributions warranted a riverfront plaza bearing his name (Costa 1926; Menezes 1952). However, in later years, he was represented as an exploitative, land-grabbing, murdering demon by a ninety-year-old woman who remembered nighttime raping and burning (Valadares 1978). The coronel was reputed to have expelled the people living on São Pedro Island in 1878. In a 2000 interview, the coronel's great-grandson, who became a justice of the Brazilian Supreme Court in 2003, explained that the memories of those who accused the coronel of atrocities must have been mistaken — that it had, in fact, been the coronel's brother, Francisco "Chico" Porfírio de Britto, whom they were remembering as an ogre. According to family lore, Chico had been a truculent, authoritarian, violent political boss. He was from the "other" side of the family.[8]

LIBERATION THEOLOGY ARRIVES IN THE SERTÃO

On the day in 1971 when Raimundo lost his case, he joined the newly founded rural workers' union, and three months later, a key witness against him, another one of the sharecroppers, also joined the union (M. R. d. Oliveira 1979). In addition to being the second year of one of the worst droughts of the twentieth century, 1971 also marked a change in administration of the Britto properties, with Elizabeth's son, João, taking the place of his brother, Antônio, who was known as an easygoing administrator. João Britto changed this "softer" approach and rapidly became known as an administrator "of iron and fire," with tales that he had violently forced his workers to vote for certain candidates and that when those candidates lost, he had increased the persecution.[9] At this moment, during the most repressive period of the Brazilian military regime, a young seminarian from Pernambuco, Enoque Salvador de Melo, known as Frei Enoque, moved to the sertão of Sergipe. There, at the end of 1970, almost a decade before students, professors, and urban intellectuals took up the cause of squatters and the landless,[10] Frei Enoque assembled a team of pastoral agents to carry out the training, based on liberation theology doctrine, that he had received at Dom Hélder Câmara's Theological Institute in Olinda, the seat of the Recife archbishopric to which Dom Hélder had been moved when the military came to power in 1964.[11] The first bishop of the new Propriá diocese, Dom José Brandão, had brought Frei Enoque to Sergipe and ordained him at the end of 1971.[12] These two men would shortly become representatives of liberation theology and key figures in the history of the region.

As a young man, Enoque defied his family's desire that he attend law school and instead entered a monastery in the sugarcane region in 1966, where people would come to hide from security forces and gunmen still hunted down remnants of the peasant leagues. At the end of that year, he took a vow of poverty and transferred to Olinda to study philosophy and theology at the new Theological Institute. There, for the first time, Carmelites, Franciscans, and other orders, as well as young men and women who were not seminarians, were brought together by Dom Hélder Câmara's vision of the meaning of the Second Vatican Council, which was informed by his friendship with Pope Paul VI. At the end of 1968, while Enoque was at the institute, General Costa e Silva issued the repressive AI-5 in the harshest crackdown on civil society of the military regime. In spite of the issuance of AI-5, Dom Hélder continued to support student demonstrations. This led to a series of repressive acts that culminated in the assassination in May 1969 of a twenty-eight-year-old priest whom Dom Hélder considered to be like a son (Piletti and Praxedes 1997:354–55). It was one of the first open acts of repression against the Catholic Church, which worsened after the inauguration of General Emílio Garrastazú Médici as president later that year.

At the time, Enoque, the same age as the murdered priest, was studying at the institute and working in the countryside, already putting into practice what he was learning. During his time at the institute, Enoque was most drawn to Joseph Comblin, the Belgian priest who was a major architect of the Medellín vision of liberation theology. Comblin was expelled from Brazil by the military shortly after Enoque left for Sergipe in 1970. So when Frei Enoque arrived in the sertão of Sergipe as a Franciscan friar during the worst drought in over a decade, he already had experience with repression and knew what it would mean to continue his practice even as the authorities in Sergipe took note of his arrival. They immediately began harassing him and his team of friars, nuns, and lay religious workers, because, as Frei Enoque has noted, "this was a different way of being a priest. We would go into the streets, talking, discussing, and taking positions. So there began to develop, in a [small interior] city like Porto da Folha, groups of people going to demand things from the mayor. You can imagine in this terrible, sad moment . . . one of us was imprisoned and we were labelled communists" (Melo interview 1997). All of this was going on as they prepared to minister to the poorest people in the poorest counties of Brazil.

As the Catholic Church in Brazil was turning to liberation theology and

Frei Enoque (photograph by the author)

deciding to support indigenous rights, as discussed in the previous chapter, Frei Enoque, the tall, powerful, charismatic new priest, was beginning to visit Raimundo, Maria, and their neighbors. He learned of the mission church on São Pedro Island, and with the support of Bishop Dom José Brandão, he began researching the history of the mission, its priests, and the people who had once lived in its environs.[13] Frei Enoque, a native of the northeastern state of Pernambuco, was himself dark skinned and not very distinguishable from the peasants to whom he ministered. None could be identified as typical Indians for observers who had always assumed that to be an Indian was to look like those in the Amazon, with "pure Indian characteristics . . . straight hair," to quote the first elected chief of the Xocó, José Apolônio (Apolônio interview 1998). For Frei Enoque, and for the Xocó themselves, the retrieval of historical information about the indigenous peoples who had once lived in the area served as both impetus and justification for the assertion of their newfound identity in the late twentieth century.

Frei Enoque's arrival was marked by immediate conflict with the Brittos (Mota 1997). When he arrived, Frei Enoque already knew he was going to minister to the peasants of the area and reject the close relations priests traditionally maintained with landowners. He chose to stay in the modest homes of the sharecroppers (Mota 1997:23; Melo interviews 1997, 1998). This caused problems for the bishop, Dom José Brandão, who was close to the Britto family. He had been "their" bishop since his arrival in 1960. Although João Britto had torn down the old houses and allowed cattle to graze on São Pedro Island, Frei Enoque reopened the old mission church, and there the Brittos' sharecroppers began talking about their indigenous past (Mota 1997:23). When this happened, João Britto forbade his workers from receiving Frei Enoque in their homes. Dolores Apolônio (mother of the first chief) defied the order, and she was called to the landowner's house. Although frightened, she went and was greeted by Britto, who was "very nice and invited us to drink some wine." Her nephew was afraid the wine might be poisoned, but she drank it to no ill effect. When Britto asked if she knew that he had forbidden their hospitality to Frei Enoque, she said she did but that she would not allow him to sleep outside with the mosquitoes and bats. Her response to Britto's question—aren't you afraid of being punished?— was no. Dolores's nephew got angry and asked Britto if he would beat the workers like slaves. "Britto was impressed and just stared at us. Then he said that, no, he just wanted to know what we thought of Frei Enoque and we said we liked him very much. Then he told us to go." Despite the cordial appearance of the interaction, "that was not the end of the story, for subsequently, Britto decided to turn his rice fields into pastures" (Mota 1997:24). This act marked the beginning of the struggle.

"AFTER THE CONFLICT CAME THE HISTORY"

History is popularly assumed to be facts from the past that create the bedrock for the present. Xocó history, however, belies this assumption. History is malleable. No one living as a Xocó Indian today—including the former chief, Apolônio, two of the more recent chiefs, and the shaman (Raimundo, of the 1971 labor lawsuit)—denies that until Frei Enoque started interviewing the old people, they had no idea they might be considered Indians or descended from Indians.[14] Even in 1983, Raimundo is reported to have said, "We were just *meeiros* (sharecroppers), miserable workers" (Mota 1997:23). In 1998, Apolônio, the first chief, expressed the sequence as "after the conflict came the history." Implicit in these representations of the Xocó story is the assumption that by building the mission church and gathering the region's Indians on São Pedro Island, the Church denied them their Indianness, stripped them of their religion, language, and cultural practices, and replaced them with Catholicism. Apolônio's view on this subject, which he expressed in public as well as in our interview session (Apolônio interview 1998), made this explicit:

[The Catholic Church] would have to pay in double for the misery and destruction they caused in this territory and in the culture of the Indians. Why does Apolônio not speak his language today? Why do I not have the characteristics of a pure Indian? Why are you not conversing with Apolônio today all painted with straight hair and a perforated nose and ear . . . an authentic Indian, a truly pure Indian? . . . It would be much easier for Brazil to pay its foreign debt to the International Monetary Fund than for the Catholic Church and the Brazilian authorities to pay the cultural debt they owe the Indians. . . . The Catholic Church is to blame for this because the state invaded the territory and the Church invaded the human being; it extracted my pure blood and brought in other blood that mixed with it. Now this blood will never be separated, the blood that my ancestors mixed with blacks, mixed with whites themselves. In the same way that I will never stop being an Indian just because I do not have those characteristics.

Paradoxically, the Catholic Church came to serve a preservationist purpose. Because the Church began to support indigenous survival, it provided, and itself became, proof of Xocó existence.

The year after João Britto's brother, Antônio, became mayor of Propriá, João informed his sharecroppers that he had decided to end rice cultivation and turn the rice fields into pasture (Melatti 1979; *Antônio Clementino de Melo v. Britto* 1979). This was bad news for the workers; in fact, it was essentially expulsion, because rice cultivation had been the basis of their survival for many generations, along with the sale of pottery and the subsistence plots they cultivated with corn, beans, manioc, melons, and squash (Apolônio interview 1998). It is likely that the lowering of the river due to the upriver hydroelectric dams played a part in his decision.[15] However, it was not the only reason for João Britto's decision to cut off his workers in 1977.

By Dom José Brandão's own account, beginning in 1975, the Propriá diocese was being carried along with the leftward, proworker shift of the Church in the Northeast and the newly defined doctrine of liberation theology. As described earlier, Dom José recounted his "conversion" to the cause of rural workers at Betume, a ranch that was taken over by the government with irrigation as its goal. In the process, an entire community was expelled from the land. The small monetary compensation provided to them was not enough to reestablish their community in humane conditions (Brandão de Castro 1985). Dom José Brandão's public support of the Betume workers marked the beginning of his vilification by politicians aligned with the government

Apolônio and Dom José Brandão de Castro upon recognition
(collection of Dom José Brandão de Castro)

party, including Antônio Britto. Dom José Brandão received national attention for his testimony before the legislative assembly of the large and powerful neighboring state of Bahia on land theft through document forgery.[16] As
a result, he was again denounced as a communist, this time in the legislative assembly of Sergipe. He was called a "red bishop" and was interrogated
about communism in a local newspaper. Dom José denied any affiliation
with communism but stood up for his defense of the poor and landless[17] and
was vigorously defended by the opposition party.[18] This, taken together with
Frei Enoque's agitation among João Britto's workers, reflected the shift to
the left of the Propriá diocese. João Britto recognized that the local Catholic
Church, which had always been a close ally of his family, now threatened his
family's interests as landowners and political leaders. This polarization is a
likely motivation for João Britto's decision to end the workers' ability to make
a living on his property.

As João Britto ratcheted up the economic pressure on his sharecroppers,
what had begun as a labor dispute became a land conflict. Considering the

diocese's interest in land reform, it is not surprising that the problem became a land conflict, but this land struggle took a decidedly different turn from the others brewing in the diocese. Frei Enoque and the elderly people he interviewed living on the Brittos' property were producing knowledge that could justify their claim to the land as descendants of Indians. They were being encouraged to remember things their parents had told them about living under the tutelage of the last Capuchin missionary on São Pedro Island, Frei Doroteu de Loreto. Some said that the Brittos had expelled their grandparents from the island upon Frei Doroteu's death in 1878.[19]

As early as 1974, Frei Enoque and his team were beginning to discuss the history of the mission church on São Pedro Island with the Brittos' sharecroppers. There is no written evidence of those early discussions, and by the time I reached the island in 1998, the old people were no longer alive. However, there is a painting on the wall of the church of a man in religious garb, with a long white beard, a book in his hand, São Pedro Island behind him, a church on the island, the São Francisco River behind the island, the mountains of Alagoas on the other side of the river, and a characteristic bright blue sky. In the lower right corner is the signature of the artist: Frei Juvenal, and the date, 1974.[20] To the left of the priest is a scroll with the following words painted on it: "This land belongs to my caboclos—Frei Doroteu."[21]

While Dom José Brandão and Frei Enoque were producing information that would be used to justify the indigenous status of the Brittos' workers, Sergipe scholar Beatriz Dantas was working on a master's degree in São Paulo. Her adviser was anthropologist Manuela Carneiro da Cunha (later to become professor of anthropology at the University of Chicago) and founder of the Pro-Indian Commission in 1978, an NGO (Carneiro da Cunha 1998). Dantas had done no historical research on the Xocó until stories appeared in the national press in September 1978 that São Pedro Island had been invaded by rural workers claiming to be descended from an indigenous tribe. She had been researching traces of other indigenous groups in Sergipe when Carneiro da Cunha asked her to look into the history of indigenous peoples in the area who might be identified as Xocó, a name that had come up in local discussions because of the Kariri-Xocó, a tribe recognized in the 1940s downriver in Alagoas.

It was at this point that Dantas met Dalmo Dallari, a progressive lawyer known for his defense of indigenous peoples, and together they wrote the book, *Terra dos Índios Xocó* (Land of the Xocó Indians), published by the Pro-Indian Commission in 1980. As soon as Dantas gathered the material in 1979, it was sent on to FUNAI, the agency responsible for recognizing Indian tribes. The book is included in all the court records and FUNAI administrative files as key evidence in the Xocó case for the Brittos' mainland property. As one example of the operation of governmentality in this context, the collaboration of nongovernmental actors (the Church, a secular NGO, an anthropologist, and a lawyer) developed the knowledge required by a government agency, FUNAI, to begin the legal process that would identify, verify, and recategorize these rural workers as Indians.

By the time stories were being collected by anthropologist Clarice Mota, in 1983 (Mota 1997), the old folks had already recounted them many times. The stories had become streamlined and coherent, making it difficult to know the sequence of knowledge production (that is, the role of Frei Enoque in reconstructing memories and the impact that the promise of land and better times may have had on the process). However, from the transcripts of interviews conducted by Frei Enoque after 1978, it seems clear that a mutual production of knowledge about the past was taking place in the homes of the old sharecroppers. Frei Enoque conducted many interviews in the shadow of the mission church, a reminder that Indians were once subject to a "civilizing" process at this very place. It did not matter to the workers whether their acculturation had occurred in the nineteenth century, as a result of the 1850 land law that declared any unowned land to be up for grabs, as proposed by Dantas and reiterated by some elderly informants (Mota 1997:21) or whether they were already mixed into the general population in the eighteenth century.

By the end of the nineteenth century, official registries no longer made reference to Indians in Sergipe but instead referred to *mestiços* and *caboclos* (categories that carried no rights to land or services) (Oliveira Filho 1997). Everyone knew that little remained of their identity and that "their rituals, ceremonies and beliefs [were] a mixture, in various degrees, of indigenous, European and African elements" (Pierson 1972, 1:149).[22] Nonetheless, these *sertanejos* chose to pursue their rights to land as Indians rather than attempting to obtain title through land reform procedures, as other communities in the diocese were doing. Such a choice did not exist for them, in part because the legal conditions for land reform were not present, but, more important, because the alliances that had grown up around their struggle were thoroughly intertwined with the new international indigenous rights movement, which had been, to some extent, instigated by Catholic Church institutions. The alliances that supported these backland rural workers in their transition to Xocó identity were links in a "chain of equivalents" (Laclau 1996), a set of discursive dynamics surrounding the particular conditions of possibility that led to connecting indigenous identity to a political struggle for land.

INVASION OF THE ISLAND, INJUNCTIONS NOTWITHSTANDING

On September 13, 1978, more than twenty families[23] crossed the small canal between the Brittos' mainland ranch and São Pedro Island and, with wire purchased using the proceeds of a cow, cordoned off part of the island, declared it unowned, and claimed it as theirs. Three days later, the state military police arrived to control the situation. Lawyers provided by the trade union federation and the diocese arrived three days after that. On that same day, the Brittos informed the governor that they had already received an injunction ordering the families to leave the island. In the exchange that took place in the press, the Brittos asserted that the island was part of their mainland property, while Frei Enoque told the press that in 1971 João Britto had marked off a small area of the island and then abandoned it because there was nothing of value on it. The workers began to see the island as available because "everyone knew that it belonged to no one, much less the Brittos." Raimundo insisted that when they cordoned off their piece of the island with wire, they had respected the area already marked off by João Britto.[24] The logic asserted by Frei Enoque and Raimundo made perfect sense under Brazilian land law, which allowed, and still provides, unused land to be expropriated and given to people who have squatted on it and made it their home. This long-standing logic of land reform informed the beginnings of the bid for Indian identity, land, and recognition.

In a shift away from the land reform argument, so as not to rely solely on a legal argument based on the Brittos' abandonment of part of the island, Frei Enoque told the press that the invaders had the same right to the island as the Brittos since they were "direct descendants of the old natives of this land." Pedrito Santana, one of the key leaders of the invading sharecroppers claiming to be Xocó, combined the two arguments: "We gathered together, we have no place to work, saw this part of the land not producing anything, land that belonged to our grandparents, and we thought we could cultivate it, since the brother of the mayor of Propriá already took a piece for himself."[25] In a common reaction to land restitution claims, Mayor Antônio Britto said he was perplexed at how a ranch that had belonged to his family for ninety years could be lost. "We will prosecute the invaders and those who have caused this," he said (Valadares 1978). This was seen as an implicit threat against the diocese because the bishop had announced, in the *Jornal de Sergipe* (1978), when the island was invaded, "If anyone were to have a claim to possess the land, it would be the Church, which has been there since Capuchin missionaries erected a church and founded a mission." With the Church's new commitment to indigenous rights, such an assertion was a slap in the face to the Brittos, who had been the bishop's most important supporters. Within a month of the invasion, the Church, acting through the bishop, began its campaign against the Brittos, who in turn threatened local Church leaders. The powerful Britto family viewed the pivotal role played by the bishop in the Xocó claim to their land as a betrayal that could not be forgiven.

Because the avowed purpose of invading the island was only to plant subsistence crops, at the advice of their lawyers and with the hope that the court would be convinced of their claim to the island, the workers, now identified in the press and in their self-presentation as descendants of Xocó Indians, returned to the mainland, for the time being. The preliminary injunction won by the Brittos against the invaders began a series of legal actions against and by the workers over the course of the following year. During that time, the undercurrent of law was ever present in the tactics, plans, hopes, and discourse of the participants. In response to the injunction one week after the workers claimed the island, Dom José Brandão invoked the Indian Statute of 1973, which he explained nullified any act or deed by non-Indians purporting to lay claim to indigenous land. In their earliest gestures, the matter that concerned the newly identified Xocó Indians most, they pleaded, was that their children were facing hunger, illness, lack of education, and misery. The author of an important article, Pedro Valadares (1978), who in later years would become a state politician but at the time was one of many leftists supporting rural workers and the Church's progressive line, "nourish[ed] the vain hope that the men who make the laws can legislate in their [the Indians'] favor, otherwise their only consolation will be to wait, agonizing, to the death."

In these early days after the invasion of São Pedro Island, the Church began its campaign against the Brittos in full force, bringing to bear the authority that only a bishop in a fully Catholic setting can exercise. Dom José Brandão instructed his priests not to baptize children of landowners for whom Mayor Antônio Britto would serve as godfather. The first time a priest denied baptism, the mayor's brother threatened the priest, saying, "In Propriá I would shoot you; I'm not firing on you now out of respect for the chapel."[26] This was not the first time that the bishop and the priest had been threatened by landowners. In October 1978, one month after the invasion of the island, on the anniversary of Frei Doroteu's death and in defiance of the injunction, the diocese sponsored a land pilgrimage to the island, the first in a series of annual pilgrimages to land struggle sites that are still being held thirty years later.[27] The 1978 pilgrimage took place just as the families were consolidating their origin story as Xocó. As a Catholic religious event, in addition to affirming the families' new identity as Indians, the pilgrimage cemented their devotion to the Catholic Church. However, it also aggravated the rift between the Brittos and Dom José Brandão. Shortly after the pilgrimage, and one week before the state gubernatorial election in which the government party won, a letter appeared in the Sergipe newspapers in which Carlos Ayres Britto, a prominent legal scholar, attacked Dom José Brandão for slandering the name of his great-grandfather. He was quoted in another article confirming that "the people who invaded the Island are not and never were indigenous" (Britto 1978).[28]

Elizabeth Britto herself published letters in the newspaper to Dom José Brandão and Frei Enoque two months after the invasion (November 1978), citing her constitutional private property rights, placing the responsibility for damages on Frei Enoque, and threatening unspecified "disagreeable" consequences if the religious leaders were to continue encouraging meetings, festivals, and pilgrimages. Her son, Mayor Antônio Britto, filed a complaint with the federal police against the bishop accusing him of violating the National Security Law for acts of subversion, echoing the "red finger" pointed at Dom José Brandão four years earlier in a letter written by a Sergipe politician to military president Ernesto Geisel.[29]

COUSINS ACROSS THE RIVER: RIVALRY AND ORIGINS

The sense of threat to private property, whether in the name of land reform or Indians' rights, was undoubtedly exacerbated by a land invasion by another group of Indians on the same day as the pilgrimage to São Pedro Island in October 1978. On the other side of the river and about 100 miles to the east, in the state of Alagoas, the Kariri-Xocó occupied a small piece of government-owned land, claiming it as the traditional site of their annual religious ceremony (Mata 1989:65).[30] Unlike the people who claimed Xocó identity in 1978, the Kariri-Xocó had been recognized since 1944 when an indigenous post was founded on the site of a Catholic mission. That recognition was one of a handful by the SPI, predecessor of FUNAI, of groups identified by Padre Alfredo Pinto Dâmaso, who was mobilizing labor for new agricultural policies (Arruti 1998b:103). In 1960, U.S. anthropologist Hohenthal

(1960a; 1960b) identified them as Xocó.[31] In 1964, Brazilian folklorist Alceu Maynard Araújo referred to them as "Cariri" (Araújo 1964b:47). The group began calling itself Kariri-Xocó, possibly to increase its chances of laying claim to potential Xocó land in Sergipe.

Perhaps due to the establishment of federal government protection at a relatively early date for the Northeast, the Kariri-Xocó have retained some Indian features, such as a dance known as the *toré*, songs with some non-Portuguese words, and annual *ouricuri* festivals in which only members of the tribe are permitted to participate. These "secrets" are considered by the Indians and their anthropologists, Vera Mata (1989) and Clarice Mota (1997), to be significant indicia of Indianness. Knowledge of the proper preparation of and getting the benefits from the drinking of *jurema* (a hallucinogen prepared from bark) were said to be available only to those with "indigenous blood" (Araújo 1964b:47). In the early years of the Xocó land struggle, facilitated by Frei Enoque, leaders appealed to the Kariri-Xocó for help in regaining their cultural heritage and tribal leadership structure. As will be seen below, a cordial relationship between the two groups was not in the cards.

The origin stories of the two groups are intertwined because the Kariri-Xocó trace their modern genesis from the expulsion of the Xocó from São Pedro Island upon the death of Frei Doroteu in 1878. As with the Xocó, the Kariri-Xocó date their land claim to a voyage up the São Francisco River in 1859 by the last king of Brazil, Dom Pedro II. During that trip, the king is said to have given land to both indigenous groups, even though he wrote in his diary that he had seen "descendants of a race already very mixed with feather plumes, bows, arrows . . . and jackets!" (Pedro II 1959:111). About his stop at São Pedro Island, Dom Pedro II wrote that there were Indians and many Portuguese people, and that Frei Doroteu complained that the Indians were indolent and that when the Indians refused to plant, the Church let the poor folk plant there without collecting rent (Pedro II 1959:133). The implication here is that the people who today claim to be Xocó are in fact the descendants of the "poor folk" referred to by Frei Doroteu.

Travel reports are often used in evidentiary claims for indigenous land (Gardner 1841). Hohenthal (1960b) and Pierson (1972) also reported the presence of "civilized" Indians on São Pedro Island in the 1950s. Also considered persuasive were the stories appearing in newspapers from the first half of the twentieth century in which individuals traveled to various cities to appeal to the government for help in reclaiming São Pedro Island.[32] For example, the FUNAI administrative proceeding recognizing the Xocó contains a document prepared by Frei Enoque based on interviews with an elderly resident, who told the story of "some caboclos who went on foot to the capital with their bows and headdresses to request government protection from the Brittos" in the early twentieth century. They brought back with them a letter requiring that the land be returned to them, but before they arrived they got drunk and the letter was destroyed.[33]

Donation of land to Indians by Dom Pedro II has often served as the basis for indigenous land claims in Brazil, despite a lack of written evidence of the king's generosity (Mata 1989).[34] People claiming land as Indians may believe that the only possible successful appeal is one that reaches to the natural law of a supreme sovereign. They may believe this to be necessary because, beginning with the 1850 land law, a series of government actions declared land not yet titled to be up for grabs. Within a few years, all indigenous groups in the region were declared to be extinct on the ground that they had mixed with the general population. As such, they had no claim to land. This is said to have resulted in both the loss of the Kariri land in Alagoas and that of the Xocó in Sergipe, which was sold by the government to the Britto patriarch in 1878, suspiciously, the year of Frei Doroteu's death (Dantas and Dallari 1980:167). When the Xocó were expelled from the São Pedro Island mission in 1878, as explained to a FUNAI anthropologist a century later, some of them went to live with the Kariri in Alagoas[35] and the rest stayed on the mainland, working for the Brittos and mixing with descendants of African slaves brought by the Dutch. As the anthropologist pointed out, this would have explained replacement of indigenous with black features (Melatti 1979:8).

In an effort to encourage solidarity, the diocese issued newsletters about ties between the two groups, saying that when the Xocó were expelled from the island in the late nineteenth century, two brothers split—one settling in Caiçara, the Brittos' mainland property, and the other in Alagoas. However, the relationship between the two groups has for many years been marked more by competition than by brotherly devotion. In May 1979, the chief of the Kariri-Xocó wrote a letter to the president of FUNAI: "We are not against the right of families in Caiçara to struggle for better days but they should struggle as squatters, because we are the true owners of São Pedro Island. We have lived for many years with the hope and desire that one day we will return to the island which is ours."[36] Recent manifestations of the competition include suggestions by the Kariri-Xocó that the Xocó do not know how to prepare jurema—a serious accusation considering folklorist Araújo's note that only those with indigenous blood can benefit from it.

FUNAI anthropologist Delvair Melatti wrote in her first report, based on a short visit in June 1979, that Kariri-Xocó informants alleged that the people who had invaded São Pedro Island were no longer Indians due to the high degree of miscegenation. Members of the Kariri-Xocó tribe were received coldly on São Pedro Island when she was there and were refused genealogical information. When Frei Enoque tried to bring the groups together, he was unsuccessful because the families on the island said that the Kariri-Xocó had not helped them when they were hungry. Shortly after the island was definitively occupied by the Xocó in September 1979, CIMI sponsored an indigenous assembly on the island with representatives of tribes from around Brazil—with the exception of the Kariri-Xocó, who refused to attend.[37]

As far back as the mid-1960s, the government had done an assessment of the island at the request of a Kariri-Xocó leader and determined that there were no Indians on the island and therefore the Indians had no claim to it (Melatti 1979). At that time, the Brittos gained definitive control over Caiçara and Belém, the mainland property, which they claimed in their lawsuits included São Pedro Island. The lack of people living on the island was also a source of interest by the Kariri-Xocó, who began talking, in 1971, about occupying the island themselves. Although the idea among the Brittos' workers of asserting an indigenous identity came to fruition later than 1971 (most likely around 1974), the question of who were the proper heirs to São Pedro Island was discussed earlier. However, there is no indication that it was considered before the arrival in Sergipe of Frei Enoque. At least one anthropologist (the one sent by FUNAI) has conjectured that the Brittos' workers invaded São Pedro Island in September 1978 because they suspected that the Kariri-Xocó were planning an invasion of their own (Melatti 1979), and, in fact, one month later the Kariri-Xocó successfully occupied their own parcel of land. Certainly the presence of these indigenous "cousins" downriver contributed to decisions made by the families who invaded the island in 1978 and who were recognized as Xocó the following year. As we will see with the later relationship of the Xocó and their kin in Mocambo, different-yet-similar and solidarity-yet-competition were the operative assumptions in both situations—cousins across the river as two tribes of Indians, and cousins in the neighboring village as quilombolas.

PROMISE OF IDENTITY—OR MIRAGE OF LIBERATION?

Thus harmony did not prevail among the Indians, and the Brittos themselves were battling out their differing views on how to deal with the predicament of the workers-turned-Indians supported by the bishop. The national newspaper, *O Estado de São Paulo* (December 10, 1978), reported that Propriá mayor Antônio Britto had denounced Dom José Brandão to the federal police, but Britto also said that he was not unsympathetic to the cause of landless workers. He just believed that Dom José was using extralegal means to obtain land for them. However, his brothers, Hélcio and João Britto, took drastic measures against the Church. Hélcio threatened to shoot a priest. Then, on Christmas day 1978, João Britto interrupted Mass in the Propriá cathedral, yelling offenses at the priest because of references to the hungry residents of Caiçara. He strode to the altar, accusing Church leaders of being communists, and tried to grab the microphone from the priest's hand.

The following Sunday, the diocese held a Mass in response to the threats, with a reported 1,000 people in attendance, receiving messages of solidarity from bishops around the country. Workers from the entire county brought banners: "This night represents unity" and "Happy are the poor reunited." In an attempt to redefine the controversy, Dom José insisted that "the real problem was between the caboclos and the Britto family and not between the Brittos and the Church." Rumors then circulated that there were armed men roaming the city, and people began to take sides. As reported by *Jornal de Sergipe* (December 13, 1978), shortly thereafter, a fight broke out between the mayor and his brother João in front of the Propriá house of their mother, Elizabeth Britto, about what measures should be taken to protect the family's interests. João supported physical retaliation against the priests, while Antônio felt that resolution could only come through legal and political power. After all, the Brittos had received an injunction and were confident they would win in court. In the midst of the discussion, João shot at his brother, barely missing both Antônio and their mother. At this very moment the bus arrived from Aracaju and stopped in front of the house to allow the riders to watch the drama.[38]

A week after the turn of the new year, 1979, Elizabeth Britto filed a criminal action against twenty-nine of her former workers, including Raimundo Bezerra Lima (of the 1971 lawsuit), Pedrito Santana, and Paulo Acácio dos Santos (Paulino), in which she alleged that they had violently invaded her land and made threats against her family. Written interrogatories and oral testimony were collected. That same week, the people who were now identifying themselves as "descendants of Xocó Indians" began to receive national attention. *O Globo* published a full-page, meticulously detailed article on their struggle for land. With the growing national publicity, the best solution seemed to be government intervention. The state of Sergipe or the federal government acting through FUNAI could solve the problem by indemnifying the Brittos and giving the island to the workers.

In April 1979, in a tactical move that seems, in retrospect, out of place, given the national publicity, but was perhaps in response to an earlier suit brought by Elizabeth Britto attempting to extinguish the sharecropping relationship, lawyers for the newly identified Xocó descendants filed a labor claim in the local court (with the same judge before whom Britto's two other lawsuits were pending). The defense brief made much of this contradiction, referring to the workers/Indians as chameleonlike and implicitly criticizing the Church. Britto's lawyers used an oblique but recognizable historical/literary reference, referring to those who "are using the misery of innocents and illiterates [to promise a] mirage of liberation that can become a technocratic republic of Paraguay" (*Antônio Clementino de Melo et al. v. Elizabeth Guimarães Britto*, 1979). This refers to the Guarani Republic of Indians, also known as the Jesuitic Province of Paraguay. From 1609 until the Jesuits' expulsion from Brazil in 1759, the Guarani Indian Republic existed, with thirty villages located in southern Brazil, Argentina, Paraguay, and Uruguay. There, for 150 years, Jesuits and the Guarani Indians developed a cooperative social system. By invoking this history, Britto's lawyers were implying that the diocese of Propriá was trying to exercise secular power just as the Jesuits had done.

The Guarani Republic is alive in the Brazilian imagination. For example, in a well-known novel by Lima Barreto, *Triste Fim de Policarpo Quaresma* (The Sad End of Policarpo Quaresma) (1911), made into a film in 1998, a public functionary petitions the government to change the official language of Brazil to Tupi-Guarani on the grounds that political emancipation required linguistic emancipation and that only an indigenous language could adequately express the natural beauty of Brazil (Urban 1991). More significant, in the late 1960s, Antônio Callado published *Quarup*, a novel that told the story of the radicalization of a priest from the northeastern state of Pernambuco who tried to implement his dream of setting up an indigenous community embodying the pure communism of the Bible and modeled after the Guarani Republic. His efforts gave way to active involvement in efforts to mobilize the peasants of the Northeast (Page 1972). The resemblance to Frei Enoque is inescapable.

"AN INDIAN WITHOUT LAND IS NOT AN INDIAN"

Weary of waiting for the court to rule on the Britto lawsuit and in defiance of the preliminary injunction still in force, on September 9, 1979, a group of twenty-four families, now identified as the Xocó, again moved onto São Pe-

Xocó planting Brazilian flag (collection of Dom José Brandão de Castro)

dro Island—this time definitively. They claimed ownership "from time imme-morial" and refused to leave. This dramatic action, supported by the Church, the rural workers' union, and local activists, marked a key moment for these workers in their ethnoracial transformation. To commemorate the event and their newly claimed status in the nation's body politic, they planted a Bra-zilian flag on the shore. Although this action seemed to signify a collective aspiration to full citizenship by people who had been the objects of patron-client relations and hence marginalized from power for generations, it had ironic implications. By becoming Indians in the 1970s, these rural workers were forfeiting full citizenship rights because Indians were (and continue to be in many respects) wards of the Brazilian state, considered and treated as children who are seen as relatively incapable of conducting their own affairs (A. C. Ramos 1998).

Significantly, only after the island had been invaded and a land claim made was there talk of calling upon the government to recognize them as an indigenous tribe. As cogently stated by the chief of the tribe downriver, "An Indian without land is not an Indian." First came land, then identity, because in Brazil an Indian without land is at best "civilized" and at worst a caboclo. Land is intrinsic to indigenous identity, and recognition is a package deal: no land, no indigenous status. Even though FUNAI had sent an anthropolo-gist earlier that year for a few days, it was only after the occupation of the island that FUNAI sent a lawyer, a sociolinguist, and another anthropologist to investigate the claim. In October, the anthropologist returned to conduct a genealogical survey of the people now living on the island. In November 1979, FUNAI intervened in all the pending lawsuits, asserting that the local court lacked jurisdiction over the federally protected Xocó. This was the first official act of recognition.

Identification of Indian with land resonates with, and is translated into, the cultural evidence of indigenous identity.[39] Throughout the Northeast, where the modern presence of Indians has only recently been recognized, a key indicia of "surviving" indigenous culture is the fashioning of clay pots, as described at the beginning of this chapter. The Xocó tribe of Sergipe is no exception. Although clay pot production has been documented as a widespread, traditional sertanejo cultural practice (Araújo 1964b) predating the northeastern tribal recognitions, since the late 1970s that practice has been reconfigured in the eyes of the public, and for the Indians themselves, as a particularly indigenous practice. After the first occupation of São Pedro Island in September 1978, the local press reported that the Xocó descendants had been forbidden by Elizabeth Britto from collecting the mud needed to make their pots. Even at that time, this activity was characterized as "marking the culture" of Indians in Sergipe (Valadares 1978). Consequently, the denial of the right to collect the clay of the land was called upon to justify the taking of the land itself. The fashioning of clay, as a metaphor for land, was transformed, with the imprimatur of anthropologists, from a long-standing sertanejo peasant practice necessary for cooking over open fires to a symbol of indigenous identity. Together with dancing the toré and preparing jurema, it became one of the hallmarks of northeastern indigenous culture. During the period of Xocó identity consolidation, from 1980 to 1991, when the Brittos' mainland property became part of the Xocó reserve, clay working took on even greater significance, since there were so few cultural manifestations and many people in Sergipe were perplexed by the presence of Indians who seemed to be no different from themselves.

Before São Pedro Island was federally designated as an indigenous reserve, it was first purchased by the state under the aegis of the governor, a member of the same party as Mayor Antônio Britto. In addition to the political alliance the Brittos had forged with the governor, they pressured him by stationing hired gunmen on the island "armed to the teeth."[40] Nonetheless, the state's purchase of the island on December 7, 1979, was a tainted victory for the Xocó and the Church. The general view was that the state had overpaid the Brittos, and many people were upset that the executive decree of expropriation indicated that the land was being bought for land reform with no mention of the Xocó. It was not until May 1980 that the legislature authorized the donation of the island to the federal government and not until 1984 that FUNAI legalized the Xocó reserve. However, the Xocó claimed that the island was too small for their growing population. With the new decade, a new land struggle would begin—a bid for the Brittos' mainland property. That large piece of land was declared part of the Xocó reserve over a decade later, but only after the Brittos had sold it to the Alagoan lawyer and political boss, Coronel Jorge Pacheco, a hardheaded man with a known propensity for violence.

Setting aside their disappointment that the state did not indicate that it was purchasing the island for the Xocó, in honor of the victory of the moment, the Church sponsored a party in the county seat on the eve of that city's patron saint day. Bells rang and a band marched into the main square. The people sang a hymn (still sung today) written by a local merchant in honor of the first victory of the Xocó: "Thank God the party has begun, on the Island of São Pedro the caboclos have already won." (Graças a Deus a festa começou. Na Ilha de São Pedro, os caboclos já ganhou.) Boats were sent to the island to bring the Indians to the party. Dom José Brandão wrote, "That night was really an apotheosis."

LEGALIZING IDENTITY IN PRACTICE: THE INDIAN STATUTE OF 1973

It was the definition of "Indian" in the relatively new Indian Statute that served as the basis for the arguments of the bishop, anthropologists, and lawyers that the Brittos' sharecroppers could claim identity as Indians. The following analysis of how the statute was used five years after it was enacted illustrates an important component of the legalizing identity theory. In this section, we will see how the meaning of the law is revised as it is put into practice. Recall the discussion in chapter 1 about the reasoning behind the Indian Statute of 1973 (colonization of the Amazon region).[41] As it turned out, the category "Indian," newly defined in the statute, brought with it rights to land, federal protection, medical care, and benefits, and as it was invoked the legislative intent was subverted to allow for recognition of Indians in places like the Northeast where everyone had assumed there were no longer any tribes.

Significantly, Frei Enoque's early work with the Brittos' sharecroppers coincided with the new definition of "Indian" (Article 3): "Indian or forest dweller is every individual of pre-Columbian origin and ancestry who identifies himself and is identified as belonging to an ethnic group whose cultural characteristics distinguish him from the national society." Prior to the enactment of this provision, Brazilian constitutions had referred only to "forest dwellers," and neither had used the word "Indian" nor provided a definition. A statutory definition was not necessary because lawmakers and anthropologists alike assumed that the only indigenous groups in Brazil were isolated Amazonian tribes, each with its own language and cultural practices.

In addition to providing the new definition, the statute codified previous anthropological assumptions about indigenous peoples. Depending on the degree of contact with Brazilian society, Indians were classified as more or less assimilated or integrated into that society. If they were considered fully integrated into Brazilian society, they were considered no longer to be Indians. The indigenist goal that was reinforced by the language of the Indian Statute was the eventual integration of all Indians into "civilized" society. Since the mid-1980s, some anthropologists (Oliveira Filho 2000:210; Oliveira Filho 2005; A. C. Ramos 1998) have come to see this formulation as a continuation of Portuguese colonial practices and the mythical dichotomy between "wild" and "tame" Indians. According to this ideology, Indians were placed on an evolutionary scale distinguished by the degree of contact they maintained with society: isolated, intermittent contact, permanent contact, and eventually integrated, as codified in Article 4.[42]

However, in the process of its application, as exemplified by the case of the Xocó and the many other northeastern Indian recognition proceedings, the definition in Article 3 of the statute came to be used independently from the provisions of Article 4, which defined the stages of acculturation. Such an independent application was more along the lines intended by the anthropologists who had assisted the lawmakers in drafting the statute. They had drawn on the work of Darcy Ribeiro, who had not completely rejected the stage approach to the contact and assimilation question but was an early proponent of shifting the definition of Indian from Brazilian anthropology's perspective on unassimilated groups on the basis of descent to a focus on self-identification as indigenous, some cultural characteristics, and an attempt to distinguish the group from national Brazilian society (Carneiro da Cunha 1986; Oliveira Filho 2005:235).[43]

During that time, while the military government's indigenous policy was undergoing revision and the statute was being drafted, many anthropologists, including Ribeiro, were reconsidering the meaning of ethnicity. In the first decade of the twenty-first century, thirty years after the statute's enactment, anthropologists still use a version of the Article 3 definition. Even João

Pacheco de Oliveira (2005:235), former president of the Brazilian Anthropological Association (ABA) and one of the first anthropologists to address the
issue of legal opinions justifying Indian status for new northeastern tribes
(Viveiros de Castro 1999), closely follows the statutory definition. In one of
his few articles translated into English, he states: "An indigenous society [is]
every collectivity that, first, through its categories and circuits of interaction
distinguishes itself from national Brazilian society, and, second, claims itself
to be indigenous (that is, descendant—whether in genealogical, historical,
or symbolic terms—from a population of pre-Colombian origin)."

New thinking about ethnicity can also be seen in the first anthropological
report filed with FUNAI in the Xocó case. Hildegart Rick, in her defense of
indigenous status for the families who had invaded São Pedro Island, despite their long history of mixing and lack of continuity as Indians, began
by revisiting the question of relations between Indians and whites in Brazil.
The question of "acculturation" had long been the subject of Brazilian anthropology (see, for example, Cardoso de Oliveira 1964; J. W. Warren 2001).
Influenced by the work of anthropologist Fredrik Barth (1969), a new way
of thinking about ethnicity opened the door for the identification and recognition of Indians in an "acculturated" setting. Barth is best known for his
revision of ethnicity theory. He critiqued the traditional notion of "cultural
traits" as the defining characteristic of ethnic groups and instead proposed
that boundaries and identification in opposition to other groups were key
concepts in understanding how ethnic groups are constructed and maintained. Boundaries are constituted as people and cultural information cross
them, whereas the character of the boundaries differs, depending on which
differences are being emphasized in a given situation. For Barth, ethnicity
was the social organization of difference and, hence, had to be differentiated
from a bounded notion of "culture" and culture traits.

Barth's 1969 revision of the theoretical landscape of ethnicity produced
practical consequences in Brazil, and Jonathan Warren (2001), in his book
on newly recognized Indian tribes in the central south of Brazil, dubbed it
the "Barthean Break," which he points out created options for caboclos that
had not existed under previous theoretical paradigms. Warren rejects the
1973 Indian Statute as a product of "savage anthropology" and argues that
the "legal definition of Indianness remained unaltered" (2001:215). He does
not, however, reflect on the opportunities provided by the new definitional
provision, nor does he consider how the implementation of the statute has
changed the nature of Indianness in Brazil since its enactment. I contend
that with the new emphasis on self-ascription and subjective perceptions of

sameness and difference, the ethnic identification of indigenous Brazilians came to be seen as flexible and contextual. Because I view law in Brazil as an expandable and prismatic phenomenon, always subject to the process of postlegislative negotiation, I consider the statutory definition of "Indian" as presenting an opportunity that was used and acted upon and whose meaning has remained elastic. Moreover, assimilated people gaining state recognition and land rights as Indians is a crucial step toward broadening discussions and strategy debates within indigenous rights movements in Brazil and internationally (Chernela and Pinho 2004; Conklin 1997; Garfield 2001; D. Maybury-Lewis 2002; T. Turner 1991). In addition to increasing the sheer number of people entitled to land and government assistance, this change in standards for recognition challenges the necessity of proving alterity and continuity of descent to successfully assert indigenous identity.

It is worth noting in this context that the 1973 Indian Statute, as it was written, assumed that Indians had cultural distinctiveness but did not explicitly mention any "racial" characteristics as conditions of Indian categorization. As seen above, Article 3 uses the language of "pre-Columbian origin and ancestry," self-identification with an "ethnic group," and "cultural characteristics." In practice, since its enactment, the "origin and ancestry" clause of Article 3 has been finessed, at least in part because of the universal Brazilian belief that almost all rural people (and maybe all Brazilians) have some Indian ancestry, along with African and Portuguese. Paradoxically, in light of the spate of indigenous recognitions of groups that could be classified as "integrated" under the terms of Article 4, it is precisely Article 4, with its potential and legally permissible transformation of ethnic Indians into non-Indians, that requires the "origin and ancestry" clause of Article 3 to be virtually ignored as a potential racial requirement. If some people can cease being Indians, there is no impediment for others to become Indians. Because ethnicity, in the form it takes in the Indian Statute, has not been linked to race, the statute actually facilitates the decoupling of ethnicity from the notion of "race" as tied to "blood" and biology. The Indian Statute therefore became available to serve as the basis for recognitions of indigenous groups that had long been considered assimilated.

By the time anthropologists were called in to examine the nature of Xocó identity, the struggle for land and governmental support had begun to cement the differentiation of the invading families from surrounding communities. In spite of their simultaneous claim as "workers" under federal labor legislation, in May 1979, the headlines read "Indians in Misery" and the newspapers reported that the Church had reaffirmed its position in favor of land for groups claiming indigenous status. The question of identity was being fought out in the courts and in the press. As a result of the increased pressure, FUNAI sent anthropologist Delvair Melatti to the area to investigate, as mentioned earlier. She spent three days there in June and reported back that very little history was available from the Church. (This was before Dantas had produced her research, which was delivered to FUNAI after Melatti's report was filed.) A few months later, another FUNAI anthropologist opined that the people who invaded the island were Indians even though they were "culturally discharacterized" and thus no different from the rest of the population. Nonetheless, she wrote, the tribe's "members share specific cultural values and want to revitalize their ethnic identity" (Rick 1979).

In other words, wanting to "revitalize" their ethnic identity was sufficient for FUNAI to send another anthropologist to investigate further. Melatti's report, which served as the basis for legal recognition of the Xocó, produced after returning to the island for a week in fall 1979, provides evidence of the unusual nature of indigenous recognition policies in Brazil beginning to take shape at that time. That report was filed in every court proceeding to show that the statutory definition of "Indian" was met. Melatti (1979) explained that the people who invaded the island did not have even the remnants of an indigenous language and were strict adherents of Catholicism. She also observed that it was "possible that facts of identity were manipulated by some of the families out of fear that they would be removed from the Island if they did not have indigenous ancestry" (Melatti 1979:20). Even with these observations, FUNAI and the courts recognized the Xocó as Indians under the 1973 statute, cited in all the briefs and opinions. These events underline the surprising result that even as indigeneity is desired, although not fully (re)constructed, government agencies affirm that people with such desires can be considered Indians. This is a long cry from indigenous recognition proceedings in the United States, where continuity is key (Clifford 1988).

INDIGENOUS ASSEMBLIES AND CONFRONTATIONS WITH LANDOWNERS: IS THE FUTURE PAINTED BLACK?

After recognition as Xocó Indians, and over the course of the following decade, Xocó identity was forged as the families on the island fought for the rest of the Brittos' land. The 1980s saw the end of the military regime, increased political activity in Sergipe, a democratic constituent assembly, and the resulting new federal constitution. For the Xocó, the decade also saw drought, violence against their leaders and supporters, anthropologists' visits, Xocó occupation of a government office, federal litigation, and eventually the legalization of the additional land they claimed.

FUNAI anthropologist Melatti was sent back in 1985 to consider the Xocó claim to the mainland property. Comparing her 1985 report to the one filed six years earlier for recognition, the number of houses on the island had grown to forty and the population had grown from 169 to 203, with the majority under age thirty. She estimated that there were another forty Xocó living elsewhere who intended to come to the area once all the land was legalized (this was one of her arguments for increasing the size of the reserve). As the Brittos' former workers engaged in the task of becoming full-fledged Indians, they found someone to fashion a statue of a "primitive Indian" with a feather headdress, which they placed in front of the church (Melatti 1985:4), a monument that is now a bit shabby but still there thirty years later. Between the legs of the figure is a snake with an open mouth, which they say represents living in the forest. The figure itself is in a position of shooting an arrow, but even by 1985 the wooden bow had disintegrated.

Melatti (1985:4) conjectured that the statue was erected to demonstrate and ratify their indigenous descent, which she believed had become essential for the self-affirmation they needed to fight for the rest of their territory. The Xocó also institutionalized their leadership structure once they settled on the island, with Raimundo Bezerra Lima, of the 1971 lawsuit, as the first shaman and José Apolônio (who changed his name to Apolônio Xokó — a gesture similar to the naming systems of some Amazonian Indians) as the first chief, completing their individual transitions from sertanejo rural workers to Indians. That transition for other individuals and for the group as a whole required differentiation from their neighbors, and there were particular events involving their new relationship with the government that deepened their commitment to being Indians.

This was confirmed in a very personal, and tragic, way a few years after the invasion of the island. Gracinha, the thirteen-year-old daughter of Pedrito Santana, a key Xocó leader, fell in love with a fourteen-year-old member of a non-Indian family that owned land next to the Brittos' property and served as the Brittos' foremen. Their land was expropriated in the 1990s to add to the Xocó reserve. The young man's older brother, João Batista dos Santos (better known as João de Egídio), had testified on behalf of Elizabeth Britto in the lawsuits filed in 1979 against the invading families, including Gracinha's father. When Gracinha married the boy in both civil and religious ceremonies, she moved off São Pedro Island to his family's land. (The Xocó had adopted a rule that when a Xocó woman married out of the tribe, she had to leave the island; a man could bring a non-Xocó woman to live with him.) At the end of 1983, Gracinha shot a nephew of her husband and killed him; the Xocó say it was accidental (Xokó 1985). She was charged with murder. Frei Enoque arrived and successfully argued that since she was both a minor and an Indian, she could not be held criminally responsible, one of the benefits of the system of government wardship of Indians.

The victim's family swore to avenge the murder of the boy, and Gracinha's family kept her sequestered in their small house on the island (Mota 1997:93). The word put out by the boy's family was that Gracinha had killed the boy to avenge the cause of the Xocó against his family's employers, the Brittos (Melatti 1985:46), or more likely because his uncle had testified against them. A full year and a half later, the revenge was exacted when Pedrito Santana, Gracinha's father, was shot in the back at a party in Mocambo by João de Egídio's other brother, Cícero, who was apprehended and sent to prison. The chief and other Xocó leaders claimed publicly that Cícero was a gunman of the Brittos sent to take a Xocó leader out of commission (Zanetti 1985). Pedrito Santana was paralyzed, and at the request of the Xocó leaders, FUNAI transported him to an Indian hospital in São Paulo (Xokó 1985). When Santana learned that he would not recover, he returned to São Pedro Island to live out his final days, cared for by his daughter (Mota 1997:94). In 2004, Gracinha, whose Xocó identity was responsible for her freedom from prosecution, was still living on the island in the house next to her mother's (her mother is the daughter of one of the elderly residents who helped Frei Enoque construct the stories that served as evidence for FUNAI recognition). Gracinha is a full member of the Xocó community, raising her children as Indians.

In Sergipe, after 1985, the year of the first democratic election for president in Brazil since 1964, a virtual war over land, ideology, and politics began. FUNAI began the long process of demarcating the Xocó land, a decision that met with resistance by landowners. In the state more generally, the Workers' Party (PT) was founded,[44] land invasions by squatters began apace, and a committee of academics, students, lawyers, and Church progressives was formed to support land movements, including that of the Xocó (Magno da Silva and Lopes 1996). The following year, Elizabeth Britto sold the mainland Caiçara property to Alagoan lawyer Jorge Pacheco, coordinator of the Association in Defense of Landowners in the Lower São Francisco, while João Britto retained Belém, the other part of the mainland. At the end of 1985, the Union of Indigenous Nations was paying attention to the situation in Sergipe, because Xocó leaders Apolônio, Raimundo, the FUNAI agent posted on the Island, and the boatman Paulino Acácio were in São Paulo.

They complained that the new governor refused to meet with them, yet had received Pacheco and Britto, because the governor was of the same party as former Propriá mayor Antônio Britto, still a political power in the area, and Propriá could deliver 40,000 votes (Zanetti 1985). Pacheco had purchased Caiçara knowing that it was the subject of possible expropriation and made it clear from the beginning that he was against ceding his land to the Xocó. Being a savvy negotiator, once he knew the expropriation was just a matter of time, Pacheco would not budge and continued taking extreme measures to keep the Xocó off the land until he received full indemnification in the mid-1990s.

In the sertão of Sergipe and Alagoas, operating outside the law with gunmen and private police and engaging in political violence in the 1980s was still reminiscent of the legendary bandit, Lampião, whose legacy represented the confusion between legitimate and illegitimate authority. Banditry, political patronage, and violence served as the backdrop and in some ways as a counterpoint for the often almost-violent encounters between the newly recognized Xocó Indians and the gunmen of Pacheco—a counterpoint, because in the late 1980s, the Xocó leaders did not allow themselves to be intimidated by Pacheco's tactics. More than once they occupied his ranch house, went to Brasília to appeal to government officials, and held meetings of northeastern tribes (with thousands in attendance) on São Pedro Island. In September 1985, the Xocó hosted such a national indigenous assembly, and Pacheco was accused of placing a "battalion of eighteen gunmen in Caiçara" (Zanetti 1985). When the FUNAI team arrived, Pacheco threatened them, saying that he had 200 men armed with rifles.[45] He also brought a lawsuit in state court and obtained an injunction against people entering the area.[46]

In 1987, as recounted years later by labor lawyer José Alvino Santos Filho, he and Rosemiro Magno da Silva, a professor and leader of the support committee for land struggles, went to a meeting on São Pedro Island to express support for a planned occupation of Caiçara. When they arrived, the Xocó leaders informed them they were going to invade Pacheco's ranch house the next day and wanted the lawyer to stay with them (Alvino was twenty-one at the time, newly graduated with no experience). Rosemiro left him there to return to Aracaju to contact the press about the impending occupation. Alvino slept in the old mission church with the bats and was rousted at three in the morning by a group of Xocó, some of them armed, and they proceeded to the ranch house. Pacheco's employees (Pacheco himself was not there) left without resistance. Then the entire Xocó community, including the children and old folks, moved into the house and slept in hammocks on the veranda.

Alvino learned from two-way radio conversations with Frei Enoque that the police had surrounded the area, allowing no one to enter. At the house, "there were many meetings and they spoke about indigenous identity" (Santos Filho interview 2000).

When a few federal police officers arrived, the Xocó told them they intended to stay, even though there would likely be legal consequences, and the federal police left. A few hours later, in a cloud of dust, the state military police arrived, 400-strong, with heavy, high-caliber arms, in buses and trucks, to enforce another injunction against the Xocó.[47] The Indians had placed logs in the dirt road, so the police had to arrive on foot. They were greeted by the women and children at the gate of the house, waving a large Brazilian flag and singing the national anthem. The police broke down the doors, shot over their heads, and began hitting people. An explanation for this offered by Alvino was that João Britto had sponsored a barbeque for the police with alcohol before they proceeded to confront the Indians. Only when the officer in charge recognized Alvino as an old friend was there a break in the situation. The negotiation was made difficult, however, because Jorge Pacheco himself had led the troops in, carrying two revolvers, appearing to Alvino like "a character from an American western sporting a ten-gallon hat, like a Texas rancher" (Santos Filho interview 2000).

Alvino was worried that he would be taken prisoner for invading private property with the Xocó, but he was not arrested because of his friendship with the state police officer, an evangelical Protestant who had aligned himself with the progressive religious movement. Alvino met with Xocó leaders about whether to stay or go. In a division of opinion that foreshadowed a later shift in leadership and ideology, chief Apolônio wanted to stay and confront, while Girleno (a military policeman who lived across the river and who became chief a couple of years later) was in favor of backing off. They eventually compromised and left the house but remained camped on the mainland, and the immediate confrontation ended. Alvino returned to the capital by boat that night, transported by FUNAI boatman and Xocó leader Paulino Acácio.

It was shortly after this aborted occupation of the ranch house that Apolônio visited the federal attorney in Aracaju to plead for federal intervention by way of a lawsuit. In the same month that the new constitution went into effect, October 1988, the federal attorney was moved by Apolônio's dedication, the story he told, and the documentation produced by Beatriz Dantas. The federal attorney, a follower of Kardec spiritism, felt a spiritual tie with the cause of the Xocó (Campos interview 2000). Within a few days,

Editorial cartoon: "Just one minute, Xocó . . . 'BLACK' Ready! Your future is already painted." (*Jornal de Sergipe*, December 6, 1979).

he had filed a thirty-eight-page brief in federal court, arguing for the Xocó right to Caiçara.[48] The original lawsuit brought by Pacheco was transferred to federal court, and it took from January 1988 until well into the 1990s for the court to determine the rights of the Xocó and the amount of indemnification due each of the thirty landowners in the area that were expropriated.

The pressure exerted by the federal attorney was not sufficient by itself to move the government to give the Xocó all the land they demanded. On April 3, 1989, forty-seven Xocó Indians occupied the regional office of FUNAI, remaining camped in the halls of the office building for four months. On Christmas eve 1991, the former governor of Alagoas, President Fernando Collor, signed the decree ratifying the demarcation of Caiçara and São Pedro Island and declaring the area to be set aside for the "traditional and permanent occupation of the indigenous group Xocó" (Oliveira Filho 1993). That same year, the Brazilian census bureau added "indigenous," along with "black, white, brown, and yellow," as a possible response to the newly rephrased question: "What is your race or color?" (Nobles 2000:121).

Despite physical appearance, newly recognized northeastern Indians often defined themselves in contrast to being black. Being indigenous was better than being caboclo or sertanejo, categories that carried no legal rights, and most definitely better than being black. Such a perspective is exemplified by a cartoon, published the day before the governor purchased São Pedro Island from the Brittos, which reflects public skepticism about Xocó identity while at the same time opining on the chances of Xocó success and survival. It contains a double entendre that inadvertently anticipates the next ethno-racial land struggle in the area. For two decades, beginning in 1971, São Pedro Island served as the crucible of a struggle that began in the darkest days of the military regime and continued through the democratic opening that led to a constitution with expanded rights for Indians. The 1988 Constitution also contained an unprecedented clause assuring land to communities of descendants of fugitive slaves, which served as the opening for another struggle for land and identity in the neighboring village of Mocambo.

Constructing Boundaries and Creating Legal Facts

A LANDOWNER DIES AND A QUILOMBO IS BORN

When the quilombo clause was enacted in 1988, no one expected it to have much effect.[1] In fact, the clause, which provides that "survivors of quilombo communities occupying their lands are recognized as definitive owners, and the State shall issue them titles to the land" (Linhares 2004:818), was placed in the transitory section at the end of the Constitution because it was assumed there were very few quilombos and that all would be identified and granted land within just a few years. The Palmares Cultural Foundation, formed in 1988 under the Ministry of Culture, with a very small budget, was assigned the task of identifying potential communities, arranging for anthropological certification, proposing presidential recognition, and granting land titles, until its power was shifted to the National Institute of Colonization and Agrarian Reform (INCRA) in 2003.[2] However, as this chapter will explain, with the new emphasis on antiracism in Brazil and the process of postlegislative negotiation in full swing, the number of identified quilombos has grown exponentially.[3]

Public interest in quilombos dates to the 1970s, when the figure of Zumbi of Palmares, the king of the largest and longest-lasting quilombo in Brazilian history, was introduced to the Brazilian public. In existence for almost the entire seventeenth century, Palmares had a population estimated at 11,000 (Schwartz 1992:123) and has been termed "an African State in Brazil" (Kent 1965). The Palmares quilombo was celebrated by nineteenth-century writers and was appropriated and publicized in the twentieth century by Brazilian black movement activists, such as Abdias do Nascimento (1980), who developed the ideology of "quilombismo," relating modern black activism to "the spirit of resistance of the ancient quilombos" (Véran 2002:20).

By 1988, the Palmares quilombo and its king had obtained a place in the official history of Brazil. Zumbi, as a "living presence in the resistance" by oppressed black people in Brazil, was identified as an "ongoing source of inspiration for the political actions of contemporary Black Brazilians" (Pereira and White 2001:137). Since the 1995 national celebration of the 300th anniversary of Zumbi's death and the destruction of Palmares, November 20 has been adopted by the government as Black Consciousness Day to replace May 13, 1888, the date on which slavery was abolished, which had for a century served as a national holiday. Over 3.5 million Africans were imported to be slaves in Brazil, beginning in the mid-1500s, leading to Brazil's status as the country with the largest number of African-descended people outside Africa. It is not surprising, therefore, that when a new agency was created to protect the interests of Afro-Brazilians it was named after Palmares. However, rural struggle as descendants of slaves did not come to the Northeast for a couple of years, and when it did, it built on the effervescence of redemocratization in the 1980s leading up to the long-awaited Constitution.

During those exciting days of the 1980s, land struggles throughout the Northeast were on the upswing, instigated and supported by the Catholic Church's Pastoral Land Commission (CPT) and the Landless Rural Workers' Movement (MST). In Sergipe, the Workers' Party (PT) was founded in 1980, and in 1985 a support committee of academics, students, trade unionists, journalists, lawyers, and lay religious workers was formed to support land struggles. When the diocese joined the committee the following year, Frei Enoque received death threats from landowners and a nun coordinator of the CPT was beaten by hired gunmen (Magno da Silva and Lopes 1996). The Xocó demand for the Brittos' mainland property became more intense, with occupations of the land itself and of the FUNAI regional headquarters. Once the newly independent federal attorney's office exercised its new constitutional power to sue on behalf of indigenous groups, the expropriation decree came shortly thereafter, and demarcation of the full Xocó reserve was finalized in 1991. However, land issues still remained, particularly for neighboring Mocambo. When a new dispute arose in 1992 over the land located between the Xocó reserve and Mocambo, no one suspected that it would lead to the rethinking of ethnoracial identification of the relatives of the Xocó in Mocambo.

The process that resulted in legal recognition moved more rapidly in Mocambo than it had for the Xocó twenty years earlier. However, just as with the people who became the Xocó, the Mocambo residents who chose to start down the path of quilombo recognition to resolve a land dispute had no idea of a history that was constructed as legal requirements ebbed and flowed. It did not take long for them to realize that the use of the quilombo clause, which brought with it the possibility of land ownership, also meant reconsidering ethnoracial self-identification and political and personal alliances.

This chapter narrates the genesis of that land struggle. It charts the transformation of Mocambo identity through a series of legal categories, each carrying particular obstacles and rights, thus illustrating the first component of legalizing identity: the experience of revised identities as laws are invoked and rights are put into practice. As will be shown, this process can happen in stages and in this case was complicated by the landowners' identities, how decisions were made in relation to the Xocó, disappointment in land reform, and the availability of a new law.

The centerpiece of this chapter is a contextualized explication of the interpretation of the quilombo clause during the key years for Mocambo, which, like the 1973 Indian Statute, provides a prime example of postlegislative negotiation. I highlight the legitimating role of anthropology in redefining the quilombo concept as an illustration of governmentality and its effects. In this case, legalizing quilombo identity was a product of goading by Xocó neighbors combined with liberation theology, legal expertise, and anthropological theory. It is sometimes tempting to tell a story such as this from a celebratory perspective. This chapter, however, shows that a narrative of unity, often insisted upon by the participants, is an incomplete explanation for the changes in Mocambo. Instead, I focus on local disjunctures and the sometimes disruptive effects of the politics of recognition. Neither the changes, nor the disagreements, would have come into being without the law and its constant reinterpretation.

NEW GENERATIONS: LAND AND LIBERATION

One year after Caiçara was added to the Xocó reserve, Mocambo was involved in a dispute with the landowner whose property served as the boundary between it and the Xocó. Even though the Xocó had received Caiçara, they were still asserting rights to that border property, which had recently changed hands upon the death of its owner, Darcy Cardoso. His landholdings had been divided among his children. Two had had their parcels expropriated for the Xocó in 1991, and Neusa, the youngest, had received the border parcel that became the focus of the Mocambo struggle.

Darcy Cardoso was born and raised in Mocambo, the son of a poor family of boatmen and day laborers. In contrast to the landowners against whom the Xocó had fought, Cardoso had started life with nothing but had, by 1960, when he fulfilled his dream of owning the land next to Mocambo, achieved wealth through trading goods up and down the river and cultivating political and personal ties. The transition from villager to landowner did not keep

Darcy from visiting Mocambo regularly and being involved with local politics, feuds, and intrigues. From 1960 until his death in 1982, Darcy Cardoso also made sure that his childhood friends in Mocambo always had work on his land. Until his estate was finally settled in 1986, his heirs continued to allow the Mocambo residents to work as sharecroppers on the land. As the Xocó heated up the pressure for Caiçara, neighboring landowners became skittish about the possibility that their workers too would aspire to take their land.

The land bordering the other side of Mocambo and deep into the interior was owned by the former senator and governor of Sergipe, João de Seixas Dória, who received it as a gift from his father in 1960 (Seixas Dória interview 2000). While João held public office, his father managed the land and is said to have gravely mistreated the workers who lived on it, including chasing them off, which forced them to move to Mocambo (Arruti 2002:229). This was viewed as an irony by many because, in contrast to his father and their cousins, the Brittos, Governor Seixas Dória was considered a benevolent landowner. He was a champion of land reform, and after only a few months in office, on the day after the military coup in 1964, he was imprisoned for a year as a subversive, despite his conservative party affiliation (Seixas Dória 1965). Years later, when Mocambo was recognized as a quilombo, Seixas Dória offered to sell his land to the government for the benefit of his former workers, citing his support for land reform and his reputation as a progressive politician. As with the Brittos and the Cardosos, Seixas Dória's decision was tied to a generational shift—in this case, impending. In his eighties, Seixas Dória knew that his sons would not want to give up the land, so he asked them out of respect for their aging father to accept payment from the government, and they agreed. Technically, he was paid for the "cultural patrimony" in the form of the buildings and their contents. No payment was received for the land itself. Seixas Dória took pride in pointing out that he was the only landowner in Brazil to have voluntarily relinquished his land to a quilombo.

Another generational shift had taken place. Ironically, as the Brazilian state was being democratized, the role of the Catholic Church in progressive political projects was beginning to diminish. The social mission of the Church, initially sponsored by bishops and priests in the early 1950s, with opposition from the military government in the late 1960s, had "become cemented into the self-image" of the Brazilian Catholic Church (Bruneau 1974:220). Even as the Church was influencing the political liberalization that led to the restoration of democracy in 1985 (Serbin 2000:2), the Vatican

Padre Isaías and Maripaulo Acácio dos Santos (photograph by the author)

was beginning its "counter-offensive" against liberation theologians in Latin America (Löwy 1996:123).[4] However, as can be seen in the sertão of Sergipe, the influence of liberation theology doctrine and practice remains powerful, particularly in relation to land movements and the struggles of Indians and Afro-Brazilians for social justice (Burdick 2004; French 2007).

Mariza Rios, the nun and lawyer, arrived in Mocambo in mid-1992, together with a former nun, Inês dos Santos Souza, at the request of an activist priest in the diocese, Padre Isaías Nascimento. Born in the interior of Sergipe, Isaías was the forty-second child of his father and the eleventh of his mother. (His father's fourth wife had thirteen children; his father was forty-four years older than his mother.) When he was fourteen years old, his family (at that time consisting of his parents and the twelve children still at home) moved to the state capital to escape the effects of the drought of 1970. Their move came on the heels of his father's religious conversion, which precipitated his father abandoning a business with forty employees to lead a contemplative life in relative poverty. The family of fourteen moved into a two-bedroom rented house, where they lived for the next ten years. Isaías became an "office boy" at a bank and at the end of the 1970s joined a youth group run by Capuchin friars, who were called "communists" by the authorities. In 1982 he moved to the progressive diocese of Propriá, which was headed by Dom José Brandão de Castro.

The following year, Isaías went to study at the same liberation theology seminary that had trained Frei Enoque almost twenty years earlier. Before Isaías returned to the diocese, Dom José Brandão fell ill, and he retired in 1987, after which the political climate for the progressive wing of the Church in Sergipe seemed to change. Some activists accused the new bishop, Dom José Palmeira Lessa, of shifting the diocese's emphasis away from the dispossessed and toward the interests of the elite,[5] although Frei Enoque pointed out that Dom Lessa continued giving support to land struggles, but from a smoother, more negotiated stance (Melo interview 1997). Two years later, in 1989, Isaías returned to the diocese to be ordained, and he became the parish priest of Porto da Folha for four years.[6] Thus Padre Isaías ended a long period in which no priest had been in Mocambo. He began to visit the village regularly, performing weddings and baptisms and encouraging Mocambo residents to struggle for their rights to food and land, continuing with the liberation theology training he had received at the seminary (Nascimento Filho interview 2000). In early 1992, Padre Isaías was visiting the area of Mocambo to pass out food and learned that a number of families from Mocambo who had been working as sharecroppers on the land of Neusa Cardoso had been expelled and their rice destroyed by Cardoso's cattle. Inspired by what Frei Enoque had accomplished for the Xocó, Padre Isaías decided to help them gain access to Cardoso's land. He called upon the CPT, with Mariza Rios, Inês dos Santos Souza, and a lay religious worker, Margarette Lisboa Rocha, to mobilize the Mocambo families and provide them with legal assistance.[7]

Mariza Rios was born to a poor family in the south central state of Espirito Santo in 1958, the youngest of nine children. Mariza identifies herself as "a real Brazilian." Her mother, she is quick to explain, was the daughter of a Portuguese and an Italian; her father was the son of a black-Indian man and a Guarani Indian woman. She often recounts that her father's grandfather "came on a boat from Africa." In the Brazilian manner of constant, never-tiring amazement at the tricks that genetics play on skin, hair, nose, and body type, Mariza once explained to me that because of the combination of her ancestors, she has blond, white siblings, while she herself favors the black and indigenous side. After returning from a stint as a nanny at the age of eleven while she attended school, Mariza worked in a shoe factory and attended high school at night. In her teens, she became involved with a youth group run by a congregation of nuns, and by the time she was twenty-one, she had taken her vows.[8] After two years as a missionary among onion workers in the interior of Bahia, she went to Rio de Janeiro to study law.

Mariza Rios (photograph by the author)

Later, while in Sergipe, Mariza kept in touch with her law professors for advice and tapped these resources when she first heard of the quilombo clause (Rios interview 2000).

Inês dos Santos Souza, born in 1956, moved to Sergipe from a town in the south of Brazil where descendants of immigrants still spoke only German. In her hometown, Inês experienced discrimination because of her relatively darker skin — she explained that there she was considered black, while in the Northeast she is considered *morena* (a term that can mean, depending on the context, anything from brunette to brown-skinned).[9] Her father's family had always been left leaning, and when she was young, she had belonged to a revolutionary youth group. Because of the Church's resistance to the military government, Inês found liberation theology to be the best way to help the poor and advance the cause of social justice. She was a nun for ten years, studying liberation theology in Italy and France in 1987. As the Church hierarchy moved to the political right, Inês became frustrated. She left her congregation and moved to Sergipe to work with the CPT in Propriá, where she married and started a family.[10]

On July 22, 1992, Inês and Padre Isaías arrived in Mocambo for the first meeting the CPT would have in what would become a long relationship with that community.[11] At the second meeting, held less than two weeks later, Mariza was introduced to the workers as the lawyer of the CPT, whose task it

Inês dos Santos Souza and her son, Marcos (photograph by the author)

would be to advise the workers of their rights. In addition to the CPT, Padre Isaías also mobilized the Rural Workers' Union.[12] Within three months, lawsuits had been filed by landowner Neusa Cardoso against the workers and by Mariza on behalf of them; a commission had been formed in Mocambo to lead the struggle; and delegations had been sent to the area to garner support, for hearings, to meet with the judge, and to complain to the police about threats of violence by the landowner's gunmen. The story of how the fight began was written into legal briefs; was recounted to INCRA, to convince that body to institute expropriation proceedings; appeared in the press; and was included in CPT documents as well as in the report filed by the government-contracted anthropologist five years later to justify Mocambo's recognition as a quilombo.

<h2 style="text-align:center">UM BELO DIA (ONE FINE DAY):
REVISING HISTORY AND ITS DISCONTENTS</h2>

The story, as it is still told, begins with the legal settlement of Darcy Cardoso's estate in 1986. In that year, the new generation, in the person of Neusa, with the help of her brother João, denied work to the Mocambo families on Darcy's land where they had always planted. Six years later, in 1992, however, the caretaker of Neusa's property permitted them to plant. But then, as

Mariza tells it, "*Um belo dia*" (one fine day) Neusa Cardoso decided to release her cattle to graze on the ripe rice planted by a group of Mocambo families on her land, destroying their harvest and leaving them destitute (Rios interview 2000), because working on Neusa's land was their only means of subsistence.[13] The prevailing narrative of the Mocambo land struggle invariably begins with the action of the new generation of landowners. Having taken over from their father, who always provided for his old neighbors, they behaved arbitrarily and forced the families who had planted on their land for over forty years into hunger and poverty.[14]

The struggle over Neusa Cardoso's land that began in 1992 would eventually lead to alterations in self-identification by two-thirds of the population of Mocambo and a ferocious feud with friends, family members, and many of the Xocó (now allied with some former enemies, such as the Egídio family involved in killing the Xocó leader, Pedrito Santana, described in chapter 2). My interest in understanding just how the struggle began led me to review contemporaneous meeting reports, court documents, and depositions and to interview many of the people involved in the events of the early 1990s. One question seemed to be inadequately addressed, even in the anthropological report written five years later (Arruti 1997). Why, if the landowner began excluding the Mocambo families from planting in 1986, did they wait until 1992 to take action? Even when Padre Isaías first appeared on the scene and began talking to them about improving their situation in 1990, the people in Mocambo did not organize themselves to invade the land or even to bring a labor claim.

What had been "forgotten" in the Mocambo story was the integral role of the Xocó in the decision made by the Mocambo families to pursue their rights. In fact, the two struggles were intertwined, as was the ancestry of the two groups. Rather than being simply a rupture caused by the landowner's arbitrary decision, the precipitating events might more accurately be seen as an indication of the persistently ambivalent relationship of Mocambo residents to the Xocó struggle and of members of the Xocó community to the incipient quilombo campaign. Once the Xocó struggle began and the Indians began to consider themselves separate from other communities in the area, stories were developed to explain the indistinguishable physical characteristics of the people who invaded São Pedro Island and the people who lived in Mocambo. For example, when FUNAI anthropologist Melatti visited the island immediately after the invasion, she heard that "the inhabitants of Porto da Folha are descendants of the Dutch who brought many slaves, placing them on the islands in the São Francisco River. The Xocó expelled these slaves that were placed on their lands, but in spite of this many blacks married caboclos, hence their negroid traces" (Melatti 1979). Differentiation was important to the Xocó, who may not have wanted the standard comments about racial mixing to raise doubts about their legitimate claim to Xocó identity (Arruti 2002:273).

However, the standard narrative involves a recollection and invocation of "ties of solidarity" between the Mocambo families and the Xocó. Once Neusa Cardoso initiated the dispute, the Xocó rose to the defense of Mocambo, the story goes. The assertion of unity by community members, NGO mediators, and the anthropologist who first heard the story in 1995 (Arruti 1997:30) may have been necessary to soften the impact of competition for limited resources between two poor communities — to present a united front to the outside world. However, when placed into the context of the time, and in light of subsequent events, an explanation that focuses on separation, the politics of recognition, and legal requirements may be more elucidating of both the motivations of those who retell the stories and the emotional impact of new identities.

At the first meeting with the CPT in Mocambo a few days after Neusa Cardoso released her cattle onto the rice in July 1992, fifteen Xocó were among the eighty participants.[15] The report on that meeting reveals that what had actually provoked Neusa's decision was the invasion less than a week earlier by a group of Xocó who had set up camp near the rice lagoon where twenty-three Mocambo families were preparing to harvest their crop. When Neusa's brother, João, came with the police to expel the Xocó, he saw them fishing with the Mocambo workers and he exchanged angry words with them. As part of the renewed invitation by Neusa to work on her land, the Mocambo families had intended to share the crop with her, as had been their practice for decades before 1986, the year of Darcy Cardoso's estate settlement, when planting was prohibited. That was the year, as well, when the Xocó began actively to assert their claim to Caiçara and the Cardoso parcels through land invasions. In the years between Darcy's death and the settlement of his estate (1982–1986), Neusa had engaged the workers of Mocambo to plant. She even supplied them with seeds, as is required under a sharecropping relationship. Beginning in 1986, the Cardoso heirs found themselves with Xocó families camping on their land, neither working nor paying rent and threatening to petition the government to include their land in the Caiçara expropriation. That year, members of the Xocó community invaded Neusa's sister's piece of the estate and destroyed the rice crop by opening the floodgates so they could fish.[16] This was the reason why the Cardosos denied access to any of the workers in 1986.

Neusa's sister and brother each lost their land to the FUNAI expropriation that became the full Xocó reserve in 1991 (it included Caiçara, these pieces of the Cardoso property, and a number of small properties owned by individuals, some of whom had been cowhands or foremen for the Brittos). Since Neusa's land was not expropriated in 1991, she relaxed a bit and invited the Mocambo families to reenter into the old sharecropping relationship. Then, in the aftermath of the release of cattle onto the rice, in a fit of anger over the Xocó, Neusa offered to pay the workers for some portion of their share of the ruined rice harvest—an offer accepted by two of the families. After all, sharecroppers are always disputing with landowners in small ways, not necessarily obvious to outside observers, such as shortchanging on the crop or planting their own vegetables on the land, and the Mocambo workers would have been no exception (Scott 1985). From Neusa's point of view, if the Xocó would just leave the property she could continue her relationship with the Mocambo families and all would be fine, so long as the Mocambo workers did not talk back. But this was not to be. What changed in 1992 was a chance for the Mocambo villagers to succeed in a way that had never presented itself before—and the Xocó Indians were keeping track of Mocambo's potential success.

According to Xocó leader Paulino Acácio, at an early CPT-sponsored meeting to discuss alternatives, the people in Mocambo had not wanted to participate in the struggle of the Indians, and now that the last piece of land was at issue, either the folks from Mocambo should assert their right to it or the Xocó would take it (Rios interview 2000). Over the next years, there were moments when some Xocó expressed a desire to help out and in the early days went to court to testify on behalf of the families damaged by the actions of the Cardosos.[17] However, the spirit generally was competitive and rife with jealousy. The ultimatum issued by Paulino, on behalf of the Xocó, was reminiscent of the threat expressed over a decade earlier by the Kariri-Xocó that provoked the Xocó invasion of São Pedro Island.

These events might be analyzed as a simple case of competitiveness between relatives, the desire of the Xocó for as much land as possible, or their insecurity about being newly recognized Indians in a system where the label "Indian" in the popular imagination was reserved for isolated tribes in the Amazon. The Xocó may have been acting out of a desire to solidify their identification as full-fledged Indians, and certainly the events of 1992 were part of an ongoing process of differentiation and boundary creation by a newly recognized ethnic group. This process of separation was taking place, however, between people whose forebears, and who themselves only a few years previously, had shared family ties, everyday lives, work, and an identical relationship to land and landowners. Beginning with decisions made in the early days of the Xocó struggle by family members and other residents of the area not to participate, resentments survived and intensified. Such resentments are expressed only in highly emotional settings when the issue arises of who "is" an Indian and how that status was determined. Some of the older people in Mocambo (all with relatives on São Pedro Island), for example, recall that the Xocó did not want them involved, while many Indians assert that their Mocambo neighbors were not interested, implying a lack of courage.

Another example involves people who are considered neither Indians nor quilombolas. Maria José is a sister-in-law of João de Egídio, the man who testified against the Xocó in 1979 and later moved to Mocambo with his family in 1999 once he had received payment for his plot of land that was included in the Xocó reserve. Maria José's husband had not owned land, so was not entitled to the proceeds of expropriation, but was also not an "Indian" and thus not entitled to live on the Xocó reserve. In a heated moment, Maria José expressed the view that everyone in the area is part Indian, asserting some kind of conspiracy against those who were not "chosen" by FUNAI to be Xocó (Maria José Bezerra Santos interview 2000).[18] Even Neusa and João Cardoso (interview 2000) expressed similar sentiments. After all, they said, their family hailed from the area for many generations. Moreover, as relatively small landowners, the Cardosos were convinced that the Brittos had conspired with the government and the workers who claimed indigenous status to cheat them out of their land and then out of adequate compensation for it.

The Mocambo family with perhaps the most complex and ambivalent relationship to the Xocó struggle was the family of Xocó leader Paulino's "other" wife, Maria das Virgens Santos, known as Dona Maria, the matriarch of one of two families leading the campaign for quilombo status. In the 1950s, Paulino had married two young women—Lindonor, who lived in Caiçara, and Maria das Virgens, in Mocambo. The first was a religious marriage, the second was both religious and civil. In Brazil, it is very common for couples who are not married in a civil ceremony to call each other husband and wife. Paulino had a child with each wife right away and then had one other daughter with Lindonor in Caiçara and five other children with Maria in Mocambo. Even with his commitment to Maria, he always lived on São

Dona Maria and her eldest daughter, Lourdes, dressed up for
Election Day in October 2000 (photograph by the author)

Pedro Island with his Xocó wife. Maria's first child died young, leaving as
the eldest in Mocambo a son, Maripaulo. Knowing that people were talking
about their marital situation and wanting to assert in no uncertain terms the
paternity of her children, Maria named three of her five surviving children
with some variation of hers and Paulino's names: Maripaulo, Paulameire, and
Paulomary, another practice not uncommon in Brazil.

As a teenager, Maripaulo helped his father in the Xocó struggle, much to
the chagrin of Dona Maria, who feared for her son's life when the police and
hired gunmen of the landowners threatened the families who had invaded
São Pedro Island.[19] Maripaulo developed an allegiance to Paulino's family,

who were Maripaulo's Xocó grandmother, aunts, uncles, cousins, and sib-lings. He was Paulino's only child in Mocambo who was old enough to be involved with the Xocó recognition process; at seventeen he would sneak away to participate in the meetings and land occupations. Dona Maria's three middle children had good relations with, and fond memories of, their father and his Xocó brothers and sisters but grew up knowing that they were not entitled to the benefits of being an Indian (for example, health care, housing, access to land).

As Maripaulo began self-identifying as a quilombola, he began referring to his mother as Paulino's "black" wife, although it is not clear that such a description was used before the Xocó struggle. These days, common wisdom has it that the people in Mocambo were historically called *negros do Mo-cambo*, but it is just as likely that such an appellation would have included those who eventually self-identified as Indians. It is equally possible that this is a post facto appellation in light of the necessity to have a specific "history" for purposes of legal recognition. With the advent of the quilombo recogni-tion campaign, Maripaulo was the only one of Paulino and Maria's children who self-identified as both an Indian and a black person.[20]

FROM NO RECOURSE TO RIGHTS: SHARECROPPERS TO SQUATTERS TO QUILOMBOLAS

As a result of the Xocó challenge to the ownership of Neusa Cardoso's land, the nature of the sharecropping (*meeiro*) relationship and the legal status of the Mocambo workers were contested and transformed by legal require-ments. Lawyer Mariza Rios explained to the villagers in August 1992 that they might have some right to work on Neusa's land under a form of ad-verse possession as *posseiros* (sometimes translated as "squatters"), which provided people living and working on land in good faith for a certain period of time the right to continue on the land and to collect damages if the titled owner expelled them. Mariza spelled out that possession of land as posseiros carried with it a set of rights distinct from the contract rights of meeiros. This difference would also permit villagers who were not among the families working on Neusa's land in 1992, but had done so at any time since Darcy's acquisition of it in 1960, to claim access to the land. After explaining this at the meeting, Mariza and Inês withdrew, leaving the decision of whether to bring a lawsuit to assert posseiro rights to the fifty residents in attendance. Once they made the decision to pursue their rights to possession and damages in court, over one hundred villagers went with the CPT delegation to the contested area to see the Cardosos' cattle eating the rice.[21]

The earliest reports indicate that the people in Mocambo considered themselves to be meeiros. When Mariza asked them to describe their system of work, they explained that for rice, the landowner provides the seed and the workers do all the work and deliver one-half the harvest to the door of the owner. All expenses other than the seed are paid by the workers. Other vegetables and roots they grow are shared, one part to the owner and two parts to them. From July until October 1992, when she filed the complaint in which she carefully used the word "posseiros" to describe the people of Mocambo, Mariza explained the difference in rights between the two on a regular basis (Rios interview 2000). "Posseiro," roughly translated, means "squatter" or "homesteader," but without the U.S. legal, sociological, and political connotations (homesteaders live on public lands over which they have usufruct rights; squatters are illegally present on privately owned land). In Brazil, posseiros are people who do not own the land in question, but live on, improve, and hold usufruct rights to the land.

There are legal and historical differences among workers with some control over land, such as meeiros; wage laborers who neither own nor enjoy even limited control over land; and posseiros (B. Maybury-Lewis 1994:244). Because of these differences, Mariza coached the Mocambo workers to use the proper word in court and with authorities. Maripaulo recalled that it was difficult for the Mocambo residents to remember to refer to themselves as "posseiros," since they had referred to themselves as "meeiros" their entire lives. Mariza had to teach them a mnemonic to help them remember ("posseiros like Poço Redondo," she said). Although seemingly a simple change in terminology, the importance of this shift in legal category was not lost on the leaders of this crucial first stage of struggle. Almost immediately after the introduction of the notion that being posseiros meant possibly obtaining rights to land (even Neusa's small property), delegations of Mocambo leaders went to the county seat to meet with officials — the earliest of many engagements with local, state, and federal government that were to insert Mocambo, a previously unknown sertanejo community, into the governmental framework at all levels. Placing Mocambo on the map and on the radar of the government also increased the stakes for its residents in terms of access to food, land, and electricity, as well as in local politics, factional fights, and family feuds.

For the people of Mocambo, the shift of labels was the difference between having no recourse and having rights. Learning to say the word "posseiro" in reference to who they were was a step in the process of identity transformation. Having "Doutora" Mariza, the appellation of lawyers in Brazil, on their side was like being given a present of the law. After she filed the lawsuit against Neusa Cardoso claiming possession of the contested land for the Mocambo "posseiros," the Xocó continued to camp on the property, while Mocambo residents continued to traverse it and work on it. The judge, known for his prolandowner bias, took no action on Mariza's lawsuit. Five months later, in March 1993, Neusa filed a suit against both the Mocambo posseiros and the Indians and was immediately granted a restraining order from the same judge, expelling them all from the land. In his order, the judge did not acknowledge that another suit was pending against Neusa, and when the order was challenged in August, the judge reissued it, this time as an injunction, again prohibiting Mocambo residents from being on the land.[22] By the time the appeal from the second expulsion was filed, however, the people who started the lawsuit in 1992 as posseiros were representing themselves as "the black community of Mocambo . . . pursuing in a court of competent jurisdiction, its request to be recognized as a descendant of a quilombo" under the Constitution.[23] Within the year, the state secretary of justice was cited by Mariza in court papers as stating that he recognized strong indications that "the black community of Mocambo *is* a quilombo."

POSTLEGISLATIVE NEGOTIATION OF THE QUILOMBO CLAUSE

How did the quilombo clause originate and find its way into the 1988 Constitution? Why and how did the negotiation over its postlegislative meaning and usage take place? And how did it find its way to Mocambo? The answers to these questions are key to understanding the new assertion of quilombo identity and the insertion of a tiny village on the São Francisco River into the political life of the nation.

As noted at the beginning of this chapter, when the quilombo clause was enacted in 1988, prospects for its enforcement were bleak. In fact, problems arose almost immediately in relation to its application, centering around the definition of "remanescentes das comunidades dos quilombos" (descendants of communities of fugitive slaves), the term used by the Constitution. Since there have always been rural black communities that deny ties to slavery with origin stories about escaping prior to enslavement and communities that are, in fact, descended from groups of slaves who acquired possession of their land through gifts from their slave owners or from the Catholic Church, a definitive meaning for the words of the Constitution was elusive (Vogt and Fry 1996; Baiocchi 1983; Magno da Silva 2000). Moreover, technically, quilombos no longer existed after 1888 when abolition was declared, but the term continued to be used as a symbol of black resistance (Ayer de Oliveira 2001:31). Consequently, the definition of "remanescente de quilombo" has been debated, narrowed, broadened, and attempted to be narrowed again, and only with a 2003 decree, when it was broadened again, have some technical issues relating to the process of identification and land grants begun to be addressed, but the postlegislative negotiation continues, with a new IN-CRA regulation in September 2008 that again makes land grants to quilombos more difficult.[24]

The debate over the legal definition of "quilombo" mirrored the debate over its historical meaning and the multiple and varied claims to the legacy of its historical reality. The concept of "quilombo" was already losing its strictly historical significance when it was thrust into the public sphere during the early twentieth century as a metaphor for cultural resistance, representing the desire to search for and preserve the traces of Africa in the "black culture" of Brazil. For the next fifty years, the dominant view of the meaning of "quilombo" was the search for an "understanding of the world of Africa among us" (Peixoto 2000:123–25). It was assumed that when slaves escaped and formed their own societies they reverted to African cultural practices, which were forbidden by their masters. An alternative to a cultural interpretation—that of political resistance—arose in the mid-twentieth century. By the late 1950s, this alternative was associated with the rise of leftist movements that used quilombos as a representation of resistance against domination with a hint of socialist political organization among the runaway slaves. This political strand was also tied to a resurgence of criticisms of the national ideology of racial democracy (Moura 1981).

An incipient black consciousness organization, focusing on the resurrection of Palmares as a symbol, was founded in 1971. It was the first to propose November 20 as an alternative to May 13. In 1978, the Unified Black Movement against Racial Discrimination (MNU) was founded and took over the drive to have November 20 marked as Black Consciousness Day (Anderson 1996:546). A new generation of militants, inspired by the black power and civil rights movements in the United States, assumed as its symbol Zumbi of Palmares (Nascimento 1980). During this period and into the 1990s, the federal government was moving to declare Serra da Barriga as a historical monument in Alagoas, location of the Palmares kingdom. The combination of public representations of "quilombo" as historical resistance continuing into the present and the government's interest in "quilombo" as national patrimony to be preserved and incorporated into Brazilian history and culture led to the opening for inserting the quilombo clause into the new Constitution.

The centenary of abolition in 1988 saw increased activity by the black consciousness movement in the immediate wake of the political opening that had begun in the early 1980s.[25] Prior to that time, black movement activity was carried out under conditions of severe repression (Nascimento 1980). The transition to democratic government became official in 1985 when the military lost control of the presidential election. The opposition succeeded in splitting the vote, and the first civilian president was elected, albeit in an indirect vote, since the military coup in 1964. Two years later, a large constituent assembly was democratically formed and began discussions and hearings, which lasted for a full year. A subcommission of the Social Order Commission on Blacks, Indigenous Populations, Handicapped Persons, and Minorities held eight public hearings in 1987. The subcommission was led by Benedita da Silva, a black shantytown dweller who had risen to political prominence. After the enactment of the Constitution, she became a senator and then governor of the state of Rio de Janeiro, a post she was still holding in 2003 when she was named a minister in President Lula's government.

The subcommission issued a report listing concerns of the black population of Brazil, including discrimination, the need for monuments and historical preservation, educational equality, and the criminalization of prejudice. The report also proposed constitutional provisions, among which was the quilombo clause, approved by the Social Order Commission on May 25, 1987, and appearing in the Constitution as Transitory Article 68. Most of the attention in the commission meetings was given to the status of indigenous populations. Amazonian tribal representatives appeared at the hearings and lobbied vigorously for changes in the law, which found their way into the new constitution (Allen 1989). In fact, compared with the level of lobbying and demonstrating in the streets of Brasília conducted by indigenous activists, there was relatively little public manifestation of concern regarding rights of Afro-Brazilians.

A review of the minutes of the constituent assembly hearings and the legislative history records in the national library of Congress reveals that there were no discussions of the quilombo clause prior to its enactment. Only two articles appeared, and those were in newsletters devoted to reporting on the constituent assembly. Both discussed ways the Constitution could prohibit discrimination and improve conditions for Indians and Afro-

Brazilians. In the article published prior to the subcommission's report, attorney Carlos Moura, future president of the Palmares Cultural Foundation, defended the participation of black members in the constituent assembly against charges of reverse racism — centrist forces said that they were trying to "invert the pyramid" through an "Afro-Brazilian Parliamentary Bloc" so that those who had historically been dominated would now dominate.

Invoking Palmares in a way that might surprise non-Brazilians trying to grasp the shifting significance and use of the term "quilombo," Moura pointed out that such accusations were particularly absurd in light of "our tradition and natural disposition and temperament to enjoy intimacy, familiarity and close relations among all types of people, with the best example being Palmares, where whites, Indians, and blacks gathered in one space to escape persecution by the Dutch and Portuguese crowns."[26] This is completely in keeping with the insertion of Palmares and quilombos into the Brazilian imaginary of the historical coexistence of multiple races, colors, and ethnic groups living together in peace and intermarrying, thus creating the Brazilian nation. In this respect, incorporation of Zumbi of Palmares into the history books (one of the demands of the subcommission and the black movement) served not only, as one would expect, to elevate the virtue, strength, and pride of blackness, but, ironically, also to illustrate the multiracial character of Brazilian society.

In the immediate wake of the passage of the quilombo clause, some policymakers were concerned with historical accuracy and promoted the goal of identifying only communities that could trace their ancestry to fugitive slaves through documentation, archaeological remains, and evidence of cultural survivals. Others, primarily those active in the MNU, pushed for the broadest possible interpretation, to include even urban black communities in the definition. This debate was carried on within the multiple organizations of the black consciousness movement and the government. Movement activists had come to serve as leaders of the Palmares Foundation and a few had been elected to Congress. The year 1994 was a watershed for bringing the meaning of "quilombo" from the past into the present. Up to that point, the need for historical and archaeological evidence to identify rural black communities as actually descended from specific communities of fugitive slaves was successfully defended by those who supported a strictly preservationist perspective. In fact, in mid-1994, an architect from the Palmares Foundation and two technicians from the Institute of Cultural Patrimony visited Mocambo and reported that it was most likely not descended from a quilombo because it had no records, because the architecture of the village indicated that it had been built only in the 1940s, and because there was a marked "absence of African traditions" (Arruti 2002:303). An anthropologist would be needed.

That same year, 1994, the Palmares Foundation hosted a seminar, "The Concept of Quilombo," in which Glória Moura, a black activist and academic and one of the originators of the quilombo clause, suggested the expression "contemporary quilombos" to characterize the constitutional term. She proposed that the term be defined to include rural black communities that group together descendants of slaves who live on a subsistence level and where cultural manifestations have strong ties with the ancestral past. This tie to the past, she continued, would have been chosen by the inhabitants as a form of maintaining identity. This identity would not have to be defined as racial, but instead as ethnic, since in those communities identity already was independent of color and African origin.[27] Her earlier work had focused on the communal nature of subsistence and decision making and was incorporated into educational materials published by the Palmares Foundation (Arruti 2002:16). Culture remained an important component of the definition but was no longer tied specifically to the notion of African cultural survivals.

To expand federal benefits and land grants to rural black communities, the Palmares Foundation, to the chagrin of the radical sector of the black consciousness movement, opted for a definitional shift from race to ethnicity. The use of the term "remanescente" in the clause (loosely translated as remnant, remaining, survivor, or descendant) has been compared to the use of the same term to justify recognition of northeastern indigenous groups, such as the Xocó. In those cases, advocates successfully argued that, despite "cultural loss," the descendants of indigenous tribes should be given rights to legal status and access to land. Arruti (2002:23) has argued that, unlike northeastern Indians, who merely consent to their status as remanescentes (and, I would add, lament the "loss of culture"), black communities that have begun to self-identify as "remanescentes de quilombos" since 1988 wear that mantle as a badge of struggle and militancy (the opposite conclusion from Jonathan W. Warren [2001]). "The use of the term implies for the people who assume it the possibility of occupying a new place in relation to their neighbors, local politicians, governmental organs and policies, in the national imaginary, and in their own imaginary" (Arruti 2002:24). This difference may be attributed to the historical disparity between images of Indians and blacks: romantic notions of the noble savage living communally without need of modern technology versus Africans brought to Brazil in bondage disconnected from their roots and assimilated into the general population of the rural poor. A desire to validate rural black land struggles through a comparison to successful recent indigenous recognitions was a key reason that communal land use became a defining characteristic and nonnegotiable requirement of recognition as a quilombo.

The shift from race to ethnicity was also encouraged by members of the Brazilian Anthropological Association (ABA) who had spent time with rural communities. Those communities had struggled for years as sharecroppers or squatters, had been categorized by earlier generations of scholars as the proletarian peasantry, and had fought for services and access to land in peasant leagues and under agrarian reform laws since the 1950s. Anthropologists and Church activists were learning that people in these rural communities were less concerned with their "negritude" or history of slavery than with fulfilling the requirements of whichever law would give them respite and rights; they did not yet identify themselves as "black," and many people were resistant to that label (Baiocchi 1983). For rural Brazilians, the appearance of an anthropologist often signified the possibility of change, because, as noted in the introduction, many anthropologists were known for their commitment to social justice and an inclination to find ways to use their professional knowledge to advance the cause of the poor. The legitimating force of anthropology in the context of quilombo recognition became even more apparent in 1994.

The category of "rural black community" had become an object of study in the early 1980s, building on peasantry scholarship of the 1960s and 1970s and producing monographs that helped form the ABA's perspective (Baiocchi 1983; Almeida 1989; Queiroz 1976; Candido 1964). Shortly after the Palmares Foundation seminar, in October 1994, the ABA formed a Working Group on Rural Black Communities.[28] This was done under the presidency of João Pacheco de Oliveira, who had engineered the 1987 exclusive contract between ABA and the federal government, requiring the government to engage only ABA anthropologists as experts to produce the reports required by law for indigenous tribal recognition. In the wake of the working group meeting, ABA was contracted to do the same kind of work for the Palmares Foundation. At that point, Eliane Cantarino O'Dwyer, a member of the ABA working group and proponent of a broadened view of modern-day quilombos, visited Mocambo in 1995 to arrange for an anthropologist to research its possible quilombo status.[29]

The ABA working group issued a statement that defined "remanescentes de quilombo" through a series of negatives: "The term does not refer to re-

sidual or archaeological relics of occupation in time or of biological proof . . .
not as isolated groups or of a population strictly homogeneous . . . not necessarily formed by insurrectionary or rebellious past." Rather, the document
went on, "remanescentes dos quilombos"

> are groups that developed practices of resistance in the maintenance
> and reproduction of their ways of life characterized in a determined
> place. The identity of these groups is not defined by size and number of
> members but by the lived experience and the shared values of its com-
> mon trajectory and of its continuity as a group. They constitute ethnic
> groups conceptually defined by anthropology as an organizational type
> that confers belonging through norms and methods employed by in-
> dicating affiliation and exclusion (Barth 1969). As to territoriality, the
> occupation of land is not by individual lots, with common use predomi-
> nating. The utilization of these areas obey seasonality of activities . . .
> characterizing different forms of use and occupation of space that take
> for their base, kinship and neighbor ties based on relations of solidarity
> and reciprocity.[30]

Even prior to the adoption of the quilombo clause, anthropologists were
defining rural black communities in ethnic and territorial terms, focusing
primarily on modes of land use and the creation of ethnic groups by the
practices of slavery, with color (not race) as a marker of such ethnicity. Rural
black communities manifested their ethnicity through communal land use
and were considered "objective expressions of resistance and ethnicity"
(Bandeira 1990:21).[31]

In May 1993, when Mariza Rios first raised the possibility of petitioning
for quilombo status at a meeting in Mocambo, archaeological, historical, and
anthropological evidence of fugitive slave ancestry was still a requirement
for recognition (Andrade 1994, O'Dwyer 1993). At this meeting, two things
were discussed: the upcoming court hearing scheduled for October 1992
in the posseiro lawsuit brought by Mariza on behalf of Mocambo residents
(seventy of them attended that hearing);[32] and the possibility of struggling
for the land by petitioning for recognition under the quilombo clause.[33] This
was the first time that people in Mocambo heard that being descended from
fugitive slaves might lead to the acquisition of the land that separated their
village from the Xocó reserve. They also learned that making a claim as a
quilombo might entitle them to even more land than Neusa Cardoso's small
ranch.

However, it was only after the ABA working group endorsed a broader definition of "remanescente de quilombo" to coincide more with that of the black consciousness movement that the residents of Mocambo were able to seriously pursue the alternative. Liberation theology groups were also supportive of an expanded view of modern-day quilombos, in part because they were looking for ways to ameliorate the losses suffered by proponents of land reform in the final version of the Constitution (B. M. Fernandes 1999). The patrimony architect's report was no longer relevant to the Mocambo claim. Residents who supported the quilombo alternative set off in quest of evidence of their own history, leading elderly villagers to recall family stories and search out old house posts and markers in the area that could be used to show the presence of their ancestors. Padre Isaías searched Church records, but without the assistance that Frei Enoque and Dom José Brandão had received from old anthropological and travelers' reports about indigenous presence in the region.[34]

Eventually, the reconstruction and resemanticization of the story of generations of sertanejo peasants in the lower São Francisco Valley won the collaboration of the anthropologist sent by the Palmares Foundation to prepare the expert report, José Maurício Arruti. Although there is little doubt that some of the people who lived along the São Francisco River were descended from enslaved people (Africans, Indians, or both), no direct evidence indicates that they were descended from a community of runaway slaves. Mocambo residents, in fact, did not talk about slavery at all before the quilombo clause entered the picture. Once it did, as will be expanded upon in chapter 6, "slavery" became a metaphor for the suffering of their great-grandparents at the hands of the landowners for whom they had toiled at the end of the nineteenth century, as the institution of slavery was being abolished.[35] In the years since his report was used to validate the authenticity of Mocambo as descended from a quilombo, Arruti (2002:238) has written that "this [when Mariza introduced the quilombo alternative] is the moment, and not before, that narratives [in Mocambo] point to as the 'time of slavery.'"[36] As with the Xocó, the constructed nature of Mocambo as a former quilombo did not keep the government from granting recognition, and then land, to the community.

In the same month that Mariza first raised the quilombo possibility in Mocambo (May 1993), national news reporters were visiting Rio das Rãs, the first community to claim quilombo status in Bahia. They found that "the struggle for land came to define itself by new categories that valorized being black. With this, what was maintained as invisible, by the force of negative stigma, was becoming positive" (Steil 1998:22). Also during that month, a caravan traveled to Brasília, including representatives of Rio das Rãs, rural worker unions, religious organizations, black movement activists, and members of Congress, to demand that the quilombo clause be put into action (Steil 1998:23). All of this activity raised for Mariza the distinct possibility that the people of Mocambo might demand the same treatment if only they could make an effort to reformulate their struggle as the people in Rio das Rãs had done.[37] Mariza knew there were lawyers and government officials available to give advice if the Mocambo residents were to decide to pursue this uncharted course. At that time, not a single community had been granted title to land and only a few had been recognized as quilombos.[38] In a telescoped version of Rio das Rãs, Mocambo decided after only one year to claim quilombo status.

WHAT MEMORY HAD NOT TOLD THEM

In the wake of the May 28, 1993, court hearing, attended by seventy Mocambo workers, in addition to union activists from the region and the state capital, another meeting was called by the CPT to discuss the next steps. Around that time, a new CPT face appeared in Mocambo — Margarette Lisboa Rocha, daughter of rural workers from a neighboring county. Margarette's family had fled to Propriá in 1970 when she was a girl to escape from the same drought that had brought Padre Isaías's family to Aracaju. Margarette's father, who had spent his life working on other people's land, was offered a construction job on the bridge being built from Sergipe to Alagoas. Once there, he became involved with Church activities and attracted the attention of the bishop, Dom José Brandão, who later offered Margarette a job with the diocese. She became one of four cadres of the Sergipe CPT. Over the years, she has often been approached about becoming a nun but has decided that contradictions she perceives within the Church would make such a life difficult for her, although she is a very spiritual person. She sees both her political activism and her decision to pursue a university degree while working full time for the Centro Dom José Brandão to be inextricably tied to her commitment to Catholic beliefs and liberation theology.

Margarette learned, probably at that first meeting she ran in August 1993, that she was related to at least one of the Mocambo residents. This was not uncommon in tiny Sergipe, where she was also related to a family that had invaded land near Propriá in 1987, a CPT project from the early days of her

Paulameire Acácio dos Santos (left) and Margarette Lisboa Rocha (right)
(photograph by the author)

career.[39] Margarette's own racial and national identification was a subject of one of our first conversations on the day I arrived in Sergipe. I noted on that first day that she was short and slender, with light brown/copper skin, curly black hair, dark brown eyes, and high cheekbones. As we stood outside my hotel room, she explained to me, speaking rapidly and intensely without being prompted, that she considers herself sergipana and sertaneja, and that she had recently discovered that she has an uncle who is Xocó. Although her mother would not like to hear it, she also considers herself to be black. On her father's side, she revealed, she has Dutch ancestry, and she remembered that her great-grandfather was white with light eyes. She said that she would not want to declare herself one thing or another, because she would not want to give up any of them.

Having consulted with Mariza before the meeting, Margarette presented to the twenty-six residents in attendance the three ways they could proceed, explaining that they were not required to choose but could pursue all three routes at the same time. First, since the landowner had not yet paid them, the workers could reenter the property and continue to plant (essentially a suggestion that they invade the land). Second, they might have some hope of qualifying as a quilombo, with the understanding that this would take a long time and was untried and that it was still unclear whether the Palmares Foundation even had the authority to grant land titles. Third, they could pursue with INCRA legal expropriation of the land through the land reform law that permits the taking of unproductive land not serving a "social use" (Araújo 1999).[40] The following morning, Margarette went with the residents to see the area they had "conquered, with the beautiful planted rice."[41] The visits to the contested land were an integral part of the relationship developing between the CPT and Mocambo, always keeping the focus on the land itself.

At this point, things began to happen very quickly. With the agreement of the Mocambo residents, Mariza began pursuing the quilombo alternative by contacting the federal attorney and transferring the pending lawsuit to federal court. An important reason the villagers initially agreed to pursue this route was that, under land reform rules, they would get only Neusa Cardoso's small piece of land, which was inadequate for the entire village to sustain itself. If, however, they were to succeed under the quilombo clause, they would gain access to a very large parcel of land that included the entire ranch of former governor Seixas Dória and thirty-nine smaller, privately owned parcels. The need for more land was becoming urgent because the rice lagoons were drying up. Hydroelectric plants upriver were going on line every year, and by the mid-1990s the level of the lower São Francisco River had fallen to such an extent that all the lagoons had completely disappeared. This ecological problem, as well as the fertilizer being used upriver, also drastically reduced fishing and increased the concentration of bacteria, making the water unsafe to drink.[42]

As one of the three tactics Margarette had outlined, with the goal of gaining the attention of government agencies and hoping to plant that year, a group of Mocambo families invaded Neusa's land and occupied her house on the ranch (she was living in Propriá). Neusa quickly perceived the drawn-out problems that confronted her as owner of contested land involving multiple federal agencies and found a buyer for the property at a discount. To get the land at the reduced price, the buyer took over the litigation and released Neusa from any obligation.[43] The land occupation continued until the local judge ordered that the Mocambo invaders evacuate the land on the last day of 1993. Things heated up even more, and the new owner passed the land along to his daughter, who, not wanting to deal with the extended dispute, sold it to an infamous landowner from the city across the river.[44]

Alagoan landowner Paulo Monteiro, like Jorge Pacheco in the 1980s with the Xocó land, bought the disputed property (by then called Fazenda Rosa

Cruz) in May 1994, knowing it was in dispute. He bought it for the purpose of collecting on the proceeds from the expropriation proceeding to be initiated by INCRA in the coming years. Renowned for his use of gunmen and trading on the national reputation of Alagoas as an outlaw state (for example, in 1998 there was a shoot-out in the legislative assembly), Monteiro maintained a house on the land and refused to accept anything less than its full value. The result was that the land the Mocambo families had invaded and from which they were expelled by judges in 1993 and 1994 remained off-limits for planting for years after they were granted land as a quilombo. Monteiro's reputation kept Mocambo supporters of quilombo recognition from setting foot on the land in whose name the struggle had begun. Even after the land was expropriated, Monteiro resisted by appealing the amount to be paid by INCRA. In 2008, the case was still on appeal and Mocambo residents were still being excluded from the land.

The other two tactics Margarette described in August 1993 were pursued vigorously over the years that followed. Letter writing, testifying at court hearings, attending meetings in the state and national capitals at government agencies and black movement events and facing Monteiro's gunmen became a common part of life in Mocambo. The CPT cadre and black activists from the state capital visited regularly, and government engineers marked off the strip of land along the river that legally belonged to the federal government so as to provide the villagers a safe place to plant. The state secretary of education attempted, unsuccessfully, to purchase Monteiro's land to make a monument in honor of Zumbi of Palmares. The state secretary of justice visited Mocambo and gave statements to the newspapers. All the while, Mariza was defending and pursuing lawsuits by and against the landowners. The two-year period from the first expulsion from Neusa's property to the first visit by the Palmares Foundation and the arrival of the government-sponsored anthropologist in 1995 was a time of great activity with a steep learning curve.

However, during this period, Mocambo still had no electricity, running water, irrigation, seeds, agricultural technical assistance, or adequate medical care. The people in Mocambo would have to wait more than a decade for that kind of help from the government. Over the course of those years, the stories examined and reconsidered in this chapter developed their own trajectories and elisions. The narrative supplied by Mariza to use in court that begins "um belo dia" (one fine day) serves as a starting point for the story of the Mocambo struggle, but it also serves to erase what came before the moment when the landowner released her cattle onto the ripe rice of her sharecroppers. The specific history of the multifaceted relationships that led to the moment of mobilization was too complex for the law. As any good lawyer would do, Mariza replaced history with what the law required. In so doing, she and the leaders who were to tell and retell the story of the first days sought to place agency in the hands of the Mocambo activists. When the quilombo clause began to require a historical rendering of Mocambo's past, the *negros do Mocambo* would find a new narrative—and it would find them.

4

Family Feuds and Ethnoracial Politics

WHAT'S LAND GOT TO DO WITH IT?

Mocambo's decision to pursue recognition as a quilombo and the land that was promised to come with it was made in the context of challenges by competitors, as it had been with the Xocó in relation to the Kariri-Xocó. Boundaries that had been porous before the law was mobilized swiftly became the subject of dispute, as did the grounds on which identity claims were either accepted or rejected. Unlike the Xocó, however, the people in Mocambo did not reach a consensus about the need for quilombo recognition. As recognition became a reality, Mocambo revealed itself to be less a unified community than a disputatious, fractured, contingent enterprise, subject to unexpected twists and turns in its endeavors and fortunes, an illustration of how "community" gets called into question as the legalization of identities proceeds.

"Talk of community" (Beyers 2008) works to reduce and deny social differences and power relations within a particular group. Moreover, it is often used to paper over the fractures, feuds, and cleavages that are always present, constituting and reconstituting, that make a community a dynamic, processual space and place. In fact, "incompletion" is the principle of community, "an uninterrupted passage through singular ruptures" (Nancy 1991:74). At the same time, the relations among the factions in Mocambo revealed themselves to be moments of articulation, times when one can see the factions taking shape in relation to one another, in the "play of the juncture" (Nancy 1991:74).

In Brazil, the word "comunidade" is associated with Catholic liberationist Base Ecclesial Communities (CEBS) so that there is also a religious connotation lurking behind the everyday use of the term. Because of this liberation theology practice, the word "community" has come to signify a site of struggle and solidarity. In the case of Mocambo, the invocation of "community" became a flash point over whether it could still mean the entire village or whether it had become something that needed to be joined or rejected. Its use as a definitional term, tied up as it was with religious belief, as well as the movement and the potential for land, carried new meanings once the land was granted to the quilombo community association. Paradoxically, the invocation of "community" also became an invocation of exclusion. To underscore another of the many paradoxes and contradictions that nourish the transformation of these ethnoracial identities, I explore the circumstances under which "enemies" are willing to share the same space. In what follows, I consider particular religious and political events in the two villages, their similarities and differences, in order to illustrate the unifying role that national citizenship played, just as acrimonious relations between quilombolas and Indians were at their worst.

In this chapter, I also analyze the interfamily and intrafamily feuds and their impact on the politics of quilombo recognition, with an emphasis on the struggle over naming the village and its residents. Understanding the feuds is important because a situation in which poor rural workers who have the opportunity to gain land through a reconsideration of their identity and choose not to do so challenges a strictly instrumentalist approach to ethnoracial identity formation—it is not only about land but also has to do with local political positions, loyalty to existing identities, and fears associated with identifying as only black without the mixture so often considered integral to a proud sertanejo, and Brazilian, identity. My analysis of the feuds, therefore, is also concerned with how the disagreements themselves played out as sensitivities to race and color. Woven throughout the chapter are highlighted moments that reveal the simultaneous importance and unimportance of race and color to the people of Mocambo.

FEUDING AND THE POLITICS OF QUILOMBO RECOGNITION

In the mid-1990s, when the quilombo movement was gaining momentum, it became clear that there were people in the village who were opposed to the tactics espoused by the CPT and who did not agree with the families who had decided to pursue recognition. In Mocambo, people either "assumed" a "remanescente" identity or not (until the 2000 land grant, quilombo movement supporters referred to themselves as remanescentes). Those who disagreed with the decision and absented themselves from the process were referred to from the beginning as "os contra" (those who are against).[1] While the movement for recognition was gaining speed, with visitors from Aracaju and Brasília and a constant stream of meetings and disputes with landowners, a group of contras became solidified, led by a wing of Dona Maria's family, a leading family in the quilombo initiative. Although the opposition participated in the quilombo endeavor for a time in 1994, there came a point when disagreements over tactics and power struggles within the family led to an ever-increasing split.

Unearthing how the feud began, why it continued and became entrenched, and why a significant portion of the population of Mocambo and almost all of the outlying community of Ranchinho (part of the quilombo) were opposed to recognition are elusive topics—difficult for members of the communities themselves to explain and even more difficult for an outsider to grasp.[2] Two years after the movement hit full stride, in May 1996, the brewing intrafamily disagreement blossomed into a full-fledged feud when the question of whether the already-existing community association could be designated to hold title to land. At that time, Mariza, the lawyer, advised quilombo supporters that they needed a new association to be formed explicitly to take title to land, since the Palmares Foundation had indicated that only communal land title would be given, unlike the individual titles given in land reform situations. With Mariza's help, they formed a new community association, the Antônio do Alto Association, named for the great-grandfather of one of the leaders of the movement. It would not be far-fetched to suggest that a preexisting power struggle was being acted out through the quilombo movement and was, perhaps inadvertently, being exacerbated by this move to form a new association. A few years later, when the extended family of Britto foreman João de Egídio moved to Mocambo because they had been expelled from the Xocó reserve, they became allies of the opposing faction in Mocambo (the contras).[3] This group, which represented about a third of Mocambo's population, opposed quilombo status and supported the political status quo in the area. They obtained the support of many Xocó, who already had an ambivalent relationship with the quilombo supporters in Mocambo who were laying claim to the boundary land.

Seriously exacerbating the feuding was the rancorous legal dispute between a quilombola and an Indian. When Xocó leader Paulino Acácio died in 1996, his two wives, Dona Maria, the matriarch of the quilombo movement, and Lindonor, a Xocó woman known among Dona Maria's family and friends in Mocambo only as "a outra" (the other), initiated a fierce legal battle over which one would get his government pension. Paulino had been an employee of FUNAI for almost twenty years, so his pension was substantial and each of the women had a daughter who was still eligible as a minor to receive pension funds as well. The stakes were high. After a long, contentious battle, the court decided that since Dona Maria and Paulino had had a civil as well as a religious marriage, she would receive two-thirds, leaving one-third for "the other." This was the decision, even though Paulino had lived his whole life on São Pedro Island with Lindonor, visiting Dona Maria on a regular basis but always identifying himself as an Indian. The negative feelings and side taking generated by this legal dispute lasted for a long time, with half brothers and half sisters not speaking and with speculations that "mistakes" had been made by lawyers on purpose. In addition to the quilombo clause, other legal provisions, such as pension laws, also linked law and identity.

From the moment that Mariza drafted new bylaws creating the Antônio do Alto Association, there were two community associations in Mocambo, each led by a member of Dona Maria's extended family. Her nephew Dede was the president of the existing Community Association of the Village of Mucambo, and her son Paulomary was president of the new Antônio do Alto Association. The relationship of these cousins had always been strained, and some saw this as an escalation of old rivalries. Some attributed it to family jealousies and long-standing disagreements, others to politics (status quo versus the Workers' Party [PT]) and to ideological or political differences between priests. Padre Isaías had left the diocese in October 1994 to study in Rome, partially because of the stress he felt from his involvement with land struggles and from dealing with constant police violence. He returned in late 1995, convinced that his work was with the poor in Sergipe and not at a seminary in Rome. He joined the PT and in 1996 ran for mayor of Porto da Folha, losing by only 600 votes (the county of Porto da Folha has a population of about 30,000).[4] The parish priest who took over from Padre Isaías allied himself with the contras, and he and they supported Padre Isaías's rival in the election, Dr. Júlio.[5] There was some speculation that João de Egídio, who was also allied with the contras, moved his extended family to Mocambo to bolster support for the political status quo and to strengthen opposition to the quilombo effort and PT influence, which were seen as connected. That same year, Frei Enoque ran for mayor of neighboring Poço Redondo, the poorest county in Brazil, on the ticket of a party allied with the state government, and won. Padre Isaías became the parish priest of Poço Redondo when Frei Enoque became mayor.[6]

Whatever its initial explanations, the feud in Mocambo was fueled by at least two sets of decisions that were made and put into effect over time. On the side of the quilombo supporters was the decision to make membership in the Antônio do Alto Association conditional on participation in the struggle, belief in the quilombo movement, and the assuming of a black identity. The contras, for their part, decided to support Dr. Júlio for mayor of Porto da Folha, from whom they expected and received favors. Personalistic politics has traditionally been the best way to acquire services, jobs, medical care, and other needs from the local government. Therefore, election time in Brazil has always been the best time to get things done for oneself and one's community. This defines a certain rhythm of life—the dry between-election years (referred to as *entre-safra*, or between harvests) and the plentiful year immediately before an election. Votes are used as items for barter—exchanged for specific improvements to the life of a particular place (Queiroz 1973). In Mocambo, the contras were reluctant to give up a system they knew well for promises made by a federal government that had never done anything for them and, in the case of some, had expelled them from their land to add it to the Xocó reserve. Moreover, the PT (aligned with the quilombo movement) campaigned on the premise that, unlike other parties, it did not give favors in exchange for votes.

To what extent the feud was also exacerbated by a general reluctance to self-identify as *negro* in a society where such an appellation had for generations been considered a curse and where people have striven to be considered "whiter" or lighter than they physically are is an immeasurable but evident partial explanation. However, even among those who identify themselves as "contra," the movement has produced a change in the perceived value of "being black" in Mocambo, although there was certainly a reticence about such self-identification. It is about "learning to be Black. Learning to come into an identification" (Hall 1991:55). In Brazil, with its myth of racial democracy, to look at what lies beneath that "culturally produced reticence" is considered un-Brazilian and a "betrayal of an unspoken but universally understood etiquette" (Sheriff 2001:184). An example is the dark-skinned woman who tended Mocambo's church when I was there, Maria José Rodrigues Travasso (known as São José). It was often said of her that she denied being black because she refused to participate in the quilombo movement. Although in the beginning she found the movement interesting, before long she had sided with the contras and may have felt that the movement was betraying the etiquette by forcing people to discuss race openly.[7]

São José told me she considered herself black but did not believe in the quilombo movement. She felt there were more effective ways to gain services and improvements to the village and preferred to be on the side of the local politicians (Travasso interview 2000). For her, being black did not require an identification with the movement, and it is likely that such a self-designation was not within her repertoire of identities before she decided that she needed to take sides. On the other hand, because of the promise of land and because she knew I was associated with the quilombo families, she may have felt it expedient to explain that she considers herself to be black.[8] It was apparent to me that the lines in Mocambo were not being drawn on the basis of race or color, but instead on other grounds, including political affiliation, personal allegiances, family relations, and varying perspectives on effective development strategies, illustrating another element of legalizing identity—experiencing identity as an effect of struggle. The significance of "black" in such a context is clearly contested terrain (B. F. Williams 1989).[9]

After the Palmares Foundation issued land title to the Antônio do Alto Association in mid-2000, the contras, who were considered by the government to be members of the community and entitled to remain in what was becoming known as "Quilombo Mocambo," challenged the legality of the land grant, because they were afraid they would be forced to leave. The fear of being expelled from Mocambo can be explained by the connection many people made to the neighboring Xocó situation. Because non-Indians are not permitted to live on reserves,[10] all those who had been living on what was to become Xocó land prior to expropriation were forced to leave (and eventually, years later, were paid for their land). Some of those, including the Egídio family, had moved to Mocambo and expressed the notion that the same would happen there, perhaps hoping that it would, so they could be expropriated and indemnified again. Government lawyers explained that this might be true for nonremanescentes, like the Egídio family, but that the "black" inhabitants whose families had lived there for a long time were guaranteed a place in Mocambo. Only the "white" newcomers, the Egídio family, would be relocated to another property.[11]

"White" is a relative term in this context. By racial standards in the United States, no one in the village would be considered white (Haney-López 1996). However, the notion of "white" in Mocambo is more like "not-black" than a positive identification, either by the people so identified or by those who would like to see them gone. It is also a new, politically expedient term, emerging with the quilombo movement and involving new forms of racial identification. Furthermore, the reason for the desire to expel the Egídio family from Mocambo had to do with their behavior and allegiances and not with their color. In practice, the question of who might eventually be required to leave was fluid and confusing, feeding exclusionary sentiments on both sides.

An example of the palpable distrust involves Dona Maria, the matriarch of the quilombo movement. One day, as we settled in for lunch, I commented on the new tabby kittens wandering around her house, and Dona Maria reminded me of her previous cat, whom she suspected had been poisoned,

Maria Aparecida and some of her nine children (photograph by the author)

perhaps by the contras, since my last visit. Her concern with the wily ways of the contras rapidly gave way to one of her favorite topics of conversation when I was around—genetic roulette. With gales of laughter, she repeated 'the observation I had heard from her many times. Isn't it interesting, she asked, that her previous—white—cat had given birth to black kittens? We all laughed, and this reminded her of a similar observation often made in the village. People took great pleasure in commenting on the skin hues of the nine children of one of the quilombo supporters.[12] It was considered somewhat of a wonderment that until the ninth birth, her sons were all dark and her daughters were all light-skinned. It was the new child, a son, who had broken this famous childbearing pattern—he had been born as fair as the girls. No explanation was ventured; the wonders and mysteries of genetics were the ostensible reasons for the delight taken in this phenomenon. However, in other cases of genetic roulette, the prime explanation for children with blond hair, no matter the texture, was always the same: Dutch ancestry. The area had been colonized by the Dutch for a brief period during the first half of the seventeenth century. Therefore, it was believed, a small population of Dutch families had been left behind when the area was recaptured by the Portuguese, "planting its seed," to appear in subsequent generations (Herkenboff 1999).[13]

The shades and combinations of skin color and facial features that abound in Mocambo was a never-ending source of conversation and commentary. Before long, it became clear to me that assuming a black identity in Mocambo was not about race, blood, or even appearance. Whether community members would assume a black identity had been a subject of concern since the quilombo movement began in 1994. Choosing to "assume" a black identity was a new phenomenon in Mocambo. Recognizing the fundamental importance of each such personal decision advances an understanding of how the transition from a typical sertanejo community to a legally recognized quilombo has affected racial self-identification. Stuart Hall (1991:55, 54) describes his own experience of "becoming black" in Britain after migrating from Jamaica, where, until a certain later moment, the label "black" was simply not available, even though almost everyone there was African-descended. In Britain, however, "black was created as a political category in a certain historical moment." It included South Asians as well as immigrants from the Caribbean and East Africa and was "created as a consequence of certain symbolic and ideological struggles . . . [plucked] out of its negative articulation and articulate[d] in a new way" (Hall 1991:55). This led to a "change of self-recognition, a new process of identification, the emergence of a new subject" (Hall 1991:54). In Mocambo, "becoming black" as a political process is tied up with the repeated exhortation to "assume" one's identity as a *negro*, just as the Xocó had assumed their indigenous identity. The assumption of a black identity, however, is more than "a narrative tie that connects micro-political conflicts to macro-political ideological clashes," not altering very much the micro-political terms (Arruti 2002:393). It is more than a formal nominalism that does not consider the effects of taking up a racial identification.

If, on the other hand, one were to employ Ian Hacking's notion of "dynamic nominalism" (Gooding-Williams 2001:242), it would be possible to draw a distinction between "being black" and "being a black person." The category of "black," created historically in specific situations and created by the law in some circumstances, is used from a "third-person perspective" and "results from criteria-governed practices of racial classification through application of racial labels" (Gooding-Williams 2001:241). Gooding-Williams proposes to add to the concept of racial identity a form of self-identification that "notes the ways in which individuals classified as black contribute to the construction of their own racial identities" (Gooding-Williams 2001:241).

Dynamic nominalism holds that "human acts come into being hand in hand with our invention of the categories labeling them" (Gooding-Williams 2001:242 [quoting Hacking]). This doctrine contends that our "spheres of possibility, and hence our selves, are to some extent made up by our naming and what that entails." By this token, being classified as black is a necessary but not sufficient condition of being a black person, so that one becomes a black person only if one self-identifies as black and makes choices "in light of one's identification as black" (Gooding-Williams 2001:242). Self-recognition when seen in this way can open up "a new world of new possibilities and impossibilities [that are] born when acts of objectifying racial classification move [people] to understand themselves, to formulate aspirations, and to plan future courses of their lives under descriptions of themselves as black," thus "actively contribut[ing] to the construction of their identities as black persons." This is precisely what happened in Mocambo, as quilombo supporters discovered that some of the "most politically salient modes of being a black person involve the assignment of a *collective* significance to being black" (Gooding-Williams 2001:243).

Even though the ideology of "racial democracy" has been dealt serious blows in the last few decades, with official and public recognition of racial discrimination (including measures outlawing it and compensating for it), the hegemonic worldview that underpins race and color consciousness in Brazil continues to inform peoples' everyday lives (Sheriff 2001). For example, sociologist Edward Telles (2004:54) reports on a 1995 survey showing that around 90 percent of white, black, and brown (*pardo*) Brazilians agree that whites hold prejudices against blacks and that the approximate same percentage of the same set of Brazilians agree that "race mixture is a good thing." These striking results confirm the continuing ironies of race and racism in Brazil. Returning to Dona Maria's cats, her repeated amazement about the serendipity of white cats with black kittens seemed to fit with this theme that reverberates through time and discourse. It is almost as though being wholly black includes a white component, and that rather than separating and homogenizing each race, there is an effort to encompass and surpass both. Many have complained that this ethos has kept Afro-Brazilians from organizing themselves politically. In the case of Mocambo, assuming a black identity has clearly been a successful political choice.

MUCAMBO TO MOCAMBO AND REMANESCENTE TO QUILOMBOLA: A ROSE BY ANY OTHER NAME?

During the key period, 1994 to 1996, a shift also took place in relation to the name of the village. Traditionally, the village and surrounding land purchased by Darcy Cardoso in 1960 was called "Mucambo." Former caretakers of the disputed property testified in 1995 against the invaders, referring to them as "mucambeiros" and as "people of Mucambo."[14] This was a variation on the word "mocambo," a Mbundu word for "hideout," used to denote a group of runaway slaves until another African-derived word, "quilombo," became the more popular term (Schwartz 1992:125). In this area of the lower São Francisco valley, Arruti (1998a) has traced the use of "mocambo" to mean a refuge for slaves or escaped cattle or simply a miserable habitation (this last definition is the one prevalent in the northeastern city of Recife, where the slums are called "mocambos," with no ethnoracial connotation). The use of the word "could suggest an association between the community and its identification as a remanescente de quilombo, but in truth . . . this name was attributed to this aggregation of families for the first time when a cattle ranch was established in that location" (Arruti 1998b:27). The ranch was desig-nated "Mucambo" in the second half of the nineteenth century, named for a stream in the area, with more than one stream carrying the same name.

Arruti (1997:7) has written that the proliferation of the name signifies the strong presence of runaway slaves in the region during the sixteenth and seventeenth centuries. However, he has also stated that there is no documen-tary evidence of quilombos or slave resistance in the sertão of Sergipe (Arruti 2002:234). Nonetheless, as the notion of being a community descended from fugitive slaves grew among Mocambo residents, the village name be-came a site of contestation. Documents and minutes of meetings through the first half of 1994 would often refer to "Mucambo," but, by the middle of that year, quilombo supporters and NGOs referred only to "Mocambo" and to the villagers as "mocambeiros." The semantic emphasis was needed to convince the Palmares Foundation that this community should qualify for recogni-tion and as a constant reminder of a history that was in the process of being "recovered." It was part of the redefining of rights and collective struggle (Arruti 1998a:28), as well as a reminder to themselves of their new identi-fication. The contras and their allies continued to call the village Mucambo, and they did not change the name of their community organization, which had been founded in 1989. In 2002, during the festivities of São João (one of the biggest holidays in the Northeast), there was a handmade poster at the entrance to the school that read "The Best São João in Brazil is in Mucambo" (O Melhor São João no Brasil em Mucambo). The "u" had been changed with a marker to "o" so that it clearly read "Mocambo."

Although Mocambo's recognition process began at a time when historical and cultural evidence was required to prove its status as a descendant of a quilombo, by the time title to the land was received the quilombo clause was being interpreted broadly to include any rural black community that shared a common ancestry and used land communally. The official designation of the land granted to the Antônio do Alto Association in mid-2000 as "Quilombo Mocambo" reflected a double, almost redundant, emphasis on an undocumentable, metaphorical fugitive slave history. As expressed by the activists in Mocambo when title was delivered, "This is no longer a village, this is a quilombo."

The shifting of nomenclature was evident between 1998 and 2000. In 1998, in addition to referring to themselves as "mocambeiros," the pro-recognition group had begun calling themselves "remanescentes." When I returned, in January 2000, there had been a dramatic shift to "quilombola." This change reflected the growing metaphoric and anachronistic use of the word "quilombo," as federal agencies and anthropologists struggled with definitional problems and growing numbers of recognition requests. The change to self-identification as quilombolas was also the result of regular attendance by Mocambo community members at national meetings sponsored by the Palmares Foundation and at nongovernmental coalitions, such as the Association of Black Rural Quilombola Communities of Brazil. These consistent contacts with the larger world of quilombo activism provided encouragement to the local movement. However, it also tapped into the traditional patron-client perspective of rural Brazil. These national organizations, it was hoped, could help local residents who identified themselves as quilombolas obtain land.

Communities are often in conflict over practical issues but also over matters of right and wrong. "Such debates imply fierce competition for leadership. They also involve competition for the right to name. . . . The power to name, to inscribe, to describe, to essentialize, implies a power to invoke a world of moral relationships, a power underlined in the myth of Genesis. Naming constitutes a forceful act of leadership in its own right" (Werbner 1997:239). Stabilizing the name of the village as Mocambo and then the naming of themselves as quilombolas were victories in the struggle for power. "Performative utterances, substantive — as opposed to procedural . . . are magical acts which succeed because they have the power to make themselves universally recognized" (Bourdieu 1987:838). Bourdieu is referring to a powerful, centralized legal pronouncement that creates "a situation in which no one can refuse or ignore the point of view, the vision which they impose."

In Mocambo, where the "established order" was in a state of flux, the vision imposed by the quilombola "authorized agents," even when it carried the imprimatur of the federal government, was not the last word (or name). Their vision was a "well-founded *pre*-vision" (Bourdieu 1987:839). With the law behind their prevision, the process of naming offered the quilombolas "the real possibility of achieving full reality—fully recognized, official existence—through the effect of legitimation, indeed of consecration, implied by publishing and officializing them" (Bourdieu 1987:839). More difficult was the fulfillment of obligations. Issues of individual interests superseding those of the common good arose periodically, creating rifts within the group that had otherwise agreed. For the remanescentes, danger lurked everywhere. The notion of solidarity was not simply a matter of agreeing on tactics but involved overcoming, at any given moment, fissures and fractures, outside and inside.

The rapid name shift was also a response to the contras' campaign against the quilombo movement. If there had been no opposition, it is unclear whether the commitment to quilombo identity would have been made so quickly. With the hardening of the internal boundaries, and with the distancing from the Xocó, identity change was accelerated. Through this new identity the remanescentes felt they were exerting the power that being aligned with federal and outside forces gave them—power to lead the community and to provide themselves with material improvements. Each storytelling, play, dance, and song that had become indicia of quilombo identity, as discussed in the next two chapters, was performed as much to assert that identity against their neighbors who doubted the benefits of the new endeavor as to convince the authorities that they were indeed a quilombo.

Arruti, the anthropologist engaged by the Palmares Foundation to prepare the report on Mocambo's claim to quilombo status, arrived for the first time in September 1995 and then returned at the end of 1996 to finalize his research. For over a year, the quilombolas, who at that time referred to themselves as "remanescentes," attended national meetings, met with government lawyers, and dealt with the opposition and shifting alliances. The watershed year of 1996 saw the Antônio do Alto Association formed, and with it the creation and alienation of the contras, the death of Xocó leader Paulino Acácio, the contentious pension dispute between Dona Maria and Paulino's Xocó wife Lindonor, which led to worsening relations with the Xocó, and Padre Isaías's failed election campaign for mayor of Porto da Folha on the PT ticket. All of these events inflamed the differences within the Mocambo community. During this whole time, no news about quilombo recognition came from Brasília.

In January 1997, Arruti submitted his report to the Palmares Foundation, which accepted it without debate. An excerpt of it was published in the Brazilian federal register, together with a legal description of the demarcated property that would become Quilombo Mocambo.[15] Finally, on May 28, 1997, Mocambo was recognized under the quilombo clause. As the Xocó had celebrated almost twenty years earlier, so the remanescentes celebrated when the news of recognition arrived. However, for Mocambo, land did not come with the decree, and the opposition the remanescentes experienced from their fellow villagers did not cease but instead strengthened. Recognition was, in many ways, only the beginning of the struggle to get what the law promised.

THE COMPLICATIONS OF LAND TITLE:
BEWARE, YOU MIGHT GET WHAT YOU ASK FOR

After three years of waiting, hoping, disbelieving, struggling, and feuding, in July 2000, title to all of the 2,100 hectares (5,187 acres) of land that had been promised since recognition in 1997 was granted to the Antônio do Alto Association. Formed in 1996 for the purpose of holding the land, it was named for the great-grandfather of Antônio Lino dos Santos, known to all as Sr. Antônio (pronounced Seu Antônio), an elderly leader of the quilombo movement and the patriarch of the second most important family of leaders of the movement after Dona Maria's. The land title, which was granted by the Palmares Foundation, included Neusa Cardoso's former property, Fazenda Rosa Cruz (still in land reform expropriation proceedings), former governor Seixas Dória's land, state land on which the village itself stood, and thirty-nine small, privately owned parcels. None of the landowners had been compensated. Dona Maria's eldest son, Maripaulo, who was the acting coordinator of the association, returned from Brasília with title in hand, after being called to the Palmares Foundation without explanation, surprising everyone and provoking a big party in Mocambo. It did not take long, however, for questions and concerns to surface.

There were two levels on which questions arose. On one level, there were the contras: dissident black families living in Mocambo who had not supported the quilombo movement (some had dropped out and others had never signed on).[16] They were members of the other, preexisting community association, who had lived in Mocambo for as many years as their relatives who self-identified as remanescentes. As previously mentioned, these dissidents were worried that they would be expelled from Mocambo. This fear was exacerbated by their Xocó allies, the Egídio families and the new owner of Fazenda Rosa Cruz, Paulo Monteiro. At the same time, behind the talk of fear of expulsion lurked the possibility that all the contra families might receive indemnification for their property in Mocambo, just as their friends, the Egídios, had in relation to the Xocó.[17]

Back in the early 1990s, when the Xocó reserve was finalized, some of the small landholders moved to Mocambo to be near their brother, João de Egídio, who had established himself in Mocambo fifteen years earlier (A. M. d. Souza interview 2000). He had built a bar and was quite successful. There were no complaints against him until 1997 when Mocambo was recognized as a quilombo. When the feud became a full-blown conflict in 1999, the federal police (involved in this local matter only because Mocambo was a recognized quilombo) closed down a bingo game planned for the Egídio bar. The police report contained observations that reflect the complexity of the racial situation in Mocambo: "The remanescentes have in their ranks many who are not of black origin, but they are not thinking of expelling them; on the other side, among others, is the leader of the dissidents who is a legitimate remanescente recognized as such by all."[18] However, under no one's definition were the Egídio families considered either remanescentes or Indians, although no one referred to them as "white" until quilombo land title was granted in 2000.

The fear of expulsion was exacerbated by the new closeness of the Egídio families with the Xocó, who sided against the quilombo movement, to some extent due to potential competition between the two new "ethnicities" for government attention. When the Egídio families were still living on the Xocó reserve, years before, they had become close allies of the Xocó, even though one of the Egídio brothers had shot Xocó leader Pedrito Santana, in 1985, described in chapter 2. Those political alliances were forged and then brought to Mocambo in 1999 and added to the kinship and friendship ties between João de Egídio and the president of the contras, Dede, Dona Maria's estranged nephew, who by then had married João de Egídio's sister (A. M. d. Souza interview 2000). This resulted in an intensification of the competitive relationship between the Xocó and the remanescentes in Mocambo, with the added rift among family members in Mocambo itself. The difficulty any outsider might have in understanding the complexities of the ethnoracial issues is illustrated by just a few of the interlocking relations among the "enemies" in 2000. João de Egídio's aunt (who had lived on the reserve but was not considered Xocó) was a close friend of Dona Maria's, while Egídio's brother-in-law was Dona Maria's nephew. Moreover, two of the Egídio brothers were married to Xocó women.

The other level of concern had to do with the laws that govern land and expropriation. Under Brazilian law, there are two forms of expropriation. Land reform law requires that once land has been determined to be "unproductive" through an administrative proceeding there must be an official valuation of, and payment for, the land by INCRA. The land is then available to be redistributed to individuals without land, often squatters who are already living on the land, but sometimes invaders who have been organized by the MST. The only aspect of the process that can be appealed to the courts is the valuation. This process is called *desapropriação* (sometimes translated as condemnation) and is contrasted to *expropriação* (expropriation or eminent domain), which is used by the government as a means to take land, indemnify the title holder, and keep the land as an environmental or indigenous reserve. Both processes are extremely drawn out. For example, Caiçara was officially declared part of the Xocó reserve in 1991, and the parcels of the Egídio families, which abutted that property, were included. Their property was expropriated in 1991, but they were not paid for it until 1999, at which time they moved to Mocambo.

At this second level of concern, everyone in Mocambo knew that former governor Seixas Dória had been negotiating with INCRA since 1997 and that, although he was sympathetic to the cause of the remanescentes, he was also dedicated to receiving compensation for his property. Moreover, he had divided up some of the land and given parcels to his sons, who were not as interested in the lives of their family's former workers as their father was. The question that arose when title was given to the quilombo association concerning this largest parcel was: What was the significance of the title given by the Palmares Foundation if Seixas Dória and his sons did not receive payment?[19] This was a concern, because, unlike either form of expropriation, the Palmares Foundation had decided not to indemnify any of the landowners whose titles had purportedly been superseded by the title granted to the Antônio do Alto Association.

Even more emotionally significant to the remanescentes was the status of Fazenda Rosa Cruz—the place where the struggle had begun in 1992. Paulo Monteiro, Neusa Cardoso's successor, had challenged the INCRA condemnation proceedings and was holding out on appeal for the most he could get. How would the granting of title by the Palmares Foundation affect his case against INCRA pending in federal court? This became even more complicated when shortly after title to Fazenda Rosa Cruz was granted to the remanescentes in July 2000 a federal court ruled in favor of Monteiro, either not knowing about, or choosing to ignore, the document that purported to grant valid title to the Antônio do Alto Association. Lack of legal assistance, due in part to the departure of Mocambo's original lawyer, Mariza, made matters worse.

Jumping into the legal fray, however, was a newly assigned, young federal attorney, Paulo Vasconcelos Jacobina, a well-educated, blues-loving lawyer from a small interior city in Bahia, which coincidentally bore his family name. A few years before filing his brief intervening in the suit on behalf of the quilombo association in September 2000, Jacobina had come to the job dedicated to unearthing corruption, saving the environment, investigating claims of racial discrimination, and helping the dispossessed claim their rights. The 1988 Constitution had given new powers to the federal attorney's office, which consists of hundreds of government lawyers. It now enjoys a status separate from the three traditional branches of government, which is different from the U.S. attorney general, a frequent mistranslation. In addition to its other powers of investigation and prosecution, the federal attorney's office has the authority to bring lawsuits against government institutions, including the executive branch, to protect the rights of indigenous peoples, rural black communities, and the environment, as well as to prosecute acts of corruption by public officials. In 1989, it was restructured to include a department of attorneys and anthropologists to "protect and defend the rights and interests of indigenous people, quilombos, gypsies, riverine communities, and other ethnic minorities."

Consequently, after years of relative inaction on the part of the Sergipe-based federal attorney's office, Jacobina became involved in October 1999 in the wake of an official request by Xocó leaders that the boundaries of their reserve be expanded to include Mocambo.[20] The letter they sent to FUNAI explained that the Xocó had allowed Mocambo to be exempt from the original FUNAI land demarcation even though by rights it belonged to them. Now, the letter complained, the Palmares Foundation "wants to include our area in the area they are demarcating for the blacks; we will not let go of what belongs to us, since the blacks want to expel our Xocó brothers living there." Once again, the competitive nature of the relationship between the two communities became overt.[21] Since the matter was cast as an "ethnic" dispute, the federal attorney could exert jurisdiction. Jacobina seized this moment to try to understand what was happening between two newly recognized groups and eventually to see what could be done on behalf of the remanescentes, particularly in relation to the constitutional promise of land. If the dispute had been treated as an everyday disagreement between individuals, it would have been referred to the municipal police and state prosecutor, and those with the strongest ties to the local power elite at the moment would have prevailed. Such jockeying in relation to the local authorities and the use of municipal power to chip away at one's political enemies, always temporary, but with a veneer of permanence that spontaneous emotional engagement provided, was common.

Although casting the dispute as "ethnic" delivered it into the hands of the federal government, presumably fairer and more disinterested than those at the local political level, the rhetoric of ethnicity could also have negative repercussions. In 1999, once the Egídio families had settled in Mocambo, the number of parties to the dispute had grown to at least four: Xocó, non-Xocó who were also not black, quilombo supporters (whether "black" or not), and Mocambo residents who were "black" but did not consider themselves remanescentes (those referred to as contras). Placing them into ethnic categories exacerbated and hardened divisions. Sertanejo village life is often about interfamily and intrafamily disagreements, shifting political and personal alliances, individual and family honor, and moments when people who had been enemies for a decade would suddenly come together—rearranging their loyalties for a particular purpose. By ethnicizing this particular dispute, freezing it in time, the normally fluid alliance and opposition building was undermined, thus creating a different landscape of relations and rigidifying boundaries, a textbook case of Fredrik Barth's theory of ethnicity.

This process of ethnicization was not attributable to the federal attorney alone, although governmental imprimatur was a powerful catalyst. As discussed earlier, the feuding had been going on for a number of years. However, in 1999, the character of the dispute changed. So much more seemed to be at stake with the arrival of the "outsider" Egídio families and the strengthening of their alliances with the Xocó leadership on São Pedro Island and the contras within Mocambo. Talk of an imminent land grant to the Antônio do Alto Association was now being met head-on by threats couched as defense against expulsion and "oppression" by the remanescentes, who, it was charged, wanted to run Mocambo. Almost immediately, conflicts began between the remanescentes, on the one hand, and the Egídio families and the contras, on the other. Letters to the local authorities were sent and meetings held to discuss the perimeters of Mocambo in anticipation of the title process by the Palmares Foundation. Fear ran rampant that families would be expelled from Mocambo.

Also in 1999, João de Egídio filed a lawsuit to have the property on which

his house, bar, and planting area (all admittedly property of the federal government) declared exempt from any land grant and to get an injunction
against threats to destroy his crops.[22] Around this time, Arruti, the anthropologist send by the Palmares Foundation four years earlier, came back to
Mocambo to conduct further research for his dissertation and became involved with helping the remanescentes write letters to local and federal authorities about the continuing problems, and it was in this context that the
Xocó chief asked for an expansion of the Xocó reserve to include Mocambo.
The remanescentes struggled to retain the hope that the promise of title
would soon be fulfilled. All of this contributed to the accelerated ethnicization of the dispute. As in a game of musical chairs—when the music stops,
everyone sits down—each took on an "ethnic" identification, only worsening the usual dredging up of personal grievances and slights.

As federal attorney, Jacobina entered the complex situation largely un-
aware of the history, resulting in a certain degree of mistrust of his motives
by leaders of the quilombo movement and by the Centro Dom José Brandão,
still very much involved in Mocambo's struggle. To some extent, that suspicion brought about Jacobina's initiation of a civil investigation in November
1999 into the possibility of revising the boundaries between the Xocó reserve
and Mocambo.[23] As far as the remanescentes were concerned, this was the
worst kind of government intervention at a moment when they were hoping
for title and dealing with aggression by the Xocó and obstruction by people
within their own community. It took Jacobina a few months to realize that
any statement he made could be used in unanticipated ways for ends with
which he did not agree. His good intentions were seen as mucking up the
process, largely because he thought he could stay detached and arbitrate
from a distance, an attitude that was soon to change.

Identification along ethnoracial lines was further solidified by the May
1999 workshop for elementary school teachers presented by Professor
Severo, a black activist who had written the original court document about
runaway slave settlements in Sergipe to support Mocambo's claim. When I
interviewed Severo in April 2000, he was living in a ramshackle house in
Aracaju, complaining bitterly that the city government had ordered men to
destroy his house (D'Acelino interview 2000). In a back room were piles of
papers and literary productions by him from thirty-two years of research and
activism in black history in Sergipe. Although he never completed his college degree (leaving college to become an actor), he had devoted a number
of years to writing about an apocryphal fugitive slave, João Malunga. He had
also identified over thirty rural communities as "generated by black resis-

tance" (D'Acelino 1999), hence the appellation "professor" and the respect it engendered.

The document produced by Professor Severo as a record of the May 1999 teacher workshop in Mocambo found its way to federal attorney Jacobina, who had been reading it in August 2000 when a dispute arose between Dona Maria's youngest son, Paulomary, and his cousin, a Xocó Indian who lived in Mocambo and was employed by the state to tend the school building. Accusations were leveled at Paulomary for shooting off a gun in front of his cousin's house. A former Xocó chief complained to FUNAI, which contacted the federal attorney's office. Again, Jacobina insisted that this was an ethnic dispute, even though the cousins had been having problems with each other since childhood. When I weighed in on the side of personal feuding, not at that time understanding why he had to cast it as ethnic, Jacobina cited as proof of the ethnic nature of the problem a passage from Professor Severo's document. In the early nineteenth century, he read, there were conflicts between quilombos and Indians, and at that time Frei Doroteu (from the mission on the island) used the blacks to capture "wild Indians"—an assertion based on no historical evidence. There were positive aspects of Professor Severo's workshop, such as educational discussions and films about black history (including *Amistad* and *Chico Rei*, in which Severo played the starring role). On the negative side, the workshop brought out differences between the remanescente supporters and the contras (both sides participated) and fed fears of expulsion. During the following months, shots were fired, crops were destroyed, disagreements became public, and complaints were made to the state police, culminating in court intervention.[24]

Once Jacobina had read Professor Severo's report and court records, he registered his allegiance to the remanescentes. Jacobina reported that when FUNAI called him to say there were complaints by Xocó against a Mocambo resident, he explained that he had the opposite information—that the Xocó were threatening the blacks of Mocambo. At this same meeting, at the request of the quilombo representative, Jacobina agreed to issue a directive banning the sale of alcohol in Mocambo, just as it was for indigenous reserves. The parallels between the two groups was important to his exercise of jurisdiction. As explained in the introduction, I attended these events and discussed issues with Jacobina. Since taking a side in the disputes was required of any anthropologist (or lawyer) entering the scene, I was always perceived as being on the side of the quilombo movement. At the same time, as an outsider with a known connection to the federal attorney's office, I always had a bit of room to maneuver.

By early 2000, Jacobina had come to the conclusion that the whole dispute could be chalked up to an argument between families and not a fight between ethnic groups. Once he threw his energy into assuring the quilombo's safety and continued existence, he remained involved until he was promoted to a position in Brasília four years later. Reconsidering the boundaries of the Xocó reserve was declared impossible. Those boundaries had been finally established over a decade earlier and could not be changed. The remanescentes had rights that were to be respected, even in relation to the Xocó. The only thing left for the Xocó leadership to complain about was the treatment of individual Indians living in Mocambo and, like the Egídios, the possibility that they would have to leave Mocambo, just as non-Xocós had had to leave São Pedro Island when the tribe was recognized in 1979. Once Jacobina decided that he needed to be an advocate for the quilombo, he helped extract an agreement from the Egídio families that they would be relocated by IN-CRA as soon as it could be arranged.[25] He also arranged for the federal government to contribute to a new elementary school in Mocambo, just like the one on São Pedro Island. He would often say that the Indians have protectors, but the quilombolas, the blacks, are in greater need of help from the federal attorney.

This did not mean that Jacobina's view necessarily coincided with that of the members of the Antônio do Alto Association when it came to who was considered a quilombola. At an extraordinary meeting with all parties present, including quilombolas, landowners, contras, NGOs, and anthropologists and lawyers from Brasília, where emotions ran high, it became clear that the government saw all the long-standing residents of Mocambo who were considered "black" as entitled to stay and participate in the benefits. The attorneys indicated that no one would be required to be a member of the Antônio do Alto Association and no one would be excluded from the land.[26] However, quilombo activists took the position that *only* members of the Antônio do Alto Association (those who had assumed a quilombo identity) could work on the land. The informal definition of who could be a member was not based on the color of skin or descent from fugitive slaves. It was not even based on multigenerational residency in Mocambo. Instead, it was based on who had participated in and been loyal to the struggle from the beginning. As expressed to me by twenty-year-old Sandra, who considered herself to be half Indian and half black, "They want rights but they don't want to be black."[27] Over the course of the following months and into the succeeding year, everyone understood that the contras could stay in the village but could not work on the land. This was not the image that either the

Sandra in front of her Mocambo house, which is painted in support
of candidate Dr. Júlio (photograph by the author)

federal attorney or the Palmares Foundation had projected in their discourse
about a quilombo as a refuge for rural black people who were to be given land
in compensation for their previous enslavement and rewarded for resisting
their masters by setting up their own communities.

The rest of the August 2000 meeting involved another level of concern:
that of the legality of the title granted by the Palmares Foundation in light of
the forty already-existing titles. What were the plans to pay the landowners, if
any? If not, how could the title be legal? At this meeting, a problem that had
been simmering since earlier that year became all too apparent. Although
INCRA had been on board since the early days of implementing the quilombo
clause, it was now taking a low profile and so did not attend this important
meeting. During 2000, there were incapacitating power struggles between
INCRA and the Palmares Foundation, reminding everyone that factionalism
is not confined to backland, village settings. A Palmares Foundation lawyer
visited Mocambo in early 2000 with only negative things to say about INCRA
and the NGOs that supported its involvement, which were crucial to an adequate resolution of quilombo land issues.[28] These problems reverberated in
quilombo communities around Brazil, as rural black people faced the wrath,
and often the armed private police forces, of powerful landowners, including multinational corporations, who were not in the least eager to have their

land taken from them by the stroke of a pen belonging to the president of the Palmares Foundation.

The federal attorney was also upset with the Palmares Foundation for telling the quilombo communities who were given title that those who already owned the property would have to seek compensation from another organ of the government, thus placing the problem squarely in the lap of the federal attorney's office itself. Mocambo was the only community with a major landowner, Seixas Dória, who was able to finagle money out of the Palmares Foundation, largely because of his connections with a former president of Brazil. The owners of the smaller parcels had little recourse beyond going to court to engage in years of litigation over the legal effects of an untested constitutional provision. The only other legal tactic at their disposal might have worked if the federal attorney had not decided to protect the quilombo's new title. That tactic involved the traditional control by landowners of the notarial offices (cartórios). Brazilian notaries are tied to local courts and, unlike in the United States, have extensive powers to register property, authorize lawsuits, and validate elections. In a legal culture where "official" documentation is the key to legality, notaries have much more power than would appear at first glance. Moreover, in the sertão, where illiteracy is high, the stamp of the notary is taken as proof of ownership, the legality of a contract, or the legitimacy of a child.

As the meeting drew to a close, federal attorney Jacobina decided to go to Mocambo the next day to congratulate the community and officially present the title. He was hoping this would also show the contras that they too were part of the quilombo community. A caravan left Aracaju early the next morning and arrived in Mocambo in time for lunch. The arrival of Jacobina was a big event, filling the quilombo-controlled community hall. None of the contras attended. After the ceremony, someone suggested that the quilombolas show Jacobina the area where the dispute had begun, Fazenda Rosa Cruz. About 200 people accompanied him on a half-mile procession along the riverfront to the parcel that was the site of the original land dispute. Only a handful of quilombolas had taken this walk in the previous eight years since the first confrontation with Neusa Cardoso and her brother. People marched along solemnly, reminiscing about events and struggles that had occurred since, not unlike a sertanejo religious procession or pilgrimage. There was a feeling of accomplishment, but also a certain wariness, almost disbelief, that the title could really mean that they would have control over the land.

That wariness turned out to be well founded, but for a reason unsuspected by the quilombolas. Upon returning from the walk, Jacobina asked

Paulo Jacobina visiting the land where the Mocambo struggle began
(photograph by the author)

to examine the title itself, which Maripaulo assured him had been properly registered with the local notary. When Jacobina looked at the title, he said in a hushed voice to Maripaulo and me, so that no one else could hear, that Maripaulo had been sent to the wrong notary. The title needed to be registered with the real estate notary, who was allied with the antiquilombo forces and who refused to place his stamp on the title. Three months later, after many attempts to have the title registered properly, Jacobina wrote an official letter to the real estate notary, who had insisted from the beginning that the land was already titled in the names of a host of private owners, which it was. Based on Jacobina's letter, the title was finally registered, in November 2000. Jacobina had explained that the questions of title and indemnification were separate and that the lack of payment did not vitiate the title authorized by the Constitution. The notary, at that point, realized that he had no choice and assumed that any irregularities would be fought out in court, if any landowner decided to go that route instead of trying to negotiate payment from the government.

Registration of the title was considered a big victory for Quilombo Mocambo, because as Maripaulo said, when someone doubted whether registration of the title would make a difference, if someone wanted to buy some of the quilombo property: "It's in the computer and when the notary taps on the keys of the computer, he will find our title." The faith expressed by

Maripaulo in the registration process, particularly the knowledge that the title was ensconced in the labyrinth of the computer's memory and could be retrieved with a keystroke, was all that was needed at that moment for the quilombolas to celebrate, plant beans on the land, and feel empowered to call the federal police whenever there was a problem.

However, with the granting of quilombo title the conflict between the quilombolas and the Xocó intensified.[29] In August 2000, at perhaps one of the lowest moments in this relationship, under threat issued by some of the Indians, only one quilombola attended the land pilgrimage (*romaria da terra*). This was an especially sad moment because these annual land pilgrimages had been a source of great excitement, pride, and a sense of empowerment since the invasion of São Pedro Island over two decades earlier. Even worse, from the perspective of the quilombolas, was the presence at the pilgrimage of their sworn enemy, João de Egídio, his family, friends, and political allies hobnobbing with the Xocó. Just as I became convinced that there could be no circumstances in which these people would consider sharing the same space, I was surprised by an event a little over a month later.

COMING TOGETHER FOR A DAY: TIES THAT (UN)BIND

While the division between quilombolas and Indians was growing, national citizenship was bringing people together in a surprising way. At the time of the pilgrimage, the country was preparing for local elections, to be held October 1, 2000, in which all the counties in Brazil would elect executives and members of the local legislative bodies. All around Sergipe, candidates and truckloads of people traveled along the roads, stopping in towns to campaign. On Sundays, it was practically impossible to drive through towns in the sertão, where candidates held big parties with music, dancing, food, and drink that drew families from the surrounding countryside. The roads were clogged with flatbed trucks typical of the sertão with colorfully painted railings and hard benches (*pau-de-arara*). Talk of the election was constant for the months leading up to it, and, in 2000, training on the new electronic voting machines was a good excuse to get people together to talk even more about the candidates.[30] Politicians paid people to be allowed to paint political graffiti on the fronts of their houses, and Mocambo was no exception (see figure 4.2).

It has been observed that during the period before elections, silences are often broken, disputes may take open form, and the usual controls on social life may be altered, with new and old power struggles surfacing (I. A. F.

Barreira 1998:32). Political campaigns in Brazil are "rituals of representation," with their own forms of spatial construction, including parades and caravans, both of which are symbolic activities in the sertão (I. A. F. Barreira 1998:46). These activities symbolize the "legal and legitimate dimensions of the political contract. As rituals of construction of representation and of the legitimation of political choices, campaigns may be considered as a sort of *re-enchantment of the political*, in spite of the massification and the attempt to pasteurize those choices" (I. A. F. Barreira 1998:46, my emphasis). An election becomes a form of "enchanted relationship," in which "in order to be socially recognized it must get itself misrecognized" (Bourdieu 1977:191); "an enchanted experience of culture which implies forgetting the acquisition" (Bourdieu 1984). This may help explain the effervescent character of the campaign period and the excitement of election day itself. In Porto da Folha, where Mocambo and São Pedro Island are located, 88.31 percent of the electorate voted (13,632 of 15,436 registered voters) in 2000. This outstanding statistic only begins to express the importance voters place on elections in Brazil (the national turnout in the 2000 election was about 85 percent).[31]

It may be that the only valuable property the rural poor have is their vote (Queiroz 1973). This would explain the votes given in exchange for favors (jobs, services, and money) and the pride in independence and refusal to follow through on promises to landowners to vote the way they instructed. Since each village is connected more to the county seat than it is to other villages, on election day there is increased consciousness of inclusion within the larger polity of the county. This is a moment when residents take note of their specificity as a social group by the benefits they expect from municipal power. They become aware of a larger society to which they are directly tied and in a certain way dependent on but still able to wield voting power, leading as well to "moments of the highest political effervescence" (Queiroz 1973:69, 81). For Mocambo, this was further complicated by the new ties of some and not others with the federal government, whether it was the quilombolas' relationship with the Palmares Foundation or the Xocó dependence on FUNAI. The awareness of these connections means that decisions about voting are more complex, but it also envelops the decision-making process in an election day ritual of choice, action, and respect for government and the law.

"Enchanted" certainly seemed an appropriate word to describe election day in Mocambo. At about 4:00 in the morning, I was awakened by voices, animated greetings, and music. People were arriving from as far away as Aracaju, Propriá, and towns across the river in Alagoas. Dona Maria had old friends to breakfast, those she saw only on election days. People had moved away years before but always come back to Mocambo to cast their votes. In addition to the happiness brought by visiting family and friends, the atmosphere in Mocambo was generally more relaxed than it had been in a while, almost as though a moratorium had been placed on the feuding. As the day unfolded, trucks arrived from São Pedro Island, outlying villages, and homesteads, bearing residents to vote on the new electronic machines at the schoolhouse in Mocambo. The entire day of voting had the air of a secular ritual that not only reflects social relationships but also reorganizes and even creates them, showing the "existence of social relationships or ideas and values inherently invisible most of the time" (Moore and Myerhoff 1977:14).

As each vehicle pulled up with people from the surrounding area, Mocambo residents greeted them, caught up on gossip, and discussed the election. At lunchtime, the quilombolas all returned to their homes to eat and prepare to vote. Each person over the age of eighteen, man and woman alike, dressed up in their best clothes. Women arranged each other's hair and put on clothing I had only seen them wear at weddings (see figure 3.4). Everyone put on shoes to replace the ubiquitous flip-flops. A clear sign that this was one of the most important events they could participate in was the universal wearing of dentures by those who owned a set. It had often come to my attention that people did not wear their dentures on a regular basis, and there were some whom I had never seen with their teeth in until election day. At a designated time in the afternoon, they walked in groups down the street to the school, chatted with the people who had come from elsewhere, reviewed with each other how to use the new electronic voting machines, stood in line to vote, and cast their ballots, then returned to their homes, changed back into their daily clothes, and returned to the school to continue socializing. The respect and solemnity with which they approached the election was not tied up with their identity as quilombolas or their differences with the contras or the Xocó.

Most surprising to me was the presence in the same room of Dona Maria and Lindonor, Paulino's other wife, as well as Lindonor's children, one of whom served as an election official alongside Dona Maria's son, Paulomary. Another encounter that showed the power of the election and public participation in it was between Dona Maria and the mother of Gracinha, the Xocó Indian who had been accused of killing her "white" husband's nephew back in 1983, recounted in chapter 2. Gracinha's mother, when I first met her on the island, was insistent that she had children by Paulino as well. She showed

me pictures of the children and insisted they looked like him. To my aston-
ishment, on the day of the election, Dona Maria invited her in to look at the
wedding photographs of her own daughter, Paulameire. When Gracinha's
mother left, before I had a chance to formulate the question, Dona Maria
said to me, "She claims to have Paulino's children, but I don't think so. Those
children could be anyone's." It was one of many interactions that day that
forced me to rethink the slippery categories of friends and enemies.

Up to that point, I had assumed that the lines were drawn pretty clearly
and that interactions would follow those lines. Although there were fights,
disputes, gossip, discord, fears of spying, and rancor, these people had relationships with one another that reflected how their communities were bound
by ties that unbind and at the same time bind them to one other. It raised
the question of why they all came together for the election but could not, or
did not, come together for the pilgrimage, a spiritual event organized with
the intention of bringing together people with a common history of struggle.
These were the same people who refused to be together at the pilgrimage,
and yet a month later, even with some suspicious glances, they were milling
around together in high spirits. On the day of the election, the Mocambo
schoolhouse seemed to be a sacred space — more so than São Pedro Island on
the day of the land pilgrimage, even with the bishop and all the priests lined
up to celebrate Mass.

Voting, as I witnessed it, was not just an instrumental act, one that would
decide who would win the election, but was also an expressive act (Connerton 1989:44). Election day was a time to exercise a certain independence and
power. On the other hand, the land pilgrimage, which the Church strived to
turn into a ritual or to canonize as official tradition, was more of a struggle
for control over celebratory proceedings, with factional politics being integral from the beginning. The discourse of the "tradition" of the pilgrimage
served to legitimate the local controversies over how it should be celebrated,
by whom, and with what themes (Guss 2000:15). If the pilgrimage was a cultural performance, then the threat against the quilombolas and the watering
down of the land struggle theme made the pilgrimage a "site of social action
where identities and relations are continually being reconfigured," even if
seemingly imperceptible, "appearing as a mere affirmation of the relations
that already exist" (Guss 2000:12). Paradoxically, the election, which might
naturally be seen as intrinsically factional and potentially violent, seemed to
be the only event for which people were willing to place the fractiousness in
abeyance for at least one day.

The drama and excitement of these months led many people in the area to wonder what would happen next and whether there would be further conflict. The leaders of the quilombo movement, however, seized this opportunity to assert their ownership of the land, giving very little thought to the legal status of the title and any possible rights of the former landowners. An important way they asserted their hegemony as the owners of even the land on which the village of Mocambo sat (contras, Egídios, and all) was through regular performances of dances, plays, and religious events. The same was true for the Indians. The disappointment over the land pilgrimage felt by the quilombolas was not at all the mood on São Pedro Island that day when men, women, and children danced on the ruins of the old monastery next to the mission church where their parents and grandparents first talked with Frei Enoque about an indigenous past. The dances and performances were molded to fit their conception of what it meant to be Indian or black in the new sertanejo landscape where they lived.

Cultural Moves

AUTHENTICITY AND LEGALIZING DIFFERENCE

A crucial element of the process of legalizing identity is the reconfiguration of cultural practices and their meanings. Culture in this context encompasses both "collective practices and beliefs, a repository of repetitive traditions and ready-to-hand responses" and "artistic rupture," which is "inimical to coercive regimes" and can "pry open the door for maneuvering" (Sommer 2006:13–14). As the experiences of the Xocó and Quilombo Mocambo demonstrate, cultural practices are not invented from whole cloth but are refashioned within the constraints of the cultural history of the region at a particular place and time. In this chapter, I will explain how revisions to cultural practices, considered at first to be nothing more than evidence for legal recognition, operated to consolidate new self-conceptions. This chapter will examine the importance to Indian identity of the *tore* (a dance associated with northeastern Indians), *jurema* (a hallucinogenic beverage made from the bark and roots of varieties of the mimosa tree), and *ouricuri* (secret sacred meetings), and the importance to quilombola identity of the *samba de coco* dance. It will inevitably provide grist for the claim that any perceived cultural change and innovation is purely instrumental. However, I will argue that significant cultural changes occurred once each community was recognized as a member group of a federally protected ethnicity. Those changes include revisions in the meanings of land and its uses. Cultural practices that had become synonymous with sertanejo traditions were being disentangled, standardized, assigned to, and adopted by self-designated, legally recognized Indian tribes or quilombo communities. This chapter then comes full circle to reflect on the cultural material from which these choices were made.

INVADING THE ISLAND, BECOMING XOCÓ, AND CHANGING A WAY OF LIFE

The people who occupied São Pedro Island twice in the late 1970s before being recognized as Xocó Indians had much physical and cultural work to do to build a tribal community there. The island had been purchased and cleared of inhabitants by the Brittos at the end of the nineteenth century upon the death of Capuchin missionary Frei Doroteu. All the buildings were razed except for the mission church, which was left to deteriorate. The people who had been living on the island were dispersed on the Brittos' mainland ranches and had become day laborers, known in ethnoracial terms since the early nineteenth century as "caboclos." This common sertanejo appellation included people assumed to have indigenous ancestry but who also were descended from Europeans (Portuguese and Dutch) and Africans. Other than being called "caboclos," a subaltern category that carried no cultural capital or legal rights, practically nothing remained of their "Indianness," and "their rituals, ceremonies, beliefs [were] a mixture in varying degrees of indigenous, European, and African elements" (Pierson 1972:149). Anthropologist Donald Pierson made this observation in the 1950s, while two decades later, the first anthropologist sent by FUNAI to check out possible indigenous status for the invaders of the island opined that they were "culturally discharacterized" and, thus, no different from the rest of the population in the area (Rick 1979). As described in chapter 2, despite these obstacles, she endorsed recognition because they "want[ed] to revitalize their ethnic identity" (Rick 1979).

Perhaps even more important to the anthropologists and activists who supported the Brittos' workers in their bid for a place of their own were the invasions of São Pedro Island. Braving gunmen, state and federal police, and hunger, the families who, on October 31, 1978, had made a pilgrimage to the mission church to publicize their claim, almost one year later, on September 9, 1979, closed up their homes on the mainland and brought their children and elderly to the island with nothing but the clothes on their backs and a few household items. It was at this moment that the press began to refer to them as "Indians" rather than "caboclos" (Arruti 2006:128). After planting the Brazilian flag on the beach, they installed themselves under the trees— one for each family. Some of the women and children slept in the church to avoid the cool morning temperatures, hoping that FUNAI would send them canvas since the rainy season was imminent. The twenty-four houses they left behind, torn down at the order of João Britto, where they had lived at least for a century, were built in a line along the river (Melatti 1979:10). They began planting vegetables for themselves, food they did not have to share with the landowner, on land between the river and the village. When they built their new houses on the island, they placed them facing the central plaza in front of the mission church, creating a village configuration. Greeting each other every morning across the plaza was the beginning of learning to live together in a new way.

Even before the state purchased the island from the Brittos in December 1979, the families had elected a tribal council, including a chief (*cacique*) and shaman (*pajé*).[1] As early as a month after the move, the Catholic indigenous missionary organization, CIMI, had arranged for the 13th Assembly of Indigenous Peoples to be held on São Pedro Island, the first to be held in the Northeast. This was the introduction for the Xocó to the national indigenous rights scene, which grew in importance as Brazil redemocratized over the following decade. Once the families had moved to the island, they were in a physical space that would remind them every day of an ancestral legacy they had taken as their own and had committed themselves to create and follow, for better or worse. It meant learning and creating new cultural practices, including marriage restrictions, and new forms of hierarchical community organization and self-governance.

The process, it should be emphasized, was one not so much of cultural replacement as reconfiguration. It was neither evidence of "ethnogenesis" (Oliveira Filho 1999a), nor a matter of "liv[ing] in the rubble of tradition" (J. W. Warren 2001:19). The cultural practices and ways of life of largely illiterate sertanejo peasants were and continue to be rich, although they are little understood and infrequently studied outside of folkloric investigations in the mid-twentieth century (examples are Araújo 1964b; Bastide 1944; Carneiro and Knox 1963; Cascudo 1962; Romero and Cascudo 1954). With new opportunities for improved living conditions through government recognition and, in some cases, encouragement of tourism, some of these practices have become more visible to the general public and academics. However, it is important to document that the changes were not definitive but rather additive. The Xocó never stopped being Catholic, playing soccer, or dancing the samba de coco, yet their status as Indians is not questioned by the Brazilian government.

SACRED DANCES, SECRET MEETINGS, AND ALTERED STATES

Sertanejo cultural practices have always been entwined with indigenous rituals, African and slave adaptations, and preconquest Portuguese rural customs tied to folk Catholicism. Most relevant to this discussion are some of the dances that mark sertanejo life, particularly the samba de coco and the toré.[2] On the Brittos' land before Frei Enoque arrived, the people who would become the Xocó participated in a large variety of folkloric sertanejo traditions, including dancing the toré and the samba de coco, although these dances were not considered evidence of anything more than playful fun and relaxation (*brincadeira*). Both were associated with working in the rice lagoons as part of their sharecropping arrangement with the landowners. In the first anthropological reports on the Xocó, filed in 1979 (Melatti 1979; Rick 1979), there was no mention of a "sacred dance" such as the type of toré practiced by the Kariri-Xocó, their downriver "cousins" (Mota 1997:35). In fact, even two decades later, the Xocó were being accused of not knowing the correct torés (Mota 1997:35). Nor was there mention of any other such practices that would set these people apart from their sertanejo neighbors and relatives. The general view was that the people who were now claiming indigenous identity as Xocó did not exhibit any of the hallmark character-istics associated with northeastern Indians. In fact, until this point, there had been a division between indigenous ancestry and indigenous traditions: "Although the . . . backlander often has Indian ancestry, he has no great weight of Indian traditions behind him, having inherited his language, his religion, and, indeed, most of his culture from the Portuguese" (A. W. John-son 1971:23). This is why, when northeastern Indians began to assert rights to government protection (*tutela*) and land, they were referred to as *rema-nescentes indígenas* (remnants or descendants of Indians).

To remedy this "lack" of cultural evidence, the northeastern indigenous cultural complex was introduced to the Xocó by Catholic Church intermedi-aries, such as CIMI, with its sponsorship of the indigenous assembly on the island in 1979, and Frei Enoque, who attempted to arrange meetings with the Kariri-Xocó to teach the secrets (Melatti 1985). Also, Clarice Mota, the anthropologist who had first visited both tribes in 1983, returned in 1985 and arranged and then filmed a visit by the Xocó shaman to the Kariri-Xocó, where he was taken to the ouricuri to obtain secret knowledge (Mota 1997:7,14,18). As the Xocó learned them, these practices became accretions to their Catholic beliefs and enhanced their allegiance to the priests and bishop. As explained by a Xocó woman who had just participated in the Xocó versions of the ouricuri and the drinking of jurema in September 2000, she was about to spend a week in the state capital missionizing for the Catholic Church in the city's periphery where the desperately poor live. As her "an-cestors" were missionized, so she would do the same for non-Indians. Like her fellow Xocó, her identity as an Indian did not interfere with her strong commitment to the Church.

In the 1940s, Roger Bastide (1944:50) identified the toré as part of a com-plex of beliefs and practices known as *catimbó*. Some of the components of catimbó were thought to have been associated with indigenous peoples and others with African descendants, but they had become incorporated into northeastern folk Catholicism. Folklorists of the Northeast, such as Alceu Maynard Araújo (1964a:46–47), whose research dates from the 1950s, described the toré as a magical practice that was a "mixture of Roman Catholic belief . . . and Kardecism [a form of spiritism popular in Brazil founded by a Frenchman in the 1850s], that is the bringing forth of a spirit through reincarnations." Saints were called upon, and dancers were said to be transformed through the use of the hallucinogen jurema, which "sertanejos piously believe" has "magical powers." Araújo explained that those with "indigenous blood" who drank jurema would "enter into a Catholic purgatory" where they could become "caboclos," considered a form of sanctification. Beyond being a plant with certain curative powers, jurema is today seen as part of a religio-cultural conjunction that includes songs, myths, and the consecration of space (ouricuri) (Mota and Albuquerque 2002:43), all of which is connected historically with *candomblé* and *umbanda*, both integral to the African imaginary in Brazil. In recent studies of jurema, in addition to learning that only by mixing it with another plant product while cooking will hallucinations result, scholars have examined its multivalent expressions and meanings. Its status in Afro-Brazilian religions mirrors that in the indigenous spiritual universe (Pinto 2002), as expressed in the subtitle of a recent edited collection, "From Botanical Species to Afro-Indigenous Divinity" (Mota and Albuquerque 2002; Mota 1997:48).[3]

Since the 1940s, when the toré became a "concise ritual" or "obligatory expression" of northeastern indigenous identity (Arruti 1998b) and took on indigenous religious connotations, it has involved body painting, masks, and skirts made of plant fiber. The performers chant a "monotonous and strongly cadenced music, the *toante*," with call and answer motifs (Arruti 1998b:106). The dance is done in a line snaking along, with men first, then women and children, all stamping feet, with the leaders playing flutelike instruments and some of the people shaking maracas. Spiritually, dancing the toré is essential to communicating with the "enchanted ones" (*encantados*), who are spirits of Indians that haven't died but have abandoned this world to become protectors of their group (Arruti 1999:255). In addition to their private use of the toré as part of the ouricuri and the use of jurema as a hallucinogen, all recognized northeastern tribes perform a version of the toré in public on special occasions, such as the annual Day of the Indian, or on the 500th anniversary of Brazil's "discovery" by the Portuguese in 2000.

How the toré became the primary evidence of indigeneity in the Northeast can be traced to the anthropological writings of Carlos Estevão Oliveira (Arruti 1999:255). In the early 1940s, he conducted research with the 1,000-strong Fulni-ô, the only northeastern Indians with an indigenous language, Ia-tê. The regional inspector of the Indigenous Protection Service (SPI), predecessor to FUNAI, adopted Estevão Oliveira's observations about the toré among the Fulni-ô to establish a criterion by which to judge communities that were beginning to claim indigenous identity in connection with land struggles throughout the Northeast.[4] As revealed in an interview conducted by anthropologist Rodrigo Grünewald, the regional inspector was quite aware that he was instituting a rite of passage and not a verification of authenticity of groups that were ostensibly no different from their neighbors. They were certainly not "primitive" or "uncivilized," like the Indians in the Amazon region with whom the SPI had had all of its experience until the 1940s (Arruti 1999:256). For this government official, the toré was not an expression of authenticity but rather an "obligatory expression" with an educational purpose equivalent to political consciousness-raising. The performance of the dance itself, he felt, was crucial to moving beyond a simple declaration that a group wanted to "be" Indian to showing that it intended to act as Indians as well. It did not take long for the toré to become reified as "substantive proof of ethnic authenticity" (Arruti 1999:256), which it continues to be in the twenty-first century.

Some rural folk in northeastern Brazil have clearly benefited from the opening up, through postlegislative negotiation, of the possibilities of becoming fully recognized Indians under the tutelage of the Brazilian state. At the same time, there is also loss associated with this choice, particularly in relation to the variety and meanings of local cultural practices. In the lives of the people who grew up on the Brittos' land, the toré and the samba de coco were both ludic experiences associated with rice planting, carrying no discernible religious significance. Seven years after Frei Enoque's arrival in Sergipe, he recorded and transcribed interviews with elderly inhabitants who had come to self-identify as Indians or, as the old folks still called themselves in 1978, caboclos. The transcripts are helpful in understanding the process of producing evidence for recognition. In questioning two women in their nineties, Frei Enoque raised the question as to whether they had danced the toré, and they answered in the affirmative. When he continued asking them about São Pedro Island, Dona Zefinha explained how she missed the island and wanted to be buried there. Frei Enoque asked, "Would you want to live there?" Dona Zefinha responded, "If I knew that we had São Pedro Island, I would yet dance the [samba de] coco." Frei Enoque then immediately turned to the other woman and switched the name of the dance back to the toré: "Would you dance the toré if you returned to the island?" This exchange is significant because the dance required to prove indigeneity was the toré, while the samba de coco was viewed as just another sertanejo dance. It would later become the equivalent cultural evidence for Mocambo to become a quilombo. Confirming the continuing entanglement of cultural practices despite new recognitions, the FUNAI anthropologist who visited São Pedro Island for the third time in 1985 noted in her report that the Indians regularly dance both the toré and the samba de coco (Melatti 1985:23), a combination that I witnessed on the island in 2000 during a celebration of the island's invasion that was closed to outsiders, with the exception of Clarice Mota, a campaigner for the upcoming election, and me. I was surprised when I saw a variation of the samba de coco on the island, since the Xocó would only dance the toré at public events, as Sergipe's only Indian tribe.

The toré that the Xocó performed in 2000 was the version that had been taught to them by the Kariri-Xocó, who had, in turn, been part of a chain of learning and teaching the dance that had begun in the 1940s (Arruti 1999). The local variations of these dances and songs have receded into the background, and, because of the public attention paid to the government-sponsored toré, it has become more difficult to analyze their historical and continuing meanings. The notion that the "true" dance has been lost and is now being resurrected devalues alternative meanings—the toré communicates more than Indianness to those who practiced it before laying claim to an Indian identity. The ludic, the form the toré took in this case, is not necessarily opposed to the sacred. In backland folk Catholicism, sacred festivals honoring saints, for example, are common and cherished: "The sacred can also serve to play and divert and shouldn't be exclusively characterized by attitudes of circumspection" (Grünewald 2004:23). In fact, the toré may not even have religious origins, in spite of its current use to show indigenous religiosity. It is just as likely that people danced variations of the toré, and it was only in the nineteenth century, with the development of Kardec spiritism and then the growing popularity of Afro-Brazilian religions, such as candomblé, with its caboclos and spirit possession, that the current attributes of the toré have become reified and used as evidence of an authentic Indian history (Grünewald 2004:25).

It is also important not to underestimate the influence of Catholicism on the sacred dance of the Indians (Pompa 2003), leading again to the conclusion that the toré was not a preexisting "pure" phenomenon that is being "recaptured." Just as on São Pedro Island, all over Brazil, indigenous populations were gathered into Catholic missions, which became spaces of labor and coexistence for Portuguese, Indians, and Africans. This led to "the spreading of the term toré to designate popular syncretic Afro-Amerindian rituals with possession" and extended to rites designated as "mixed torés" (*torés misturados*) in Alagoas and Sergipe (Grünewald 2004:18), precisely the home of the Kariri-Xocó and the Xocó. When observers or participants make the judgment that any kind of variation in these practices betrays an imagined authentic universal practice, even for the sake of political expediency, they run the risk of sabotaging the ability to achieve a richer analysis of the use of dance in the process of legalizing identity. The toré is a cultural practice that was mixed, combined, and inauthentic from its inception (Briggs 1996; Hobsbawm and Ranger 1983; Ranger 1994; T. Turner 1991; Vlastos 1998). Even so, it has come to occupy the legal and symbolic space of northeastern Indianness, while changing its character and meaning for future generations.

CULTURAL MEANINGS OF LAND IN MOCAMBO

Not unlike the impact on the daily lives of the Xocó when they moved onto the island in 1979, the granting of land to the quilombo association of Mocambo in 2000 evoked similar changes, but also deepened the rift in the community and revealed that the meaning of land is far from unitary. What land means to the people who live on it, possess it, own it, work it, and yearn after it is tied to the circumstances of acquisition, the nature of the title, the land's arability, agricultural practices, and the class and power position of the owners. Land can signify the ability to feed one's family or the possession of political or economic power. Moreover, the meanings of land can vary, not only in different places, such as the Brazilian South of family farms or the sugarcane plantations of the coastal Northeast (Wolford 2001), but it can also change over time and even for individuals as the context of their lives and struggles change. Culture and society should not be "expressed in an habitual past tense" or experience converted into "finished products," but rather the observer must recognize that "there is a frequent tension between the received interpretation and practical experience" (R. Williams 1977:128, 130). The changing meanings of land to peasants in Mocambo are "changes in structures of feeling," or "structures of experience." Such a "structure" is a "set, with specific internal relations, at once interlocking and in tension," and defines "a social experience which is still *in process*" and often not seen as social until analyzed at a later stage when "returned, interactively, to [the] evidence" (R. Williams 1977:132, 133). Possession of land can also be a condition that defines the identity of a group, as was the case in Mocambo. I was in Sergipe when Mocambo received its title from the government and so was witness to the effects of that event on the Mocambo residents and to the legal wrangling, concerns, and implications for power relations that ensued.

The standard narrative about the struggle for land by the Mocambo families was that they had been landless sharecroppers for generations until the day in 1992 when they were forced by the arbitrary actions of the landowner to begin a protracted struggle for land, as described in chapter 3. That narrative was disrupted for me shortly after title was granted. On July 26, 2000, the day Maripaulo, the acting coordinator of the quilombo association, thought he had properly registered the title, I was driving him back to Mocambo when he mentioned that the land we were passing had once belonged to his uncle and that others from Mocambo had also owned land around there. When I expressed surprise, he explained that sometime around 1946, land in the area had been acquired by the state of Sergipe and distributed to local peasants. A few weeks later, I had a conversation with the sister of the owner of a large house in Ranchinho on the road to Mocambo, which was considered part of the quilombo. Her brother was one of the few people in Ranchinho who supported the quilombo movement.[5] As we drove through the same area, she explained to me that her father had received land from the state in 1946. When pressed to tell the story of 1946, they expanded on it, and the story was later confirmed by some of the other older people in Mocambo.

Maripaulo explained that in 1946 a union organizer had managed to get land in the county of Porto da Folha for rural workers. Maripaulo was born after this event, which makes his knowledge of the details significant—he must have been told the story of how the Mocambo families had acquired their land as a child. The size of the land grant depended on the number of children in the family. At least seven families from Mocambo benefited, including Maripaulo's uncle and the ninety-year-old faith healer father-in-law of Sr. Antônio. Sr. Antônio was an important leader of the quilombo movement and coordinator of the Antônio do Alto Association until mid-2000. Therefore, when Sr. Antônio married as a young man, he worked on land that was owned by his wife's family and thus was not a landless peasant. Sr. Antônio's family also had their house in Mocambo, built by his grandfather around the turn of the twentieth century. Maripaulo's uncle, a man in his eighties, explained that each family was given a receipt for the land, which served as the equivalent of a deed. About twenty years later, he took advantage of his legal ownership of the land and sold it, as did most of the others. Some moved permanently to Mocambo, and others moved to the city.[6]

Also in the late 1940s, the state purchased the land on which the village of Mocambo itself is situated.[7] In the 1940s, Mocambo was one of three nuclei that served the surrounding ranches (Arruti 1997).[8] When, thirty years later, the work dried up, Mocambo was the place where those who did not leave to work in the city could find refuge. They moved into the village and built houses that shared walls with the ones that were already there, giving the two streets of Mocambo their current row house appearance, so that the demographic configuration of the area was radically changed from scattered dwellings and families living far apart to a concentrated settlement. This change in land use was instrumental in the later ability of community and Church activists to organize the quilombo movement. Although Mocambo was far from the center of national power, the democratic upheavals of 1945 and the Constitution of 1946 nonetheless had its impact on the area. Finding its way to this most local of situations, Article 156 of the national Constitution of 1946 required that squatters be given preference when state-owned parcels of land (*terras devolutas*) were distributed.

In Sergipe, at the time, the state government was also trying to reduce the concentration of land ownership. A state constitutional provision empowered the governor to distribute state-owned land to poor agricultural workers (Magno da Silva 1995:40). It was under this provision that the Mocambo families were given land in the 1940s. Arruti (1997) conjectures that the state's acquisition of the small piece of land on which the village of Mocambo is situated was a governmental response to generalized political mobilization by peasants in the Northeast. He does not mention specific agitation in Porto da Folha, nor did the men I spoke with who had received title in 1946. As they spoke about it in retrospect, it seemed that their land grants carried a sense of government entitlement, a bit like retirement benefits. Therefore, it seems likely that these donations by the state were not the result of a local collective struggle for land or social justice, or at least not in this area. The Mocambo families were beneficiaries of a government policy and the efforts of a rural union activist who was most likely involved with larger-scale efforts connected to the democratic upsurge of the 1940s (Skidmore and Smith 1992:170). As mentioned earlier, when families received land from the state in 1946, they were given a receipt that could be turned into cash when they sold the land. This did not signify a coming together, either as the result of struggle or to conserve a cultural heritage. It was a welcome windfall. Many of the people sold their land, and by the time the quilombo struggle had hit its stride, they were living in Mocambo, working as sharecroppers, or collecting their state retirement pensions. There was clearly a difference between the earlier land grants and the collective title that resulted from the quilombo movement, even though the newly titled land included the parcels once owned and sold by some of the by-now self-identified quilombolas.

There is a complex relationship between property and culture. It is not simply a question of private property as a disintegrative force in collective or communitarian sensibility and cultural cohesiveness. Rather, property ownership and restrictions on property transfer (whether they come from above, as in the case of Mocambo, or from below and voluntarily, as in certain religious communities in the United States) can act to integrate and "preserve" the cultural life of a group. At the same time, the desire to maintain a distinct cultural community through property restrictions often clashes with the right to free alienability of property, creating "tensions between goals of cultural preservation and goals of cultural development" (Stolzenberg 2000:189). To begin to negotiate this tension, quilombo advocates have encouraged the Brazilian government to adjust its pension regulations, which normally give a rural pension only to those who own land, and allow the communal quilombo title to count toward individual association members' pensions. This is a small step, and there are still disadvantages to owning land collectively in the form of an association. Nonetheless, people in the Mocambo community voluntarily incorporated their property into the quilombo.

Unlike the 1946 individual, alienable land grants, the title provided to the quilombo association carried with it meanings grounded in cultural and ethnoracial identification that had developed as the result of collective struggle and that also derived from the contested nature of the quilombo "community" and its new relationship to the larger Mocambo community. These changing meanings can also be seen in the situation of the quilombola with the large house in Ranchinho, about a mile up the road from Mocambo and part of the quilombo. He runs a bar out of his house where people in the area stop to chat and socialize on their way back from working in the fields or visiting the county seat. This man, whose son, a metalworker in São Paulo, has paid for improvements to the house over the years, decided early on that he was willing to forfeit his individual, alienable title in exchange for an untried, collective title that would leave him without the right to sell his property. By doing so, he is also risking the inheritances of his children since the question of whether children automatically succeed to the membership of their parents in the association upon death is completely unresolved. In other words, this man has exchanged a known property right for a right, the legal status of which, and its relationship to his land, is unknown. No small part of the tenacity with which people viewed the new, collective title was attributable to the opposition they faced from within their own families.

Cultural cohesion of the quilombo group within Mocambo represented by the land title imbued the title with different meanings to individuals. For example, Maripaulo's uncle, who had sold his property almost forty years earlier, was now willing to suffer the invectives of his own family. This uncle of Maripaulo, who was in his eighties, had chosen to side with his sister, Dona Maria, whose children were the leaders of the quilombo movement, rather than with his other sister, Dona Rosa, whose children led the contras. Before Dona Rosa died, at the end of 2000 (Dona Maria did not attend her funeral but her brother did), he went one hundred yards down the dirt street to visit Rosa, who berated him and made him cry. Another tragic family story involved a woman in her sixties who always danced the samba de coco with Dona Maria and put herself in the forefront of the struggle. Her husband and all but one of her children were contras and left her to live in Aracaju. This situation persisted until 2004, when she broke down, became a contra, and distanced herself from all her old quilombola friends.

In addition to the changing meanings of land as a result of the process of struggle, the requirement of communal ownership affected the way the new owners worked on the land itself. Because the government required that the land be held collectively, on the grounds that the key marker of quilombo identity was the communal use of land, during the planting and harvest of 2000 an effort was made to increase the collective nature of land use. In insisting on communal land title, the government's ostensible purpose was to give land in a way that would not disrupt presumed preexisting land-use patterns—an assumption about descendants of quilombos. However, in the case of Mocambo, most of the communal work had been done as sharecroppers, while the state-owned areas on the riverbank had been divided into individual family plots. Once they received their large parcel of land collectively as a quilombo, villagers began to work it communally for their own account for the first time.

Therefore, the government's interpretation of the quilombo clause as requiring land to be owned collectively by an association was instrumental in consolidating, if not provoking, a shift in land use that paralleled, and coincided with, the shifts in the meaning of land. However, a certain romantic notion of collective land use appeared to lie behind the directive. As I watched their early attempts at collectivity, both with cooperative milk sales (from the cows that were individually owned) and with bean planting, harvest, distribution, and sale, it became obvious that there was much to be learned to be successful collective farmers. It did not come naturally, particularly for people who had, for generations, worked on other peoples' land and lived their lives in an individualistic society, even on the banks of the São Francisco River.[9] Moreover, the land grant was accompanied by neither irrigation nor agricultural technical assistance, making the meaning of land more symbolic than a real source of sustenance.[10]

Another example of the shifting symbolic nature of land is illustrated by arguments over the Mocambo soccer field, which started before title was granted and continued for at least a year. Even though a soccer field is not often thought of as "land," because it is not agricultural, it was significant to the larger question of how the quilombo movement as a community of struggle related to the village property, technically owned by the state until July 2000 and thereafter titled in the name of the quilombo association. In this case, it was not only that the contras denied access to the soccer field to the quilombolas and that periodic fights erupted over its use, but it was also the galling action on the part of Paulo Monteiro, the new owner of Fazenda Rosa Cruz (the ninety hectares that had become the hallowed, but forbidden, ground where the quilombo struggle was born), who had sided with the contras, the Egídio families, and the Xocó majority who opposed the quilombo. In a further act of war, Monteiro made that "holy" ground available to the opposition for *their* soccer games. This came after police and the local state prosecutor intervened and tried to impose a schedule so that the two sides would not have to play on the Mocambo soccer field at the same time.

These examples of the shifting cultural meanings of land show that the existence of a right to land does not by itself provide the impetus to keep it and pass it on to future generations, or to struggle to obtain the credits, technical assistance, and irrigation necessary to make the land productive. Other factors may intervene to modify an interest in owning land that by itself evokes little affective attachment. Land, in and of itself, is not enough to provoke action or commitment. Rather, it is in the process of obtaining land and the structures of feeling that are produced through that process that also provide the meaning of struggle. A crucial stage in that process in Mocambo was, as it was with the Xocó, the transformation of a local dance into proof of quilombo identity.

SAMBA DE COCO: REVEALING LYRICS ABOUT BLACKS AND INDIANS

The process of legalizing quilombo identity in Mocambo began about a year after the families who had occupied Neusa Cardoso's land learned that recognition as a remanescente de quilombo might be possible. They started focusing on cultural manifestations that would help in their legal claim. This focus became even more important as the national quilombo debate shifted to an emphasis on ethnicity, as explained in chapter 3. A Brazilian anthropologist has noted, "The characterization of the dispute as an ethnic question changes the very instruments of struggle, legitimating dance and music, that will be incorporated in the political practice not only as expression of 'black culture' but also as a form of affirmation of social rights" (Steil 1998:23). I would add that the definition of the struggle was being changed, not only for theoretical or even practical reasons, but also because the cultural manifestations themselves were being "discovered" in communities seeking recognition. Some of those manifestations, long found in folklore literature as sertanejo cultural activities, were being reframed as evidence of quilombo history. Moreover, political mobilization was making possible an "inversion of meanings," in that a quilombo, which in the slave order had been something that delegitimized land possession, was becoming the basis, through invocation of the quilombo clause, for rural black communities to claim recognition and land rights.

Since the Xocó had a dance that proved their Indianness, the Mocambo families adopted the samba de coco for the intermediaries (Church, government officials, and NGOs) who would come to the village on a regular basis throughout the 1990s. As with the Xocó, performing a variety of dances was integral to their lives in the sertão and was often tied to agriculturally important moments. A former missionary who had been closely associated with Frei Enoque recalls that after the Xocó won São Pedro Island, there was an early attempt to mobilize Mocambo, based on the land struggles in progress in the region. At this point, in the mid-1980s, representatives of the Church tried to convince people in Mocambo to make samba de coco the principal symbol of the village to outsiders. At that point it was not tied to any sort of historical thoughts about quilombo identity—there were no rights associated with such a thing and Mocambo had never considered itself descended from a fugitive slave community. They even considered changing the name, Mucambo (at the time), to avoid an association with being black.

In addition to urging the instrumental use of the dance, Frei Enoque tried to convince Mocambo to reorganize its saint's day festival to make it less a lay celebration, with popular dancing, like the forró, and serious drinking, and more religious. He wanted the residents to dance only between the procession and the Mass and to refuse to take funds from local politicians and landowners to finance the festival. The village refused to make the changes, and, as punishment, Frei Enoque stopped performing Mass in Mocambo from 1986 until 1990 when, Padre Isaías became the parish priest (Arruti 2006:138–139). This disaffection with Frei Enoque may have contributed to Mocambo's refusal to adopt the samba de coco as the symbol of the village in the mid-1980s. However, a decade later, when the decision was made to pursue quilombo recognition, the dance resurfaced and achieved the status that Frei Enoque had prematurely wanted for it.

The samba de coco was a staple of sertanejo culture. Folklorists considered it the "dance of the poor . . . of those who possess only hands to give rhythm, to overcome the lack of musical instruments" (Araújo 1964a:239). The origin of the dance has been traced to Alagoas, the state across the river from Mocambo; yet it exists in most rural corners of the northeastern sertão and is considered "Afro-Amerindian," having strong associations with indigenous practices (E. Pereira 2004). By the time the Palmares Foundation and the local black activist, Professor Severo, visited for the first time in July 1994, the people claiming remanescente status had already begun recasting the samba de coco as proof of their (re)discovered fugitive slave history. The dance can take the form of a circle with soloists taking turns dancing in the center (as it is done in Mocambo), or it may be danced in couples like a square dance (Melo 1982:63), as it is done on São Pedro Island by the Xocó. In Mocambo, in 1998, when I first saw it performed, the samba de coco was accompanied by songs, with simple clapping, foot stamping, or banging coconut shells accompanying the rhythm of the dance.

The dance was highlighted in a short film made on the day of the final judicial expulsion from Fazenda Rosa Cruz in May 1994. The film was made with the help of the CPT to convince the government to send an anthropologist to qualify Mocambo as a quilombo. During the filming of the rice planting and dancing on the disputed property, gunmen of the landowner appeared, threatening violence. The whole thing was captured on film and forwarded to the Palmares Foundation.[11] At this point, both the Palmares Foundation and INCRA became more involved with Mocambo. Within a few months, state and federal government agencies began converging on the village, with INCRA beginning a series of a dozen meetings which would take place through recognition in 1997. INCRA pursued expropriation of Fazenda Rosa Cruz, where the struggle began, at the same time that quilombo status and land title were being promised by the Palmares Foundation. Sometimes Mocambo found itself the subject of intense governmental interest, and other times, when the agencies were at loggerheads with each other, it was abandoned—left to its own devices and subject to the whims of local politicians.

When Arruti, the anthropologist assigned by the Palmares Foundation to research possible quilombo status, arrived in Mocambo in 1995, and during his second visit in 1996, elderly women and a few younger people performed the samba de coco. In his report, filed in January 1997, he noted that they had performed the dance for him three times, once during each time he visited and always in connection with a meeting of the quilombo association. The dance was accompanied by a tambourine, with its beat marked by clapping hands and the noise of feet stamping on the floor of the parish house (Arruti 1997:14). The older people explained to him that the dance was traditionally done in the final phase of the rice harvest when the lagoon was "closed" (*fechar a lagoa*). At that time, they would dance the samba de coco to celebrate, but by the mid-1990s, they were dancing for another reason.

The president of the Palmares Foundation arrived in Mocambo in 1997 for the recognition ceremony, during which the samba de coco was performed. On the second anniversary of recognition, I witnessed the dance. The following anniversary, in 1999, Professor Severo gave a workshop in Mocambo on black culture. It was after that event that the women, who had always performed the dance dressed in their usual everyday clothing of shorts and t-shirts, began for the first time to don the garb of Afro-Brazilian religious ceremonies, such as candomblé—skirts, blouses, and turbans, all in white. This was what I saw when the dance was performed again on Black Consciousness Day in 2000. Three years after recognition, the dance had been fully transformed into a representation of a history with African roots, being danced both to celebrate the land grant earlier that year and to convince those in the community who still opposed quilombo status to reconsider their position. Mocambo had entered national consciousness as a quilombo, and there it would stay, if the quilombo association had anything to say about it.

Since the mid-1990s, when the samba de coco became associated with the quilombo movement in Mocambo, there have been times when opposition forces and the slowness of the government in granting land title have led to a refusal to dance—another example of the elasticity of newly experienced identities. Even if law encourages "people both to have and to express inner qualities" that it "defines as innate or inherent" (Collier, Maurer, and

Suárez-Navaz 1995:21), ostensibly distinguishing them from others, communities are not necessarily united around such legal opportunities. It is not uncommon for such disagreements to find expression around questions of cultural practices. When the question becomes "Whose reality is it that is being reflected? [then] . . . cultural performance will remain both contentious and ambiguous, and while the basic structure of an event may be repeated, enough changes will be implemented so that its meaning is redirected" (Guss 2000:9).

In fact, sites of cultural performance are often also sites of tension, confrontation, and contestation (Mendoza 2000:239). When I first visited Mocambo in 1998, the dance was performed for me inside a house and not out on the street in public, where I saw it performed on later occasions. When I returned at the beginning of 2000, Dona Maria, the organizer of the dance, told me she would never dance the samba de coco again. She said that her legs hurt and that the women were getting too old to dance. Not to mention that the youngsters, several complained, were not interested in learning the dance. Dona Maria was feeling discouraged about problems with the opposition, which included her sister's family. This made the political question also a family feud, because of which she had not spoken to her sister in five years. The pain of separation from her family who lived only a few houses away was apparent every time I visited her.

Some things did change after land title was granted in July 2000. Although the contras were still adamant in their opposition to the quilombo movement and Dona Maria's sister, by then dying of cancer, was still not speaking to her, Dona Maria and a large number of women were dancing the samba de coco again and with even greater enthusiasm than before. The women danced in their white clothing and turbans and had organized a group of children to perform their own version of the samba de coco on Black Consciousness Day. By the year 2000, the women and children danced in the quilombo association's community hall, a large public space used for parties, meetings, voting, and watching soccer on the communal television. In 2004, the quilombo association received a small grant to purchase white cloth, and costumes were made for the dance. The ebb and flow of occasions for performing the dance have reflected and tracked local political alliances, relations with the government, and the state of negotiation over the meaning of the law. The reconfiguration of the dance provided the quilombo supporters with an opportunity to reach for new meanings that gave them choices, as well as tools for reinforcing, opposing, or celebrating old and new alliances and feuds.

The intention here is to address the potential accusation that revisions of local culture to impress government representatives is fundamentally instrumental or strategically essentialist (Spivak 1988) and thus implicitly "inauthentic." A desire for independence from landowners and freedom from the vagaries of rural wage labor are part of the impetus to assume an identity that would meet legal requirements. However, a purely instrumentalist explanation is a denial that what it means to be a quilombola is in a state of flux for Mocambo residents. The existence of a group of residents who deny quilombo identity and refuse to "assume" their blackness belies a simple instrumentalist explanation. If being a quilombola is so useful, why are there people in Mocambo who, in the words of Dona Maria, "are, but do not assume" their black identity? In order to have robust explanatory value, it is crucial to move beyond a simple functionalist perspective (Sahlins 1999) that allows little space for local creativity, meanings of personal histories, and attachment to place, all of which find expression in the process of struggling for or against legal recognition. The process of legalizing identity is just such an analytical tool. Through its application, it is possible to honor the needs and desires of the people in Mocambo without subscribing to reified notions of identity and law. Cultural forms "express and consolidate the sentiments and identity of people who [may] come together as the result of specific economic-political condition[s]" (Cohen 1993:7).

Both the Xocó and Mocambo communities have used certain aspects of sertanejo culture to meet legal requirements, showing that political movements may constitute new ways of making cultural differences organizationally relevant. Because cultural symbols carry multiple meanings, political action can influence which of such meanings bears the highest emotional valence and which meanings provoke "emotionally powerful intuitive representations" of place (LeVine 1984:85–86). After all, the invocation of "tradition" by its very nature involves a dimension of selectivity, thus leading to the almost imperceptibly emotional, yet practical, choice of a particular identity (or rejection of that identity) at a specific juncture. A recognition that the signs and symbols of identity and self-identification can operate to invoke deep sentiment and attachment to place, as well as to serve a politically emancipatory purpose, can help explode the false dichotomy between primordialism and instrumentalism.

In an effort to further interrogate that false dichotomy, it is helpful to consider the reported lyrics of the samba de coco as performed by Dona Maria and the other women in Mocambo. The lyrics that Arruti chose to include in his expert report supporting quilombo recognition would have been quite familiar to folklorists and observers of northeastern backland music. Rather than a song with bandits, planting, or love as its theme, all common accompaniments for the samba de coco, Arruti (1997:15) chose to foreground the following set of lyrics: "Dance the samba, black, that white not come here. If he comes, he'll have to take a beating" (Samba negro, que branca não vem cá; Se vinhé, pau há de levá). Folklore literature of the Northeast, dating back to the mid-twentieth century, documents these very same lyrics being sung throughout the region (Carvalho Neto 1994:91; Melo 1982:74). Surprisingly, although he mentions it briefly, Arruti does not emphasize the contexts in which these lyrics continue to appear in other locations in Sergipe and Alagoas. The example he does mention in passing is the "lambe-sujo" festival in Laranjeiras, a colonial city about three hours from Mocambo with a population that is about 90 percent black (A. C. d. S. Lima 2000) with a strong legacy of sugar plantation slavery and quilombos. This is very different from Porto da Folha, the county where Mocambo is located, which was reported to have few slaves and no evidence of communities of slaves who had fled from their masters (Arruti 2006:187).

The lambe-sujo festival, held every October, is a regional tourist attraction. Probably dating to the nineteenth century, it is a dramatic reenactment of a battle between *caboclinhos* ("little Indians") and *lambe-sujos* (literally, "beat the dirty ones," or runaway slaves), meant to remind everyone of the defeat of Palmares, the seventeenth-century quilombo "kingdom" in Alagoas. After several defeats at the hands of the Palmares runaways, slaveholders brought caboclos from the interior of São Paulo (known there as *mamelucos*) to the Northeast to capture runaway slaves and to successfully defeat Zumbi, the last king of Palmares. All the participants in Sergipe's lambe-sujo festival are black but paint their skin to be either black slaves or Indians. The people playing the lambe-sujos paint themselves with sugarcane molasses mixed with charcoal and carry wooden scythes like the ones used in the sugarcane fields. Those portraying Indians paint themselves with red dye, wear feather headdresses, and carry bows and arrows. During the processions before and after the battle, musical instruments associated with both groups are played and there is much dancing and singing. The lambe-sujos go door-to-door asking for money to help buy their freedom. In the 2003 documentary film by Gabriela Greeb, the lambe-sujos are also asking for donations so they can slake their thirst. The lambe-sujos go on to capture the queen of the Indians, but then they are defeated and themselves captured by the Indians, who take them door-to-door asking for people to pay to free them. The festival ends with the total defeat of the lambe-sujos, the imprisonment of their king, and the delivery of the slaves to their masters. The lyrics of the song that now accompanies the samba de coco in Mocambo are also sung by the lambe-sujos ("white not come here; if he comes, he'll have to take a beating"), declaring they cannot be captured and intend to remain free. However, every year they are captured and returned to a state of bondage.

Parallel to lambe-sujo in Sergipe is a festival in Alagoas called "Quilombo," during which the same lyrics are sung. There is evidence that the festival was celebrated during the first half of the nineteenth century, but descriptions had to wait until the twentieth century (Amantino 2005). In the Quilombo festival, as in lambe-sujo, there is a battle between Indians or caboclos and fugitive slaves, with the slaves being captured. In this version, the quilombo is destroyed, the quilombolas are sold, and their queen is turned over to a leading man of the village (G. Ramos in Conrad 1983; Carvalho Neto 1994:73). Even though the runaway slaves lose in the end, the festival was threatening enough to the slaveholding elite that it was declared illegal in 1839. Participants were subject to eight days in prison and a fine, and if slaves participated their masters were also required to pay a fine (Amantino 2005). In a sense, the recapture at the end is an accommodation, so that later in the nineteenth century slaveholders could permit their slaves to participate. By allowing themselves to be recaptured, the slaves (and their descendants) were also allowing themselves to express dangerous thoughts. In all three cases (samba de coco, lambe-sujo, and Quilombo festivals), expressions of racial hostility are relegated to the past, with the present maintaining its character as a race-neutral environment, enacting the predominant view, until very recently, that in Brazil race relations are easy and without social antagonisms.

In the next chapter we will see an example of how things are changing in Mocambo, and in Brazil more generally, as discourses about blackness and Africa have become more central to Brazilian identity and struggles, since the 300th anniversary of Zumbi's death and the adoption of Black Consciousness Day as a national holiday in 1995. Mocambo's recognition as a quilombo provides a different context for the words of the song performed as part of the samba de coco. The lyrics are the same as those in Laranjeiras and Alagoas, but rather than being sung in a setting where the blacks always lose and are returned to their masters or killed, these lyrics now signify freedom from slavery. The samba de coco and its attendant lyrics were deployed strategically by the Mocambo families bidding for quilombo recognition. However, as it turns out, their song is tied to other festivals that are linked to Palmares, a historical quilombo.

To the extent that "images of the past and recollected knowledge of the past [were being] conveyed and sustained" by the "more or less ritual per-formances" (Connerton 1989:4) of the samba de coco, they were now being configured as evidence of an imagined quilombo past. To assume that the Mocambo residents' decision to advance the samba de coco, with those par-ticular lyrics, was driven only by instrumentalist motivations papers over the significance of that decision. In fact, continuity marks the cultural prac-tices they chose to advance their cause. While the mytho-history of Palmares and stories of slavery were disparaged, and sometimes censured, aspects of northeastern culture, their telling and retelling, are now encouraged by legal requirements. Through this, we learn not only that cultural moves can be made to bear on new circumstances, but also that culture moves in unex-pected ways.

6

Buried Alive

A FAMILY STORY BECOMES
QUILOMBO HISTORY

A cascade of changes in relationships and self-conceptions accompanied the recognition of Mocambo as a modern-day "quilombo." At the same time, those transformations have been guided by, and continue to be associated with, continuities in practices, beliefs, and worldviews about race, color, ethnicity, and religion that were salient prior to the invocation of the quilombo clause and that remain embedded in newly configured narratives. This chapter is about one such narrative and the changes it reflects and has generated. It chronicles the transformation of a family story into the foundational narrative of those in Mocambo who came to identify themselves as black people descended from fugitive slaves. Through variations in the family story and its appropriation by village teenagers, the story became a play about slavery performed annually to commemorate Mocambo's newly significant past.

THE PLAY'S THE THING

As illustrated by the lambe-sujo and Quilombo festivals discussed in the last chapter, performances are often intended to represent local history, but they also tell stories that link performers and their audience to a national, and even international, understanding of how the newly signified past can serve the present (for examples, see Agier 2002; Fuoss and Hill 2001; Guss 2000; Rockefeller 1998). Moreover, cultural performances have often been theorized as constructive of social identities and relations (Bauman 1992; Schechner 1988; V. W. Turner 1986). In the case of rural Brazil, with the advent of the quilombo clause, villages previously considered "rural black communities" began to associate themselves with representations of an imagined African past. Some authors and activists have come to consider such communities indispensable inspirations for the twenty-first-century black consciousness movement (Linhares 2004; Pereira and White 2001). Just as some anthropologists have argued for a connection between Brazil, as a nation, and African sensibilities, as a result of the large number of Africans brought as slaves until the mid-nineteenth century (Segato 1998), others have pointed out a certain romanticization of Africa in the context of quilombo recognition (Véran 2002). In this chapter, I complicate further the connection between "Africa" in the imagination of Brazilians and modern-day quilombos that have come to represent "myth and history" (Hill 1988) as well as the past and future of what it means to be "black" in the African diaspora (Gomez 2005). Drawing on the concept of "constrained refashioning" (R. Wilson 1995) and showing that new elements in cultural practices are forged "in the shadow of the past" (Fuoss and Hill 2001), I propose that assuming a black identity in rural Brazil does not preclude multiple identifications drawn on local, national, and international discourses.

The play mounted by the Mocambo teenagers reenacts the story of Mocambo's most renowned ancestor, Antônio do Alto, and his unfortunate end. The basic elements of the original story are as follows: Antônio do Alto, great-grandfather of Sr. Antônio, had a love affair with the niece of the powerful local landowner; when the landowner learned that his niece was pregnant, he had Antônio do Alto buried alive. My analysis of the elaboration and transformation of this story into Mocambo's foundational narrative runs along two axes: one of change that shifts in response to perceived legal exigencies and renders the story persuasive in the context of the quilombo clause; and the other of representational durability. The aspects of the story analyzed along the second axis render it comprehensible and credible by retaining preexisting structural elements of power, sexuality, family, and patronage.

As quilombo identity took shape in tandem with changes that can be traced in the story-turned-play, elements of the story's narrative have become crucial to the production of new bases for self-identification, solidarity, and conflict. In that context, the public performance of the play was an attempt to delimit the Mocambo community and reinforce the boundaries and schisms that predated the bid for quilombo recognition. The acknowledgment that community and conflict are entwined has led to a renewed rethinking of the unexamined use of "community" as an invocation of positive associations tied to an assumed communal past (Creed 2004, 2006). Therefore, in addition to illustrating how law can be instrumental in transforming local cultural practices and self-understandings, exemplifying the third component in the process of legalizing identity, the example of Mocambo adds to the unfolding reexaminations of community and illustrates the fourth component.

AFRICA AND THE CONSTRUCTION OF THE QUILOMBO CLAUSE

Despite anthropologists' efforts to restrict the identification of quilombos to rural black communities that cultivated land communally, the mass media continued to present these communities as "authentic and archaic African tribes in the midst of contemporary Brazil" (Véran 2002:20).[1] In considering the appeal of Africa as a historical reference for Brazilians of all colors, it is instructive to consider locating Africa "within the equation of the nation" (Segato 1998:129). In that formulation, the articulation of blackness and discourse about Africa "varies according to national framework" (Segato 1998:130). Unlike the United States, "traditions" in Brazil, such as Afro-Brazilian religions, which are practiced by people of all colors and classes, "have inscribed a monumental African codex containing the accumulated ethnic experience and strategies of African descendants as part of the nation. . . . This codex operates as a stable reservoir of meaning from which flows a capillary, informal, and fragmentary impregnation of the whole of society" (Segato 1998:143). The state's role can be explained through the hegemonic perspective of Brazilian national formation (intermingling of the three "races"—European, indigenous, and African), which incorporates individuals of any origin and serves as a "re-creation of Africa in Brazil" adopted by a weak state that was not consolidated enough to impose an erasure of Africa (Segato 1998:144). This inability to erase Africa from the Brazilian imaginary must be placed in the context of "the existence of a virulent racist attitude and feeling in Brazil against people of black color" (Segato 1998:148). Because of the "peculiar processes that lie behind the Brazilian form of racism," in Segato's view, the state was forced to "share this encompassing . . . function with black enclaves that actively produce and expand African culture through the nation and beyond" (Segato 1998:148, 145).

Tied to the discourse about African survival, however, a certain element of "folklorization of blackness" (Godreau 2002; Hanchard 1994) may also be involved in the government's quilombo recognition program. The Brazilian government's embrace of a quilombo project might involve a romanticization of rural black communities as "remnants of a past era," thus feeding a Brazilian version of "discursive nostalgia" (Godreau 2002:283). Connecting quilombos to a romantic notion of agricultural practices in Africa (Geipel 1997; Pereira and White 2001:136) creates a "special distancing of blackness," relegating it to communities that are isolated and "different," often through an attempt to "document the prevalence of African cultural traits or survivals" (Godreau 2002:293). As seen in the last chapter, demands to farm collectively can affect all aspects of people's lives.

In Brazil, the primary enunciated goal of both the government and black movement activists has been to guarantee that impoverished rural black communities are inserted into the nation with full citizenship rights while their way of life and cultural practices are protected—a goal of a newly conceived multicultural, pluralistic Brazilian society (Pereira and White 2001).[2] Nevertheless, even if unintentional, an effect of these efforts has been a form of folklorization, particularly when African cultural survivals are invoked to support quilombo claims. Moreover, the desires of the members of quilombo communities may not entirely mesh with the images of them as a link to the past (Véran 2002). For them, government recognition brings the promise of modernization (electricity, running water, better roads, technical assistance for agricultural production, education, and health care), all of which are part of the implicit promise that comes with recognition and land. The implementation of those promises does not necessarily comport with the expectations associated with the folkloric aspects of the requirements for recognition and can create a gap that is often filled with feuding, disgruntlement, and the exacerbation of factional fighting within the quilombos, as was the case in Mocambo.

As discussed earlier, almost from the beginning, several families in Mocambo were opposed to pursuing recognition. When an untried law is invoked, people consider potential risks as well as rewards. In this case, both residents who were for and residents who were against the quilombo path thought their route was the better way to achieve an improved life. The problem from the point of view of the contras, and perhaps the irony, was that to get such modern improvements they were being asked to identify themselves with a premodern sensibility, a slave category, and a racial category that had been reviled since the moment their ancestors arrived in Brazil. The contras and their allies had determined, from the early days of the struggle, that it was to their benefit to remain loyal to local politicians who, for years, had been the only source of promised services. The federal unproven promise did not seem as certain as the local political configurations, which were at least predictable, if often unfair or unjust. Once the land was titled in the name of the Antônio do Alto Association, named for Sr. Antônio's great-grandfather, the contras were excluded from working on the land. As can be imagined, the atmosphere in Mocambo remained tense throughout the entire decade of quilombo mobilization.

THE STORY OF ANTÔNIO DO ALTO BECOMES THE FOUNDATIONAL
NARRATIVE OF QUILOMBO MOCAMBO

In September 1995, when Arruti, the anthropologist, arrived in Mocambo to investigate its quilombo claim, he got to know Sr. Antônio, an elderly, soft-spoken, dark-skinned man, mentioned previously as an important leader of the quilombo movement. From the beginning, members of the quilombo movement and its supporters considered Sr. Antônio to be the best person for the task of "historical recuperation." For this reason, he was elected to the coordinating committee of the new association and eventually became its president. As the leader and as a man with an acknowledged talent for recounting the past, Sr. Antônio was designated to show Arruti the markers of old houses, corrals, and boundaries and to explain how the village had become consolidated as the surrounding land was turned into cattle-raising pasture in the previous century. Sr. Antônio's reputation for having more historical knowledge than anyone else in Mocambo was founded on his un-disputed talent for storytelling. In fact, respect for Sr. Antônio's leadership was enhanced when Arruti memorialized one of Sr. Antônio's stories in his report to the Palmares Foundation justifying Mocambo's recognition.

Sr. Antônio's mother had told him the story about her grandfather's fate many years before. Arruti (1997:43) included the following story of the great-grandfather for whom Sr. Antônio had been named in his report in the broadest outline:

> Antônio do Alto fell in love with the niece of the landowner for whom he worked and having found that the girl returned his interest, they maintained a relationship until the landowner discovered them. When he learned of the affair he was so enraged that he had Antônio do Alto killed, and so that the punishment would be of the same magnitude as his fury, he had him buried alive.

A notable detail about this first recorded rendition of the story is the absence of any mention of slavery or of fleeing from slavery, even though Arruti was using the story as evidence for Mocambo's claim to quilombo status. In fact, no evidence exists that Antônio do Alto or his father were slaves or that the landowner was a slaveholder, as explained further below. Another signifi-cant omission from this first rendition was any reference to the race or color of any of the protagonists, a detail whose importance rapidly became clear to the Mocambo storytellers and in later versions was remedied. This first version, rather than being a story about slavery and race, was most likely a

Antônio Lino dos Santos (photograph by the author)

story about social status and kin relations in the sertão. As Sr. Antônio was encouraged to retell the story of his great-grandfather, and as others who also claimed descent from Antônio do Alto took up the story, these and other details changed. The naming of the new community association after this ancestor, shortly after Arruti's visit, was a crucial step toward enshrining the story as the foundational narrative of Quilombo Mocambo.

Before I analyze this first version and the subsequent versions of the Antônio do Alto story, I would like to review when and how often the story has been told and presented as a play. Village teenagers first performed a play based on Sr. Antônio's story in May 1997, when the president of the Palmares Foundation came to Mocambo from Brasília to celebrate quilombo recognition.[3] For each of the Black Consciousness Day celebrations following quilombo recognition, the play has been performed in a manner reminiscent of the kind of pageant well known in the tradition of rustic folk Catholicism.[4] The play was also featured at a number of Mocambo's annual patron saint festivals since recognition and has now become the main event at the annual celebration of the anniversary of recognition. The performance I attended on Black Consciousness Day in 2000 was mounted to celebrate the land grant earlier that year.

In addition to witnessing the play, I encountered four versions of the Antônio do Alto story during my year of fieldwork. I heard Sr. Antônio tell the story to a self-identified black Palmares Foundation lawyer in April 2000. I also collected two transcribed versions: one was taken from the videotaped workshop on black culture for Mocambo schoolteachers led by Professor Severo, and the other, Sr. Antônio's narration, was transcribed at my request by a staff member of the Centro Dom José Brandão when Sr. Antônio was visiting the state capital. Partial versions of the story were told to me by several Mocambo residents, who also claimed to be descended from Antônio do Alto. Through retellings by Sr. Antônio, the recording of the story by anthropologists and activists, and the production and performance of the play, Antônio do Alto had come to be considered the founder of the quilombo.

Despite Sr. Antônio's descent from Antônio do Alto and his storytelling abilities, his stature as a leader had diminished significantly over the years. In mid-2000, he stepped down as president of the association to run for county office, only to be disqualified because he was illiterate. Maripaulo, over twenty years his junior, took over as association president and often boasted that he was more capable than Sr. Antônio because he had traveled and knew how to relate to government officials and movement organizers in Brasília. One of the ironies of this sad situation for Sr. Antônio was that he, as the guardian of Mocambo's history, was considered less capable of leading the quilombo than the younger man, who had spent time in the city and had traveled more than the average Mocambo resident. Although quilombo supporters benefited from the younger man's literacy, they nevertheless respected Sr. Antônio's family story, which by this time had become the foundational narrative of the quilombo. However, the continuing respect for Sr. Antônio's family story was evident during my visit to the village in mid-2004, when Mocambo was on the verge of gaining the legal right to use the strip along the river and finalizing the expropriation of Fazenda Rosa Cruz, the neighboring land on which the struggle had begun. The quilombo association had turned the one-room outbuilding of the state-owned school into a museum and library named for Sr. Antônio's mother. The museum housed pictures of Sr. Antônio's ancestors and items from his parents' house. Sr. Antônio, although upset and disaffected from the governance of the quilombo, sparkled as he showed off his family as the root from which the quilombo sprouted. Speaking with great solemnity, authority, and ceremony, Sr. Antônio described each museum item and how it related to his family history. His family, because of the Antônio do Alto story, has come to represent the "history" of Mocambo.

The story of Antônio do Alto is not simply a tale with some historically accurate elements. It has entered the "mythic-historical consciousness" (Hill

1988:9) of the quilombolas and the general public in surrounding areas and the capital who have heard the story and attended performances of the play. Myth and history are not necessarily mutually exclusive categories and in some circumstances may be inseparable. In this part of Brazil, for example, stories abound about slaves being punished with death for having relations with wives and daughters of their masters. As long ago as 1903, historian Manoel José do Bomfim (1903:153), who grew up on his father's plantation on the Sergipe coast before abolition around the time of Antônio do Alto's youth, described how

> not infrequently, the young mistress, who has been brought up rubbing against the sturdy slave lads [*mulecotes*], yields herself to them when her degenerated nerves awake in irrepressible desires. Then the paternal morality intervenes; the Negro or mulatto is castrated with a dull knife, the wound is sprinkled with salt, and he is then buried alive. As for the lass, with an increased dowry, she is married off to a poor cousin.

Even today, in the backlands of the neighboring state of Bahia, guides relate such stories and show visitors the places where slaves were buried alive (Jacobina interview 2002). Another myth is belied by such stories—the assertion espoused by Gilberto Freyre (1986) in the 1930s that slavery in Brazil was more benign than in the United States because of a purported difference between English and Portuguese colonizers.[5]

Algerian historian Mohammed Arkoun has described "mytho-history" (Arkoun and Maïla 2003:93) as a process by which the transmitter of collective memory (that is, the storyteller) is an "active organizer of the memory" who sacralizes past actors and events by attributing to them exemplary behavior or supernatural powers. Future generations then transform such actors and events into a "living tradition." As a mytho-historical figure, Antônio do Alto has been sacralized because of his tortured mistreatment and martyrdom as well as for defying his master for the love of his master's niece. Antônio do Alto has become the good ancestor in opposition to the evil landowner and his henchmen, allowing the quilombolas to think of themselves as a "people" deserving of recognition and land (Malkki 1995). Simultaneously, the niece seems to be a bridge between the two, perhaps representing the ambivalent relationship between the Mocambo residents and modern landowners, such as Darcy Cardoso and Seixas Dória. If one considers the Antônio do Alto story as a merging of history and myth, it provides a rubric that allows one to examine how the story has changed and why certain elements remain unchanged. The particular "organization of clues" (Silverstein and

Urban 1996:5) I propose allows for an analysis, while retaining respect for Sr. Antônio's family story as part of the history of the area that has been preserved through oral narration for three generations and has begun to be transformed into a "living tradition."

I will analyze the elements of the versions of the story along two axes. Along one axis are those elements of the story that shifted in response to perceived legal requirements and expectations of quilombo supporters, including black movement activists. Along the other axis are the elements that remained within the structure of the story's origins as a backland tale of power, sexuality, family ties, and patronage. The play, conceived of and performed by village teenagers, although based on Sr. Antônio's renderings, contains important "facts" that have been introduced by the performers. Because the play has become the public version of the story, it has been most instrumental in consolidating the specific, locally grounded form of quilombo identity experienced in Mocambo.

AXIS OF CHANGE: CULTURAL PERSPECTIVES ON LEGISLATIVE CATEGORIES

Recall the broad outline of the Antônio do Alto story as it was told by Sr. Antônio in 1995: Antônio do Alto fell in love with the niece of the landowner. She returned his affection, and they maintained a relationship until the landowner discovered them. He became so enraged that he had Antônio do Alto buried alive. Three aspects of the story were transformed over time that signal changes traceable to perceptions of legal requirements and expectations of outside supporters. The following three components were introduced in the subsequent versions: slavery, race or color, and a trip to the Afro-Brazilian cultural center of Bahia by the child born to the niece after Antônio do Alto's death.

When Sr. Antônio told the story to the black Palmares Foundation lawyer, he began by asserting, "Antônio do Alto was a slave." This is the only explicit mention of slavery. In fact, none of the versions casts the landowner as a "master," but, instead, all refer to him by his historical name, Captain Zezé Dória (an ancestor of the landowner and former governor, Seixas Dória), or, as in the play, by the generic title denoting power and patronage in the Northeast, "coronel." The implication, however, that a form of slavery was the backdrop for the story was emphasized by Sr. Antônio in late 2001 when he added a detail that had not appeared in any of the earlier versions: Captain Zezé had seized the land on which the black people of the area had lived at least since the mid-nineteenth century, when the Brazilian emperor, Dom Pedro II, on his trip up the São Francisco River, purportedly bequeathed the neighboring land to the indigenous inhabitants.[6] After seizing the land, Captain Zezé forced the "blacks" to build a house for his son in a single day. Thus, Sr. Antônio concluded, the family of Antônio do Alto had "come to be enslaved" by the captain.

Research conducted by Padre Isaías when quilombo recognition was first considered failed to locate a listing for Captain Zezé in the baptismal books as the owner of slaves, even though, calculating back from the birth date of Sr. Antônio's mother (1907), Antônio do Alto would have been born sometime in the 1870s, when slavery was still legal.[7] If the family had been slaves, Sr. Antônio's grandfather would have heard about it and more than likely would have passed that information along to his grandson. Captain Zezé, like most of the other landowners in the area, used sharecropping labor and did not own slaves (Arruti 2002:220). In fact, Antônio do Alto's father was always referred to as a "cowhand" of Captain Zezé. In the northeastern backlands where Sr. Antônio and his ancestors lived, the primary economic activities were raising cattle, growing rice and cotton as cash crops when there was enough rainfall to sustain them, and subsistence farming. Landowners often lived in a county seat and hired local families to care for their cattle and oversee their property, as Captain Zezé had done with Antônio do Alto's family. The sensibility advanced by Sr. Antônio when he referred to his ancestors as "slaves" was a result of what he had learned about the history of "true" quilombos as fugitive slave communities. Moreover, the "slavery" being referred to, implicitly or explicitly, in each of the versions of the story could just as easily have been a form of virtual slavery that many backland peasants experienced. By calling it "slavery," Sr. Antônio fulfilled what he perceived as a requirement of black activists and the government while stating what was, for his family, a general truth of their economic circumstances.[8]

Even more explicitly than slavery, skin color became an increasingly salient aspect of each of the versions of the story. Indicating that the niece was "white" became a theme, as did the use of the word "black" not only to describe Antônio do Alto but also to refer to his fellow villagers, who were ordered to bury him alive when the captain discovered his niece's pregnancy. The teenagers added the most significant "fact" involving the color of the protagonists in their dramatized version of Sr. Antônio's family story. As noted above, I witnessed a performance of the play on November 20, 2000, at the end of the Black Consciousness Day pilgrimage across the land that Quilombo Mocambo had been awarded earlier that year. The Catholic

After the play, the teenagers posed for photos, including Ingrácia (center),
the young woman who played the niece (photograph by the author)

priests who had helped organize the event hoped that this show of unity would convince some of the quilombo opponents to change their minds. In the tradition of backland folk Catholic practices, the long walk included cross bearing and stops to dance and sing along the way; in the new quilombo "tradition," some men wore skullcaps meant to identify with Africa, made by a Mocambo resident who was the uncle of one of the black priests.

When the group of pilgrims arrived in Mocambo, the crowd went to the end of one of the two streets in the village, where the church, built in 1950, stands. Significantly, the church stands at the end of the street where many of the contras and their allies live. Quilombo supporters had constructed a stage in front of the church, and about a hundred people were in attendance for the event. It began with singing and recitations by Mocambo schoolchildren about black heritage and then proceeded with the play based on the story of how Antônio do Alto was buried alive. After the usual opening depicting the romance between the slave and his master's niece, played by a young woman who was chosen for her relatively light skin and "white" facial features, the coronel forced her to reveal the name of the baby's father. The niece replied, "I will go to the city and wait to see if the baby is born white." When that turned out to be the case, the niece returned, baby in her arms, and held the child out to her uncle. She said, "Just as you wanted." The coronel agreed to raise the baby girl in his household so long as she was never

Cast of the play portraying the life and death of Antônio do Alto
(photograph by the author)

told the identity of her biological father, Antônio do Alto. This attempt to ra-
cialize the story still carries within it the seed of ambiguity toward race and
color prevalent in the northeastern backlands and in Brazilian society, more
generally.

The effects of this discursive racial polarization were beginning to be felt
beyond stories and plays in the everyday life of Mocambo. As previously
mentioned, some families had relocated to Mocambo after they were moved
off their own land when it was converted to an indigenous reserve for the
Xocó in the early 1990s.[9] These "outsider" families (such as the extended
Egídio family) were allied with the contras. I am reluctant to endorse the
appellation of "outsider" for those families, even though quilombo supporters often referred to them that way, because substantial intermarriage occurred between them and both local Xocó Indians and Mocambo residents.
Even though none of the "outsiders" would have been, or had ever before
been, classified as "white," as the feuding intensified, quilombo supporters,
including children, began referring to them as "the whites" (os brancos), thus
ratcheting up the potential racial element of the fractured community life of
Mocambo. This is not to suggest that the quilombo movement created factionalism in the village. As discussed in chapter 4, in the shifting of emphasis
to race and color and giving it a name, lines of difference became hardened
and contributed to a reframing of the concept of "community" for all the resi-

dents of Mocambo. People previously assumed to be part of the Mocambo community were now being considered "outsiders."

The third element added to the story by Sr. Antônio, possibly to provide an allusion to African-based religious observance, involved Maria, the grown daughter of Antônio do Alto and the white niece. Significantly, this addition was emphasized in the versions told in the presence of urban-based black activists, led by Professor Severo, who had organized the workshop for Mocambo's elementary schoolteachers to give them the background in Afro-Brazilian heritage they needed to teach the quilombo's children. In these versions, after Captain Zezé died, Maria learned that Antônio do Alto had been her father. She traveled to Salvador, Bahia, the center of Afro-Brazilian religion and culture, and went to a candomblé temple (*terreiro*) to participate in that African-based religion's practice of speaking to the dead. Maria saw her father, who revealed himself by possessing the body of the "father of saints" (*pai de santo*), the religious leader of the terreiro. Speaking through the pai de santo, Antônio do Alto confirmed that Maria truly was his daughter, lending an alternative reading to the notion of being "buried alive"—according to this version, Antônio may have been buried alive, but he remained alive for his daughter to meet him as a candomblé spirit. This added element further mythologized Antônio do Alto by making him powerful enough to return to this world. When the black lawyer from the Palmares Foundation asked, "What did Antônio do Alto say to his daughter?" Sr. Antônio responded, "He said he had suffered for her by being buried alive." By adding this element, Sr. Antônio was also adding a hint of subversion to the story. Maria's trip to Salvador to see her father undermined her uncle's plan to erase Antônio do Alto completely. As the revised tale goes, he may have been buried, but he remains alive, as do his black identity and legacy.

These additions to Sr. Antônio's family story are part of a process of incorporation of reified images of slavery, previously unexpressed antagonism between black and white, and the place of Afro-Brazilian religion in the politics of quilombo recognition. As such, through the revised narrative, they are defining black identity for others (Oakdale 2004:61)—for the contras and their "white" allies within the village and for people who live in the area but were not aware of the new ways of being "black" and "quilombola" in the northeastern backlands. In Mocambo, where the "traditional" and the "modern" are intertwined, embodiments of folk Catholicism (pilgrimages and pageants) serve as vessels through which quilombo identity is transmitted and they reshape the social space through which these cultural practices move (Urban 2001:24, 55).

Mocambo quilombolas have self-consciously formulated their stance vis-à-vis rights, activists, and the transnational world (Abercrombie 1998:156) through the retelling of the story and regular productions of the play. These additions have been self-consciously appropriated to improve Mocambo's standing on a national scene that has come to value descent from runaway slaves and rural black identity. Even with the land grant, much is still at stake in the field of quilombo recognition, including assistance from President Lula's government under the basic food program, agricultural technical assistance, irrigation, health care, education, and credits for cooperative farming, all of which began to arrive in 2007. In fact, the village of Mocambo is substantially better off in 2008 than it was when I first visited in 1998, with a new school, government aid, additional housing, and the right to work its own soil, even though many problems remain, as do many of the contra families and their allies.

AXIS OF REPRESENTATIONAL DURABILITY:
ANCHORING MYTHO-HISTORY IN NARRATIVES OF SLAVERY

Each of the three story elements that were changed or added could be viewed as a potential simplification of "ideas about blackness and whiteness into Manichean binaries that are easily readable to a wider audience and can move in global circuits of commoditized images" (Wade 2002:18). Peter Wade and others (for example, Agier 2002; Hoffmann 2002), however, discussing parallel instances of rural black community recognition on the Pacific coast of Colombia, point out the crucial need to consider the deep-seated complexities of race and color in the region before jumping to the conclusion that people vying for recognition as "black" are engaged in the reification of categories historically viewed with suspicion by rural backlanders. Here, I examine elements of the Antônio do Alto story that are anchored in the specificities of the region. The alterations in self-identification wrought through an engagement with legislative categories (such as "quilombo") and activists' expectations could only have been possible against the backdrop of, and in dialogue with, existing perceptions and customary modes of thinking. The story's twists and turns reveal some of the particular ways race, color, sexuality, family, and power are conceptualized in Brazil, specifically in the northeastern sertão.

Four key elements of the story remain within the structure of its local and national origins. The first element, fundamental to the foundational aspect of the narrative, is a surprising twist at the end of the play and in all versions of the story. After the protagonist has been buried alive and his daughter has been accepted by the white landowner's family, it is revealed to the audience that Antônio do Alto had a wife in Mocambo with whom he had two sons before his affair with the master's niece. One of those sons was Sr. Antônio's grandfather, hence the historical and genetic tie of Antônio do Alto to the residents of Mocambo who would, 100 years later, celebrate Antônio do Alto as the community's founder. Reflecting the sexual politics of the backlands, Antônio do Alto's stature as the founder of Mocambo is not sullied by his unfaithfulness to his black wife. Significantly, her name is not recalled, just as the name of the master's niece and Antônio do Alto's mother's name have been forgotten, even by Sr. Antônio. The story reflects the gendered nature of life in the rural interior of Brazil, where men are powerful and women nameless.

The second element, added by the teenagers in the production of the play, reflects the youths' grounding in a place where racial categories remain mutable and malleable. In a performance that has elements of racial polarization tied to a new black identity, as discussed above, a moment occurs when the narrator of the play describes Antônio do Alto's two sons by his Mocambo wife. They are referred to as "caboclos." This is a revealing choice of nomenclature because "caboclo," in the northeastern backlands, as indicated earlier, and even more clearly in the Mocambo area, most often means a person with indigenous ancestry. Therefore, at the point in the play at which the biological link is made between Antônio do Alto and Mocambo as a site of black identity, the direct ancestors of the man most identified as black among village residents, Sr. Antônio, are referred to by a term that denotes racial mixture.

The third element of the story, added by the teenagers and discussed in the previous section, involves the niece's plea to her uncle that she be permitted to see if the child is born "white," in which case it can be raised in the landowning family. In this case, an element that represents change — a new polarization based on racial identity — contains a twist that also makes it a durable element, grounded in local assumptions and cultural understandings. The upshot of the story is unquestioned: that a black slave man and a white woman could have a child born white and free under the law. The niece's gamble, added by the teenagers, albeit with added emphasis on race, remains within their life experience, because they live in a society in which black parents can have white children and vice versa and in which white children can have black siblings from the same parents. This is in direct contradiction to U.S. racial ideology, which "considers a white woman capable of giving birth to a black child but denies that a black woman can give birth to a white child" (Fields 1982:149). Moreover, the teenagers and the audience in Mocambo did not find it problematic that the "white" daughter of Antônio do Alto could lead a privileged life, whereas her dark-skinned half-brothers would live as "slaves" in Mocambo.[10] Once the child, Maria, learned of her parentage, she was incorporated into Antônio do Alto's Mocambo family, and, according to Sr. Antônio, she married a state police commander and moved to the state capital to be near her half-brother, Sr. Antônio's grandfather, one of the black children of Antônio do Alto.

This theme of racially inclusive families resonates in the lives of other Mocambo residents and even in Sr. Antônio's immediate family. His daughter-in-law, one of the most militant quilombo activists in the village, has light-skinned relatives who live across the river and who had been the employers of her parents. She was proud that these relatives did not call her parents "employees" and that they invited them to parties, unlike other people with black relatives who do not even acknowledge them, introducing them as belonging to the darker side of the family, euphemistically calling them *moreno* (a term used for physical types ranging from olive to dark-brown complexions). In fact, this important leader of the quilombo struggle referred to herself as *morena* (and not *negra*) and said of her own grandparents, "Each side had a light-skinned one with straight hair marrying a black one with bad hair." This example of the not-uncommon coexistence of a new black identity alongside the acceptance of negative assessments of darker-skinned relatives and compatriots allowed a militant black quilombola to speak unselfconsciously in terms that contradicted her militancy.

In another example, Sr. Antônio has proudly explained that he had white relatives in the city who were policemen and who protected him in his youth when there was trouble at parties. He could even carry a gun without it being confiscated (Arruti 2002:315). Adding a certain symmetry to the relationship between the landowner's niece and Antônio do Alto, in that same generation, Sr. Antônio's great-grandmother on the other side of his mother's family had a relationship with the landowner's son, with whom she had two "white" sons who went to live with their father in the city. These were the grandfathers of the white side of Sr. Antônio's family to which he was referring. This information, in conjunction with the Antônio do Alto family story (before it became a foundational narrative), reveals the matter-of-fact attitude of sertanejos toward such relationships. These anecdotes are only a few examples of the innumerable situations in which family trumps race, color, and class in the backlands.

Even though the ideology of "racial democracy" has been dealt serious blows in the last few decades, with official and public recognition of racial discrimination (including measures outlawing it) and a new racial quota system in higher public education in many states, the federal district, and other regional federal universities, the hegemonic worldview that underpins race and color consciousness in Brazil continues to inform peoples' everyday lives (Sheriff 2001; Racusen 2009 forthcoming). Unlike the United States, with its "common, colorblind myth of shared effort and meritocratic reward," Brazil's racial paradigm "is based on encompassing the other, inclusion is its strong motif, and the myth [in Brazil] is the colorblind myth of an inter-relating people" (Segato 1998:137). "'The blood is the same.' . . . Racism is repugnant [and] un-Brazilian. It poisons what is closest to the shared heart, the common spirit of Brazil. . . . To call [racial democracy] a mere myth-as-smokescreen is to miss the extent to which it is also a series of heteroglot narratives that . . . implicitly direct themselves to the future as well as to the past" (Sheriff 2001:220).

Consequently, through this analysis of the nodal points at which the Antônio do Alto play retains the structure of the continuing racial politics of Brazil, one can see that certain conceptualizations of race and color remain intact, even with the assumption of a new black identity. This transformation of identity within existing structures has been termed "constrained re-fashioning" (R. Wilson 1995:13), in which an underlying set of assumptions permits the group to be anchored while it initiates and experiences change (R. Wilson 1993). New elements are forged "in the shadow of the past. [The 'something new'] is a palimpsest on which the past is written over but not entirely erased . . . simultaneously present and absent, ineffable yet palpable" (Fuoss and Hill 2001:113n4). In Mocambo, assuming a black identity does not necessarily preclude simultaneous racial logics.

The fourth element of the story, again an aspect of the tale that has dual meanings in the context that encompasses both change and structural durability, is the reported journey of Maria to "talk to her father" in an Afro-Brazilian religious ceremony. This was most likely added under the influence of Professor Severo, a longtime follower of candomblé (D'Acelino 1999), when he came to raise black consciousness in Mocambo. In another cultural innovation in Mocambo, also in connection with Professor Severo's workshop, as described earlier, the quilombolas began performing their signature dance dressed in the white clothes and turbans worn by elderly black female adherents of candomblé, even though neither the quilombolas nor anyone else in the area practices the Afro-Brazilian religion. At the same time, no one was surprised that Antônio do Alto's daughter, Maria, a white woman, would go to a ceremony associated with Afro-Brazilian cultural practices. Adherents represent every class and racial self-identification—from senators and authors to maids and metalworkers (E. P. Johnson 2002:100).

At the intersection of these two axes of analysis—one of change, the other of durability in representation—the nature of identity transformation is clarified through the play's development from a family story and its performance to reinforce celebration of quilombo recognition and Black Consciousness Day. Observations made with respect to other rural black communities in Brazil shed light on the importance of the play in the process of quilombo identity formation. As part of a recent oral history project, Karina Cunha Baptista (2003:13) has produced a sensitive analysis of interviews with known descendants of slaves in a variety of locations in Brazil. Like the Mocambo residents before quilombo recognition, interviewees were silent with respect to any kind of racial identity, insisting only that they were peasants. Baptista concluded that, particularly when there was no memory of slave ancestry or contact with "African cultural practices," racial identity was diluted, allowing peasant identity to predominate. Moreover, she found that when the matter of racism was raised by interviewers, the "assimilationist" ethos of Brazilian national identity ("we are all one people") emerged as the primary social identity among rural Afro-Brazilians. Acting out the foundational narrative of what has become Quilombo Mocambo, although reminiscent of religious pageants and pilgrimages, is not about holy intervention. Metaphors notwithstanding, the act of struggle to achieve some degree of autonomy as it combined with an opportunity provided by the state has drawn on local understandings and worldviews to create a racial self-identification tied to a history previously untold.

CULTURAL PERFORMANCE AND LAND

Brazilian anthropologist Neusa Maria Mendes de Gusmão (1996:9) has observed that land defines who quilombolas are. The struggle for land in the context of the quilombo clause is not just a confrontation between legal ownership of land and other forms of possession but is also a matter of "individual and group definition as subjects—blacks of this or that place" (Gusmão 1996:10–11). "Land as territory is the fruit of social narrative in the context of tension in which diverse groups confront each other" (Gusmão

1996:10). In Mocambo, Sr. Antônio's family story, reconstructed as a play, is an integral component of the social narrative associated with the transformation of newly acquired land into the territory of a quilombo.

Although one is tempted to place the greatest emphasis on the land grant as instrumental in identity formation, I have tried to show here that land should not overshadow the role of cultural forms and practices in the formation of new ethnoracial identities and self-identifications made possible by legal provisions. Most significant is the crucial role that "Africa" and assuming a black identity (and how those two phenomena are linked) have come to play in the transformation of social relations in rural communities in the Brazilian backlands, historically considered to be neither white nor black in racial terms. Drawing on literature that posits the concept of "Africa" as key to Brazilian national identity (Segato 1998) as well as anthropological work in other parts of Latin America that analyzes the possible "folklorization of blackness" (Godreau 2002), in this chapter I have critiqued the general view and public face of quilombos as remnants or survivals of the past (Linhares 2004). I have also striven to make the indispensable connection between the reworking of self-identification and public self-representation by the people doing the work. In the case of Mocambo, that self-representation was conceived and performed by members of a community in the process, and under the stress, of exploring the intersection of multiple, and contradictory, discourses meant to improve their lives.

The play about Mocambo's most renowned ancestor, performed annually in commemoration of quilombo recognition, is a key "cultural performance" (Bauman 1992; Fuoss and Hill 2001; Schechner 1988; V. W. Turner 1986), a "site of social action where identities and relations" were being reconfigured and where spectators were likely "to rethink the boundaries of a community, or to reconsider issues of race and ethnicity" (Guss 2000:12).[11] As Sr. Antônio reframed his great-grandfather's story in connection with perceived legal requirements for quilombo recognition, his discourse was "fashioned for ease of detachment from a situational context" (Bauman and Briggs 1990:74), thereby creating the possibility, picked up by the teenagers, for the story to be performed in other places and times and by other people.

As a "situated performance of identity" (Agier 2002), the Antônio do Alto play itself has been deployed as a "spectacle" (Rockefeller 1998) intended to instruct the audience that gathers in the street dominated by the contras.[12] The performance in that context "simultaneously instantiate[s] contestation among competing interests and, in so doing, negotiate[s] community," reconceptualizing it "as the stakes being vied for in cultural performances rather than merely the context in which the contestation occurs" (Fuoss and Hill 2001:93, 99). In doing so, the performance of the Antônio do Alto story provides the framework for a history taught by the teenagers—a new generation committed to staying in their rural home, as black quilombolas, and exercising their newfound control over their political lives and their cultural environment.

CONCLUSION

In this book, I have highlighted a series of productive contradictions that inform the personal and political changes integral to ethnoracial identity transformation in the context of new legal rights. Choosing to self-identify in a new way, to place oneself in a category with historically negative connotations or that represents a loss of some rights in exchange for others, is a gamble that requires courage and perhaps desperation. Decisions taken and acted upon with the belief that an improved life would be the outcome may also lead to unanticipated difficulties and sorrows. A series of contradictions were brought to light in this book that preexisted, and were called into being by, the opportunities that arose as a result of the law but were contingent upon the revision of worldviews and self-conceptions. My point here is that contradictions, in this case built into the history, geography, and human relations of the northeastern sertão, provided openings for change. Such openings were also the fissures and instabilities that made possible peoples' willingness to take chances and settle for trade-offs.

The theoretical model I have proposed in this book for analyzing and evaluating ethnoracial identity transformation, legalizing identity, reveals, and takes into account, the crucial role of a variety of productive contradictions. Starting with my explanation of postlegislative negotiation, we see that law can both exist and not truly exist until it is molded and used, often by those for whom it was not intended. Identity, itself a slippery concept that has the illusion of being rock solid, is in fact a series of experiences, including that of struggle, and is mutable, allowing for counterintuitive revisions of what we often assume is immutable. Community, the word itself calling forth visions of cohesive, coequal groups of people whose common interests supersede their differences, is called into question. Cultural practices that are usually considered timeless and unchanging as evidence of heritage are shown here to be inventive refashioning of sertanejo folkways that are crucial to identity transformation. And perhaps the most difficult to comprehend for those of us who live in the United States, the stories in this book reveal that race and color may not matter, yet may still remain intertwined with experiences of poverty and discrimination, as well as the measures taken to combat those ills.

Another contradiction brought to light in this book has to do with how the Xocó and Mocambo communities have become different from one other, but at the same time have remained similar. The Xocó are different because becoming Indian places the group under a particular governmental umbrella with rights and protections unique to indigenous people. The struggle waged by the people who became Xocó Indians entailed many more confrontations with landowners and their private gunmen than did the quilombo movement. This gave the Indians "bragging rights" in relation to what they considered to be their then-complacent neighbors. There were criticisms on both sides—the Indians thought their relatives in Mocambo were not politically engaged, and, when their time came, the quilombolas saw the Indians as wasting their land by not using it and holding on to the old paternalistic political machine. The two communities now report to, and make demands of, different federal agencies, the legal status of their land is different (Indians have possession, while quilombos have collective title), and they perform different dances when they assert their respective identities in public.

However, the two groups are also similar to each other and to the surrounding sertanejo population. While the members of each group generally self-identify as either Indian or black, they all still retain the understanding that their identities are multiple. Each person, whether Xocó or quilombola, also self-identifies as simultaneously being Indian, African, Dutch, Portuguese, Sergipano, and sertanejo. In fact, it is this very perspective on heritage that permits them to be different and separate, yet similar and related. This sliding form of identification is not held against them. If we were to compare this approach to the history of mixed-race people in the United States who claim to be Indians, we can see just how different the effect of multiple identities operates in the two countries, Brazil and the United States, although both countries were built on African slavery and the decimation of indigenous people.

COMPARING XOCÓ RECOGNITION TO AMERICAN INDIANS: BLOOD AND LAW

There are at least two well-known cases of Indian tribes in the United States who have been trying for many years to be recognized by the federal government: the Lumbee of North Carolina, who remain unacknowledged by the Bureau of Indian Affairs, and the Mashpee of Massachusetts, who were finally recognized in 2007, thirty years after the trial memorialized by James Clifford (1988). In both cases, as with the Xocó, the people who constitute these groups have ancestors of a variety of ethnoracial backgrounds and have had to piece together histories based on scant documentation. Like the Lumbee and the Mashpee, the Xocó lack an ancestral language, typically Indian phenotypical features,[1] material cultural manifestations, and genetic continuity. Yet the Xocó have been recognized by the Brazilian government, while federal Indian status continues to be refused the Lumbee and, until 2007, the Mashpee were also denied recognition. Although these two North American groups are analogous in many ways to the Xocó, their trajectories differ, largely because of legal and cultural differences in the ways "Indian" has been defined and perceived in the two societies.[2]

In the United States, as in Brazil, black, white, and indigenous miscegenation has occurred for hundreds of years (Jolivétte 2007). However, in the United States, the dominant discourse on Indian identity is characterized by such expressions as "mixed-blood," "blood quantum," "only one-eighth Cherokee by blood," and "full-blood for the purpose of enrollment" (Bordewich 1996; T. P. Wilson 1992). Although not without its critics, the standard of blood quantum remains a major consideration in determining tribal status and is a source of dispute and discussion among members of indigenous communities throughout North America (Garroutte 2003; Field 2002; Strong and Van Winkle 1996).[3] Even where blood quantum is not the primary determining factor, racial ideology in the United States provides a framework for discourse about Indianness that encourages a racial standard. The focus on blood quantum is particularly noteworthy and emphasizes the salience of "blood" as a metaphor for belonging in the United States, where, paradoxically, a vast majority of those who self-identify as Indians are mixed race (84 percent of the 7.4 million people who called themselves Indian in the 1980 census, when the Xocó were being recognized in Brazil, reported that they were "Americans of Indian descent") (T. P. Wilson 1992:124). Fears that diluted blood quantum will jeopardize legal status are quite pronounced among American Indian tribes with a long history of intermarriage.

The Lumbee petition for full federal recognition asserts that their native ancestors were descendants of the Cheraw tribe, a hazy grouping that may have been the "Xuala," encountered by De Soto in 1540 (Bordewich 1996). Around 1730 the Cheraws disappeared from history, not unlike the Indians in Sergipe. The remnants of decimated Indian groups from around the area escaped into the swampy southeastern part of North Carolina, adopted English as their lingua franca and Christianity as their religion, and mingled with frontiersman, surveyors, and outlaws of all colors (Bordewich 1996:74). Legal scholar Ariela Gross (2007) points out that it is now generally accepted that current-day Lumbees "grew out of an amalgam of different native peoples . . . who mixed with ex-slaves, free people of color, and whites" (2007:480). After the Civil War, they began to self-identify as Indians rather than mulattos (2007:481) in order to avoid the inevitable categorization as nonwhite and therefore black.

Apolônio, the first chief of the Xocó, explained to me twenty years after his tribe's recognition that the mixture of black, white, and Indian that he and the others represent may have cost them recognizable indigenous features, but he insisted they "will never stop being Indian just because [they] do not have those characteristics." In Apolônio's narrative, the Catholic Church is to blame for the theft of indigenous language, belief, and physical appearance (a crime which the Church still repents). Claude Lowry, a leader of the Lumbee Indians, also remembers history as a story of white predation leading to Indians who look like whites or blacks. By the time the question of Indians in North Carolina emerged in the nineteenth century, the people who later came to call themselves Lumbees were a "demographic anomaly, dark-skinned but free, clearly not colonists yet farming, dressing, and praying like Europeans. Seeing no feathers or beads, the white authorities saw no Indians at all" (Bordewich 1996:75), a statement not dissimilar from that of the king of Brazil on his trip up the São Francisco River when he spotted the people on São Pedro Island with their jackets.

However, what is different is that in 1836 North Carolina's new constitution denied every "free negro, free mulatto, or free person of mixed blood" the right to vote, to serve on juries, to bear arms, and to attend "white schools." During the Civil War, a detachment of the Confederate army captured three Lowry brothers from southeastern North Carolina, charged them with desertion, made them dig their own graves, and shot them. Henry Berry Lowry, the youngest member of the family, witnessed it, vowed revenge, and organized a band of men, including Indians, deserters from the Union forces, a white man, and several blacks, all of whom became wanted criminals. To the Lumbees, Lowry is a martyr and a hero: "He let the white man know that they would never accept classification as Negroes" (Berry 1963:154–55).

After Reconstruction, with the enforcement of legal segregation, people who considered themselves Indians were required to identify themselves as "colored." A white friend of the group took their cause to the state legislature, which in 1885 designated the self-proclaimed Indians "Croatans" and declared that they were to have separate schools with the right to select their own teachers. Over the years, because the name "Croatan" became associated with "colored," the name was changed first to "Cherokee," then to "Siouan," and eventually to "Lumbee" after a local river.[4] Within Claude Lowry's memory, even light-skinned Lumbees were barred from shopping in "whites only" drugstores and were required to sit with blacks in the movie theaters, and newborns were barred from hospital nurseries, having to sleep in the bottom drawer of their mother's dresser. At the same time, Lumbees who married blacks were said to have "crossed the border." Lumbee "blood committees" investigated to the fourth generation the race of every child and teacher who applied to the Indian schools (Sider 1993:72). In fact, notions of blood taint remained prominent among Lumbees well into the late 1990s (Bordewich 1996:77). For example, a young paralegal with the Lumbee River Legal Services said at that time,

> People get scared when you mention the word "black." I have this thing with blood quantum. I went a long time, I wouldn't enroll. You hear all your life you're not all Indian, that you're mixed with black. You keep thinking, reckoning, if I've got any black blood there, I think I don't want to know about it. Finally, it became real important to me to know whether I really am an Indian. When I enrolled, I was really surprised to see that I had a good blood quantum—it was quite high—I was so relieved!

Established Indian tribes have refused to support the Lumbees' claim, with the most vigorous opposition coming from the only federally recognized tribe in North Carolina, the Eastern Band of Cherokees. Citing "extensive intermarriage with various races," their chief told Congress, "How then can the Indian people of this country (or the non-Indian community for that matter) seriously be expected to accept these people as full-blooded Lumbees" (Bordewich 1996:82).

Although their neighbors have accepted the Lumbees, who have received state, but not federal, recognition, as Indians, the tribe has never had a central government of any kind, unlike the Mashpee in Massachusetts. The Mashpee goal of federal recognition proved elusive for over thirty years, even though a majority of the people living in their town had been known for generations as Indians (Clifford 1988). Like the Lumbee, the image of the Mashpee Indians was complicated by issues of race, and like the Lumbee, the Mashpee had been referred to, including by the government during the case, as "really blacks rather than Native Americans" (Clifford 1988:285).

Also, like the Xocó, the Mashpee owned no tribal lands and had no surviving language or clearly distinct religion, and their kinship was much "diluted." Unlike the Xocó, however, the Mashpee did have a place recognized by its neighbors as an Indian town, whose boundaries had not changed since 1665 (Clifford 1988:289). Moreover, unlike the Xocó, who did not know they were Indians until Frei Enoque appeared in the 1970s, the Mashpee Indians had identified themselves as such for generations. Still, they were refused recognition for over thirty years, while the Xocó have had those thirty years to consolidate their indigenous identity.

The cases that were, and continue to be, made against the Mashpee and Lumbee tribes could have been made against the Xocó but were not: the Xocó community was a creation of the colonial encounter, a collection of disparate Indians and other minorities, decimated by disease and converted to Christianity, a people of mixed descent who had been assimilated into American (Brazilian) society. As with the Xocó, the category "Indian" disappeared from the Mashpee federal census records for most of the twentieth century. The people who had been classified as Indians before were now listed as "colored" or "other" (Clifford 1988:300). Similar census changes existed for the Lumbee and the Xocó. However, when the issue came before the law, the Xocó were immediately recognized and the Lumbee and Mashpee were not. Unlike the Xocó and Mocambo, where racial purity is not a consideration, in the United States even personal acknowledgment of mixture is avoided where the law is responsible for naming one's identity.

RIGHTS FOR AFRO-BRAZILIANS AND INDIANS DURING THE FIRST DECADE OF THE TWENTY-FIRST CENTURY

As I explained in this book, recognition standards for quilombos are constantly being revised. Since the 2003 presidential decree that changed the process and assigned the task of resolving quilombo land issues to the land reform agency, fourteen rural black communities in Sergipe have been recognized, although titling itself is moving slowly, especially for those quilombos that are claiming land of private landowners. For these new quilombolas, Mocambo has become the lodestar, the historical exemplar, in the decade since it was recognized. Moreover, Mocambo itself has received substantial assistance from the government and continues to host visitors from around the country and the world. However, it may be too soon to celebrate. National opposition to quilombos by landowners can be seen in rancorous editorials in major magazines, newspapers, and on the web, attacking both rural black communities being given land and the quota system for Afro-Brazilians in government employment and public universities. A bill has been introduced in Congress that would suspend operation of the 2003 decree and nullify all land grants. A major administrative rule was revised in 2008 as a result of the opposition, which would reduce the number of quilombos, as well as the size of land grants.

At the same time, and while the Brazilian Supreme Court is considering the constitutionality of both the 2003 presidential quilombo decree and the system of quotas, an important bill is said to be on the verge of becoming law. The Statute of Racial Equality would protect Afro-Brazilian religious practices; enforce quotas; provide legislative regulation of the quilombo clause; mandate the teaching of Afro-Brazilian history in public and private elementary and middle schools; and encourage the inclusion of Afro-Brazilians in the workforce. Considering that a similar proposal has been debated by Congress for the past ten years, it is difficult to say whether the optimism of its supporters is well founded. Undaunted, President Lula issued another decree a year ago that "institutes a national policy on sustainable development for traditional peoples and communities" (Decree 6040 of February 7, 2007).

Responding to an initial meeting with 350 representatives in 2006, the decree defines "traditional peoples and communities" as "culturally differentiated groups that possess their own forms of social organization and that occupy and use territories and natural resources as a condition of their cultural, social, religious, ancestral and economic reproduction, utilizing knowledge, innovations, and practices developed and transmitted by tradition" (article 3, section 1). This encompasses both quilombos and Indian tribes but expands protection, resources, and the benefits of citizenship in the broadest sense of the word to people who make their living from the land, such as communities of hunters, fishingpeople, rubber workers, and those who live a nomadic life, such as gypsies.[5] The goal is to coordinate all the government agencies that address concerns of these communities and define a coherent national policy.

Another initiative of the current executive is a program to put enough money in the hands of poor families to subsist (Programa Bolsa Família). This program includes special provisions for Indians and quilombolas, with positive results apparent in Mocambo and on São Pedro Island. In addition, the president launched a program called Territories of Citizenship early in 2008 dedicated to helping the regions with the lowest Human Development Index rating in Brazil, including 2 million family farmers, people living in

land reform communities, quilombolas, Indians, people who survive on fishing, and "traditional communities" in 958 counties, with a total investment
in 2008 of about $7 billion. The sertão of Sergipe will receive about $145 million for improvements such as electricity, clean water, and schools.[6] People
in the poorest parts of Brazil are holding their breath and hoping that their
improved livelihoods and rights will continue into the second decade of the
twenty-first century.

The passage of time and what it will tell is key to the stories told here. This
book begins and ends with generational shifts. The first shift involved the
passing of large ranches to a new generation of owners. For both the Xocó
and Mocambo, the land struggles that began their identity transformations
were tied to a transfer of responsibility to a new generation that had a very
different relationship with the land and the workers who lived on it than
had their parents. The book ends with teenagers of Mocambo retelling the
Antônio do Alto story. The effect that the legalization of new ethnoracial
identities has on the children and grandchildren of the first generation of
struggle cannot be overstated. Eight years after Mocambo received land title
as a quilombo, adolescents, most of whom were children at the recognition
ceremony in 1997, are identifying with an ancestor who is now regarded as
a slave. Perhaps even more important, the newest generation, born since
recognition, have only known a quilombola identity. I suggest that when we
apply the concept of legalizing identity, we take care to examine the generations following the shift of self-identification to obtain a full picture of how
notions of citizenship and empowerment, as well as negative implications of
resentments and racialized attitudes, are being carried on through time.

In Mocambo, the educational focus on quilombo history and culture, as
well as the proven support of the federal government, has accelerated the
movement of some contra families into the quilombo camp. Certainly, the
poisonous atmosphere of 2000 has subsided considerably as federal funds
and Church assistance have found their way to Mocambo, although the Egídio family remains in the village, perpetuating resentments.[7] On São Pedro
Island, the process is much further along, since Xocó recognition dates back
twenty years. Beginning with my first visit to the island in 1998, and with all
those thereafter, the assumption of indigenous identity by the young people
was apparent in their discourse and practices. Even though there are clear
differences between being an Indian and being a quilombola, the process of
legalizing identity is dependent upon new generations over time experiencing a new way of being in the world, which to them feels quite natural. As
these children begin to consider higher educational possibilities, the new

system of quotas (for both blacks and Indians) in many public universities in Brazil has the potential of consolidating their quilombo and indigenous identities.[8]

SOCIAL JUSTICE AND STATE RECOGNITION
OF NEW ETHNORACIAL IDENTITIES

In my view, there is no social justice without redistributive justice. Meeting the material needs of all people is required for a society to exist in which everyone can participate fully in the democratic life of the nation. To that end, "justice require[s] social arrangements that permit all (adult) members of society to interact with one another as peers" (Fraser 1998:30) to achieve "participatory parity" (Fraser 2000). As Nancy Fraser (1998:48) has explained with respect to every claim for either recognition or economic equity, it is necessary to "trace the interpenetration of the two logics"—cultural and economic. "Properly conceived, struggles for recognition can aid the redistribution of power and wealth and can promote interaction and co-operation across gulfs of difference" (Fraser 2000:109), even when ethnic differences are partly brought into existence by political maneuvering and alliance formation to take advantage of multicultural laws (see also Speed 2008; Pallares 2002:226; Postero and Zamosc 2002:14, 26; Kay 2002:46).

In the Brazilian Northeast, newly recognized quilombos and Indian tribes suggest the possibility that ethnoracial claims and class-based claims to redistributive justice can converge. The Xocó struggle, for example, united identity and material claims: indeed, it is widely viewed not just as the first successful *identity claim*, but as the first successful *land struggle* in Sergipe. This perspective is advanced and reinforced by liberationist Catholicism, which offers a powerful master frame synthesizing struggles for material resources and recognition of identity. The Church has lent continuity to struggles that were initially for land but have become successful bids for ethnoracial recognition. The liberationist language of "marginalization" identifies particular excluded identities, such as blacks and Indians, while its key teaching of a "preferential option for the poor" identifies both a specific class oppression and its material remedy.

The politics of Mocambo is a concrete example of this unification of cultural and material meanings and struggles. In practice, however, such unifications are not without complications, because groups are never homogeneous. The government recognized Mocambo as a quilombo and delivered title in the name of the community association created for that purpose.

Without a closer look, it appears that the government fulfilled its obligation and all should be well. As shown in this book, the contras (about a third of Mocambo), although considered quilombolas by the government, did not think of themselves that way, nor did the majority of the community that self-identified as descended from fugitive slaves, from the beginning. The tension was between those, on the one hand, who believed recognition must lead to some form of redistribution, and if it did not was not worth supporting, and those who considered the act of recognition a value in and of itself, a kind of "existential recognition" (Graham 2005).

Three years after Mocambo was recognized as a quilombo, the association was given title to land, and with it came local government support (which had been denied from the beginning of the struggle)—a further redistributive effect of recognition. Although celebrated by the quilombolas and their supporters, the land grant was somewhat insufficient from a redistributive perspective because the land was not arable and the people had neither resources to transform it (through irrigation, seeds, and fertilizer), nor tools (animals with plows or tractors) to work it, all of which continued to be Mocambo's demands on the federal government. Since the election of the Workers' Party (PT) at the state and national levels in 2002, however, there have been improvements in the quality of material resources allocated to quilombos and Indian tribes, as described in the previous section.

Legal sensibilities in the rural communities examined in this book are highly developed, the result of experience with law and the state, and reflect changing forms of legitimate and illegitimate authority in the region and the nation. The use of, and relationship with, law in a place where self-ascription is multiple and simultaneous reveals the mutability and multiple nature of identity and the limits of that mutability. Legal recognition can operate as an exercise of power, but its effects are far more complex. Everyday forms of domination through legal procedural precepts find their way into people's planning for survival and improvement of life situations, as well as their self-conceptions and ethnoracial identifications. The periodic successes connected with law, accompanied by the complications and defeats, have reinforced a certain hopeful skepticism. They have produced a worldview that both perpetuates the knowledge and discourse about the failure of the legal system to protect the poor and encourages hope that the law will be just and that justice will intervene.

As the politics of recognition play a greater role on the world scene through the discourse of human rights, the issues confronted in this book should not be confined to national policies tied to multiculturalism. Just as the positioning of each of these two communities has taken place within "complex, potent, shifting fields of power, including not only the nation-state, but [national and] international NGOs . . . and transnational advocacy networks" (Hodgson 2002:1040), so too might the theory of legalizing identity be used to analyze networks at those other levels. International indigenous rights movements that have developed in conjunction with United Nations declarations, Fourth World conferences, and worldwide indigenous survival networks may be analyzed through a *global* framework of legalizing identity.

In the United States, where equality before the law is both a dream and an assumption, law is believed to act upon ethnic and racial identity, which is seen as preexisting government intervention. I suggest that considering how identities are legalized in the United States would open up possibilities for reconsidering the ways in which we presume to know "what" someone "is" in this country. An example of this might be the use of the categories "Latino" and "Asian." In both cases, these labels are applied to people who in previous generations when living in their countries of origin identified themselves by reference to a particular nationality. The invocation of these new categories, Latino and Asian, calls into being identities that exist nowhere in Latin America or Asia but are key to a variety of rights in the United States. People who are now considered and consider themselves to be Latinos and Asians through a process of governmental recognition (immigration, census, affirmative action) have not replaced their national identities but instead have added or incorporated these new adopted (and imposed) identities.

Native American identity formation is another arena in which an analysis based on the legalizing identity framework might prove valuable. Rather than disqualifying peoples who are struggling for tribal recognition because they cannot prove direct descent, because they are African-descended and so do not meet the expectations of what an Indian should be, or because their cultural practices have been revised or recently adopted, thinking of their claims using the elements of the legalizing identity model could help us see recognition and identity formation as simultaneous processes. Whether identity experienced and represented as a product of struggle will be respected and validated by a governmental recognition process remains the unanswered question in each situation.

Finally, we might apply the concept of legalizing identity to the most durable category—race in the United States as it applies to African Americans. As laws were enacted governing the status of slaves from Africa and then their descendants, previous ethnic identities were replaced with racial ones. Since emancipation, racial categories have changed and continue to change, with effects that range historically from the deepening oppression of Jim Crow to the drawing of electoral boundaries, from opportunities provided by affirmative action to a growing black middle class whose children attend the best universities. Although race in the United States is the most essentialized identity, with raging debates as to its character and even as to its existence, a concept such as legalizing identity could expand the discussion to include the mutable nature of even the most entrenched identity.

In Brazil, new legal identities are combining with the lived experience of ethnoracial identification and contemporary discourses of black and indigenous consciousness to change the concepts of race, ethnicity, culture, and law. An analysis based on legalizing identity shows the effects, both liberatory and restrictive, of ethnoracial identity formation that are experienced in concert with recognition by the state and the redistribution of resources. The theory of legalizing identity reveals a creative process that evokes attachment to place, while at the same time shows how the play of cultural reconfiguration combines with the work of learning what to do with rights granted and then won.

NOTES

Preface

1 "In Brazil [the term] Indian has gone through phases of denigration and of re-generation. The indigenous movement of the 1970s and 1980s reappropriated the term and infused it with a substantial dose of political agency" (A. C. Ramos 1998:5–6). The use of the term has come to be a "dynamic element of struggle" (Garcia 2005:27). The Xocó refer to themselves as Indians.

2 Sergipe covers an area of 22,000 square kilometers and contains within its small area all of the climatic zones of northeastern Brazil. Its humid lowlands and meadows on the coast yield to a rich belt of vegetation and then in the north to a semiarid plateau. In 2000, Sergipe's population was approximately 1,784,000, out of a total Brazilian population of 185 million, with 67 percent of the population of Sergipe self-identifying as nonwhite (563,000 white; 111,460 black; 1,085,400 mixed; 9,000 "yellow" and Indian) (Table 2.1.1, <http://www.ibge.gov.br/>). The name "Sergipe" comes from the indigenous Tupi language expression "in the crab's river."

3 The state symbol, introduced in 1892, is an Indian (with headdress and grass skirt) standing next to a hot air balloon.

Introduction

1 Prior to the work of anthropologists under the leadership of João Pacheco de Oliveira Filho, it was assumed that almost all the indigenous peoples in northeastern Brazil had assimilated into the general population and lost whatever cultural differences they had once had. With new definitional structures and democratization, assimilation was no longer an impediment to tribal recognition, as it had been during the long period of indigenist ideology (A. C. Ramos 1998). Between 1980 and 1993, over 30 northeastern tribes were recognized, with an increase in population from 4,750 to 31,600 distributed in 46 indigenous areas (Arruti 1995:59; Oliveira Filho 1993). The phenomenon of "racial-ethnic reclassification" can be seen in other parts of Brazil as well. Recent findings show that "reclassified indígenas constitute nearly half (approximately 47%) of Brazil's indígena population in 2000" and that most of the growth in population in the 1990s (79 percent) is attributable to reclassification (Perz, Warren, and Kennedy 2008:27). At the end of the 2000s, there are approximately 230 peoples and 170 languages, with a total of more than 700,000 Indians, divided between indige-

nous reserves and urban areas (Comissão Pro-Índio de São Paulo, <http://www .cpisp.org.br/>, accessed June 11, 2008).

2 The booklet from which this quote is drawn, *Xokó: Grupo Indígena de Sergipe*, was published in Aracaju by the state of Sergipe in 1997. It was given to me by Chief Damião on São Pedro Island, explaining that Professora Beatriz Dantas had written this book so that teachers in Sergipe could explain the Xocó history of struggle.

3 For an example of an argument critical of affirmative action using "quilombo" as a metaphor for Brazil, as the Supreme Court decides the constitutionality of quotas, see Mainardi 2008.

4 The use of identity is "riddled with ambiguity, riven with contradictory meanings, and encumbered by reifying connotations" (Brubaker and Cooper 2000:34). A more precise use of identification can allow for the dialogical character of identity, thus calling attention to the complex processes of becoming, rather than a static condition of being. I use "identity" as a category that may be imposed by, or made available through, law as the codification of rights and enacted through new categories of personhood. Identity can thus be understood as "mediated by institutional resources of recognition and authorization—an identity that locates us and determines our part within a socially intelligible world" (Santner 2001:27). I use "identification" to indicate the process of taking up such an identity with the resulting transformation in the significance of local cultural practices and selfhood.

5 See Hernandez (2002:1168–69) for a discussion of the difference in Brazilian discourse about affirmative action between social-racial classifications, which "are characterized as fluid," and the "'Black' qualifier as a political category rather than a social one." For the notion of "political race" in the United States, see Guinier and Torres (2002).

6 A relevant U.S. example is that of the black Cherokees, who were disenfranchised in tribal elections as a legacy of Dawes Commission rolls from the 1890s that did not list Cherokees of African descent (Staples 2003) and as the result of the British colonial traders' policy of introducing enslaved Africans to southeastern indigenous groups to open a new market for slaves and to close down an escape hatch for runaways (Katz 2003). In fact, Cherokee relations with their black brethren who live in their midst and have greater "blood quantum" but have not been permitted to enroll range from tense to nonexistent (Sturm 2002).

7 Legalizing identity is a process involving a voluntary impetus for restitution and recognition by the state, which may lead to unintended consequences—liberatory, confining, or both. I have not explored the imposition of legal categories of identity intended to mark individuals for discrimination, imprisonment, or death.

8 Since there is not a tradition of judicial precedence in Brazil (unlike the common-law system of the United States and England), judges are much freer to interpret statutes on their own. They are generally not bound by previous decisions that cover similar terrain or legal provisions.

Chapter 1

1 The concept of the *sertão* dates back to Portuguese exploration of African inland regions in the fifteenth century (Souza Lima 2005:198).

2 The nine states of the Northeast are Alagoas, Bahia, Ceará, Maranhão, Paraíba, Pernambuco, Piauí, Rio Grande do Norte, and Sergipe.

3 At the end of the nineteenth century, Antônio Conselheiro gathered a crowd of poor followers as he wandered around the Northeast. They founded the religious community of Canudos. The military leaders of the new Republic of Brazil initiated a campaign to destroy the "blessed city." Intolerance and mysticism lay at the heart of this bloody conflict, which caused the death of almost 20,000 people. The subject of Canudos has intrigued scholars for over a century because of its messianism and as a model of social conflict and resistance (Arruda 1993; Burns 1990; R. M. Levine 1992; and Sá 1997).

4 In addition to Graciliano Ramos, other authors associated with the Northeast include Gilberto Freyre, João Guimarães Rosa, Rachel de Queiroz, José Lins do Rego, Ariano Suassuna, and Jorge Amado.

5 All translations from Portuguese are those of the author.

6 Dams and roads were built "to benefit properties of friends or to consolidate the political influence of some political chief of the interior" (Hirschman 1963:24). Historically, when a northeasterner was in power nationally, greater assistance was given to the region (Hirschman 1963:18–21).

7 Popular pamphlets called *literatura de cordel* (stories on a string) are wood-block illustrated booklets of poems on a variety of themes that touch on the imagined Northeast (Slater 1982). One of the most popular themes is the bandit Lampião, with others being Canudos, great droughts, magic cows, brave cowboys fighting dragons, and journalistic topics of the day (Fentress and Wickham 1992:104). Singing duels are also common in the weekly markets of backland towns and touch on all the themes associated with sertanejo living (Lewin 1996).

8 See Pernambucano de Mello (2001) for a full description and explanation of the tricornered, wide-brimmed leather hats embroidered with coins; fleurs de lis sewn in a cross; Stars of David; ammunition belts and shoulder bags made of colorful fabric, sometimes with mother-of-pearl buttons; and leather sandals with a strap at the heal.

9 Oligarchy emerged in the nineteenth century as the product of a national electoral system combined with local extended family clans, which had by the close of the colonial period expanded to absorb rural society's landed estates and their dependent client populations (Lewin 1987:17).

10 The captaincy of Sergipe D'El Rei was part of its large southern neighbor Bahia until 1823 and became a state in the federation when the end of the monarchy and the Brazilian Republic was proclaimed in 1889.

11 The power of the Catholic Church in the sertão of Sergipe is reflected in disputes in the 1850s over whether the local parish or the landowners should pay the recording fees. The provincial authorities argued that the parish had better

information about who possessed the land since it had always kept such records and the government had not. Moreover, the understanding of land ownership was tied to possession rather than to legal title, causing continuing confusion in the area (Teixeira da Silva 1999:11–12).

12 Article 198 provided for the inalienability of land inhabited by forest dwellers (*silvícolas*), guaranteed the perpetual use of the land by them, nullified any legal actions that might result in others taking possession of their land, and specifically denied indemnification from the government to landowners whose land was taken to be held in trust for indigenous peoples.

13 See Singh (2002:56–69) for a critique of the Indian Statute. Although the statute expanded the definition of "Indian," it also made demarcation of indigenous land more complicated technically (G. O. Carvalho 2000:465).

14 The success of the military's policy is also reflected in the increase of indigenous areas initiated under military rule: in 1967 only 10 percent of indigenous lands had been recognized; by 1996, 205 indigenous areas, covering 106 million acres, had been registered (Schwartzman, Araújo, and Pankararú 1996:39). The FUNAI website as of 2001 included land that had been identified for demarcation as a total of 441 indigenous areas, covering 11.58 percent of the national territory. The website (<http://www.funai.gov.br>, accessed October 5, 2008) lists 488 indigenous areas covering 12.41 percent of the national territory (of which 398 are fully regularized). Another 123 areas are under consideration. Moreover, the indigenous population of Brazil has grown from 100,000 in 1970 to 460,000 in 2008, constituting 225 peoples speaking 180 different languages. See also Hemming 2003:638.

15 Key provisions used were those that did not permit indemnification of private owners by the federal government. Under Brazilian indigenous law, demarcated land is owned by the federal government for the benefit of the tribes who have the right to possess it indefinitely, because they are deemed to have lived on it "for time immemorial" (Allen 1989:154). Under the 1969 Constitution and the 1973 Indian Statute there was no right to indemnification from the federal government because any claim on such lands was deemed null and void. This did not sit well with landowners, and consequently, according to the democratic 1988 Constitution, a right to indemnification for improvements constructed in good faith was included (Article 231).

16 The political unit known as a *município* is translated here as "county" although the nature of the two carry different political and administrative significance. A município may consist of only one city or may be relatively large, perhaps containing a capital city called a *sede* or county seat, other towns, rural villages, settlements, and individual homesteads, such as Porto da Folha, where Mocambo and the Xocó are located. The elected head of a município is known as *prefeito*, which I translate as mayor, although once again they are not technically equivalent terms.

17 The local government's installation of electricity in Mocambo coincided with its recognition as a quilombo, but many believe the two events were not necessarily related, particularly because the county government was not sympathetic to the

quilombo movement until land was granted to Mocambo in 2000.

When the 2000 elections in the United States ended in the voting machine fiasco, people in Mocambo knew the details and were quick to laugh at the advanced electoral machines that even they use — the United States is not as advanced as it claims to be, they teased. This was a big change from 1998, when people asked me if the United States was in Europe.

18 After years of disputes with the proprietor of the bar, the federal attorney obtained a court order that the bar should be demolished, on the grounds that it sat on the federally owned land adjacent to an interstate waterway.

19 The story on which the Xocó base their claim to São Pedro Island and the surrounding mainland, Caiçara, is that one square league of land was given to the Catholic Church to establish a mission for the indigenous population in return for their aiding the Portuguese in their fight against the Dutch invasion in the early seventeenth century (Oliveira Filho 1993:5).

20 *Caboclo* is used in the Northeast to mean any person who is suspected of being descended from Indians or who "looks like" an Indian. Unlike in the Amazon, where *caboclo* often means an Indian-white mixture, in the Northeast it most often means a black-Indian combination. In the Amazon, *caboclo* is often used to connote a "detribalized Indian who speaks Portuguese, but still participates in a subsistence economy with some ties to local markets and regions, and practices a syncretic religion largely based in popular Catholicism" (Saillant and Forline 2001:147). In the Northeast, in addition to the phenotypic meaning, *caboclo* may indicate a person who may be descended from Indians but has since lost cultural connection to an identity claim or "simply the person taken from the dense forest (*mato*) who originates in the forest, the enslaved or catechized Indian who has come to live in the village" (Ayrosa 1935). *Caboclo* has traditionally had a derogatory connotation, not unlike the term "negro" for black, except as it is used metaphorically in Afro-Brazilian religions, such as candomblé.

21 Especially important to Brazilians was the freeing of the African colonies of Portugal as part of the "carnation revolution" in 1974, which overthrew the fifty-year authoritarian dictatorship in Portugal without bloodshed.

22 In 1952, a group of Church leaders in the Northeast gathered to discuss the proposed hydroelectric plant on the northern border of Sergipe, including the poverty and potential displacement of people who lived on the river, as expressed in the Declaration of Archbishops, Bishops, and Prelates of the São Francisco Valley (Declaração dos Arcebispos, Bispos e Prelados do Vale do São Francisco e das Circunscrições Eclesiásticas Situadas no Raio de Ação da Hidro-Elétrica de Paulo Afonso, reunidos em Aracaju de 25 a 28 de Agôsto de 1952).

23 Until the late 1940s, Dom Hélder Câmara was a supporter of the Integralists, a radical right-wing organization comparable to the Italian fascists. By the time he founded the CNBB, Dom Hélder had switched his allegiance to a more liberal and then radically leftist position, which he retained for the rest of his life. Dom Hélder was moved to the archbishopric of Recife in 1964 as a result of the military's desire to move leftists and those they considered "communists" far from the centers of power (Piletti and Praxedes 1997:304).

24 An army Intelligence Officer told a researcher in 1965 that the MEB primer, *To Live Is to Struggle*, itself was enough to justify the coup. The primer was declared subversive and confiscated (Page 1972: 214). The literacy movement was based on the work of Brazilian educator Paulo Freire, who developed the practice of consciousness-raising while teaching people to read and write (Berryman 1987:35).

25 The "CNBB changed fundamentally after 1964, and its structure and orientation approached that of the institutional church at the very time the Second Vatican Council was committing the universal Church to almost precisely the position formerly promoted by the CNBB" (Bruneau 1982:53).

26 This comes from Comunicado Mensal da CNBB, No. 231, December 1971, quoted in "Y-Juca-Pirama, O Indian: Aquele que Deve Morrer," Documento de Urgência de Bispos e Missionários, 1973. One of the signatories of this document was Dom Tomás Balduíno, bishop of Goiás, who had also been present at the creation of CIMI and who, in 2003, as president of the Pastoral Land Commission (CPT), was made a member of the Council of Economic and Social Development by President Luiz Inácio Lula da Silva.

27 In March 1971, in Iquitos in the Peruvian Amazon, a meeting of bishops of five countries (Peru, Venezuela, Colombia, Ecuador, and Bolivia) issued a document that Balduíno (1992:84) considers the origin of the profound change happening in the indigenist missionary Church of Latin America.

28 John Hemming (2003:751) believes CIMI "evolved from the Anthropos Institute," established first in 1906 as an international review of ethnology and linguistics and then as an institute in Vienna in 1932. The Brazilian manifestation of the Anthropos Institute became active in 1965 in São Paulo and was moved to Brasília in 1971.

29 A full history of CIMI has yet to be written. Just as CIMI remains active, so the Indian Statute of 1973 remains in force in 2008. Significantly, and perhaps in response to the CNBB's creation of CIMI, President General Médici vetoed the sections of the law that would have given missionaries and anthropologists the right to give assistance to indigenous groups without prior approval by the government. See Addendum to "Y-Juca-Pirama, O Indian: Aquele que Deve Morrer," Documento de Urgência de Bispos e Missionários, 1973, in Suess (1980).

30 Evidence of this can be seen in the two most-quoted statements by the bishops of the Amazon and the Northeast, respectively, as being the most radical statements ever issued by a Catholic Church official body: *O Grito das Igrejas* (The Cry of the Churches) and *Ouvi os clamores do meu povo* (I Heard the Outcry of My People) (Löwy 1996:87; Martins 1985). These statements were issued in the wake of the 13th General Assembly of the CNBB held on the twenty-fifth anniversary of the United Nations Declaration of Human Rights (Mainwaring 1986:112). A month after the bishops' statements were issued, Law No. 5,889 was enacted (regulated by Decree 73,626 of February 12, 1974), extending the Consolidation of Labor Laws to rural workers, giving them, by law at least if not everywhere in practice, employment stability and social security (Shirley 1979:358). In 1975, the CPT was founded, and the following year the Bahia/Sergipe CPT was born

("Interview with Dom José Brandão de Castro, Transcript of Recording," *Tribuna de Aracaju*, May 22, 1977).

31 The Brazilian Church's move to the left as the result of repression was very different from other Latin American countries, such as Argentina and Chile, where authoritarian regimes weakened progressive trends within the Church (Mainwaring 1986:102). This difference has a historical explanation as well. The Catholic Church in Brazil was never as strong as in Spanish-colonized countries, with the church-state separation in Brazil dating back at least to the nineteenth century (Viotti da Costa 2000), and even to the eighteenth century, when the Jesuits were expelled from the country under the Portuguese Pombalese reforms.

32 Dom José Brandão was a member of the Redemptorist order, founded in 1732. The order arrived in Brazil in 1893 and is still devoted to "evangelizing especially the poor and most abandoned" (<http://www.praiseofglory.com/redemptorist/whysite.htm>, accessed December 8, 2005). Better known is another Redemptorist priest, Alec Reid, a facilitator in the Northern Ireland peace process, who also worked in the Basque country to achieve a ceasefire. In Brazil, the Redemptorists are known for running the sacred places to which pilgrims come each year, often from great distances (Steil 1996:77). As will be seen below, Dom José Brandão was one of the organizers of the first *romaria da terra* (pilgrimage for the land) in Sergipe, instituted around Brazil by liberation theologians to support rural land struggles, in an excellent example of a reinvention of a traditional form in support of liberationist goals (Steil 1996:272–88). Land pilgrimages continue to be used by the CPT and the MST, often together, to cement what has become a much-anticipated religio-political experience of those who struggle for land (Burdick 2004:124).

Chapter 2

1 Until the 1988 Constitution, indigenous people did not have the right to vote or run for office. They could also not sue or be sued or prosecuted. Even after 1988, Indians remain wards of the state, legally defined as "relatively incapable" (A. C. Ramos 1998:98). Although there have been proposals to "emancipate" Indians, none have come to fruition, primarily out of fear that without tutelage the government would withdraw essential services. In the United States, not only slaves but also free people of color did not have citizenship rights (Gross 2007).

2 The Rural Worker Statute was Law No. 4,214 of March 2, 1963, enacted a year before the military coup.

3 Slavery was abolished in 1888 by Princess Isabel, the year before Brazil's transformation from a monarchy to a republic. However, Brazil always had the largest population of free people of color (Klein 1986), and many people lived in an ambiguous status between slave and free (Grinberg 1994). The status of *agregado* was a personalized relationship based on cordiality, at least on the surface (Franco 1997:100).

4 The legal differentiation of church-versus-civil matrimony is important for establishing patrimony, inheritance, and pension rights.

5 Testimony in Brazilian courts is produced through an interaction between the witness and the judge, who is accompanied by a secretary sitting at a typewriter or computer. All questions are directed by the judge and are answered to her or him (even in the 1970s female judges were not uncommon). Lawyers who want to interrogate the witness address their questions to the judge, who then restates the question to the witness. After the witness answers, the judge dictates a re-statement of the answer to the secretary. At the end of the testimony, the judge, witness, and lawyers sign the testimonial document. For a description of the legal system in rural Brazil in the 1970s, see Shirley (1979). For a critique of the Brazilian system of testimony, see Kant de Lima (1995).

6 With the construction of a series of hydroelectric dams upriver, the level of the river was decreasing each year, thus reducing the fish population and abolishing the periodic flooding of lagoons along the banks that had been rice production and fishing areas. This left people without means of support, since they no longer had the cash crop they used to share with the landowner and their main source of protein, fish, was depleted.

7 In the new millennium, the plan to redirect a portion of the São Francisco River to provide water to states to the north of Sergipe has moved forward, despite the objections of scientists, the World Bank, and local residents.

8 In fact, it *is* more likely that peasants interviewed in 1978 would have remem-bered Chico, since he was still alive in 1928; his brother, Coronel João Fernan-des de Britto, died in 1916. In keeping with generational shifts of powerful, landowning families, it is interesting to note that Carlos Ayres Britto, constitu-tional scholar, great-grandson of the coronel, and son of Dr. Britinho, became a Workers' Party (PT) militant in 1985, ran for federal deputy from Sergipe on the PT ticket in 1990, and tried to run again in 2002. He also attended the celebra-tion in 1991 of the federal recognition of Caiçara as an indigenous reserve for the former sharecroppers on his great-grandfather's land. He was appointed to the Supreme Court of Brazil by President Luiz Inácio Lula da Silva in 2003.

9 Dom José Brandão de Castro, "Relação das Famílias do que se Entende por Fazenda Belém, na Marias Pretas, na Caiçara," in Propriá: Collection of Dom José Brandão de Castro [1978], p. 4; "Colonos Cercam Terras e PM Reprime," *Jornal de Sergipe*, September 20, 1978, p. 4.

10 In 1971, while Frei Enoque was beginning his work, activists in the capital were living under a cloud of government repression, made worse by the death in April 1970 of Dom Távora, the progressive archbishop of Aracaju, and the assump-tion of the archbishopric by Dom Luciano Duarte, who was unflinchingly allied with the military. Dom Luciano, in power until 1998, facilitated the complete repression of the nascent Catholic student movement and expelled a number of foreign priests from the archdiocese who supported liberation theology (J. I. C. Dantas 1997:149). What made Frei Enoque's activities possible was the support he received from Dom José Brandão de Castro. Because bishops enjoy signifi-cant autonomy, his diocese became a haven for those involved with early land struggles.

11 Frei Enoque arrived in Porto da Folha from the Regional Seminary of the North-

east in Recife, where seminarians, with the support of progressive bishops such as Dom Hélder Câmara, conducted the equivalent of anthropological fieldwork in rural communities to prepare for pastoral action (Melo interview 1997). This form of study at the seminary lasted from 1969 to 1971 but was continued as a model for priests working in rural communities after that (Serbin 1992:116) and is likely to have been the model for Frei Enoque's group of priests and lay religious.

12 In 1960, the diocese of Aracaju, Sergipe, was divided into three—Aracaju, Propriá, and Estância. In 2002, 97.85 percent of the population of the Estância diocese was Catholic (fifth highest in the nation); Propriá was 96.78 percent Catholic (twelfth highest). The percentage of Catholics in the Propriá diocese has gone down less than 1 percent since 1966. Aracaju has fallen from 97 percent in 1976 to 76.8 percent in 2002 (<www.catholic-hierarchy.org>, accessed May 21, 2005), a trend that is repeated in major urban centers around the country—in Rio (54 percent), in Recife (62 percent), and in São Paulo (68 percent)—according to the 2000 census (Jacob, Hees, Waniez, and Brustlein 2003). In fact, the São Francisco River valley that runs through the Propriá diocese, then through Bahia and into Minas Gerais, is known for its loyalty to Catholicism, with percentages of Catholics remaining in the nineties (Jacob, Hees, Waniez, and Brustlein 2003:15). It is significant that, although church growth is slower than the growth of the overall Brazilian population, 125.5 million people declared themselves to be Catholic in 2000, the largest number of Catholics in a single country. As of 2005, estimates have increased to over 151 million Brazilian Catholics (BBC News In Depth, April 1, 2005, news.bbc.co.uk/1/hi/world/4243727.stm, accessed June 29, 2008).

13 One of the religious lay activists that formed part of Frei Enoque's group in Porto da Folha, Raimundo Eliete Cavalcante, has explained that two radical seminarians, Juvenal and Angelino, who had come to the area just before Frei Enoque, brought with them the idea of visiting São Pedro Island because they had learned of the mission from the history of the Franciscan order in the Northeast (Arruti 2002:123). However, these two seminarians left the diocese before the events described in this chapter, because of federal police repression (Arruti 2002:126).

14 Chief Heleno Bezerra Lima issued a call in 2000 that appeared as a small item in an Aracaju newspaper for anthropologists to help the Xocó reconstitute their culture. As for Raimundo Bezerra Lima, he became shaman of the Xocó shortly after they invaded the island and was holding that post when I met him in 1998; as of 2008, he was still shaman.

15 "Dom Brandão," *Jornal de Sergipe*, October 22 and 23, 1978.

16 "Deputados Denunciam Bispo de Comunista," *A Tarde*, May 11, 1977; "Falar Sobre Terra na Bahia Virou Comunismo," *Jornal da Bahia*, May 15, 1977.

17 "Entrevista com Dom José Brandão de Castro," *Tribuna de Aracaju*, May 22, 1977.

18 "Gilvan Rocha, Carlos Teixeira, Guido Azevedo, Jackson Barreto e Jonas Amaral Defendem Bispo," *Fase*, June 13, 1977.

19 There are conflicting accounts of Frei Doroteu's death. A local newspaper in

1978 reported that he had died mysteriously, implying that the Britto family was responsible. Others say that he drowned on a beach in Alagoas. The Capuchin history reports that he died of illness when going to Bahia.

20 Frei Juvenal was part of Frei Enoque's team of priests in the early 1970s.

21 This is my translation of "Esta terra pertence aos meus caboclos Frei Doroteu." Since sometime in the 1980s, there has been a rectangular urn holding the bones of Frei Doroteu with the inscription "Frei Doroteo de Loretto 30-10-1878." The bones were transported to the island with much pomp, and those involved with church works celebrated Frei Doroteu as a helper of the Indians (D. Santos interview 2000). There may have been some dissension on the part of those who felt that the church was responsible for their original oppression and loss of identity. However, out of respect for Frei Enoque, no overt objections were expressed (Apolônio interview 2000).

22 In September 1978, the diocese bulletin devoted its monthly issue (two-page mimeo) to the demarcation of the island, with a drawing of an Amazonian Indian as the illustration ("Para a Gente Pensar," in *Boletim*, Year III, no. 27, Diocese of Propriá, September 1978). Northeastern Indians who are overwhelmingly mixed race often are referred to as *descaracterizado* (having lost their character as Indians), which can refer to physical or cultural characteristics.

23 The first FUNAI anthropologist to visit the island recorded twenty-four families from Caiçara, four from Belém, one from Taperinha, five individuals living in São Paulo but intending to return to the island, four families in Mocambo identified by her as being Xocó, and two individuals living on the Ilha do Ouro (Melatti 1979), at least one of whom moved to the island later. Another contemporaneous source indicates that thirty-three families were involved, of which twenty-eight were from the mainland, four from Mocambo, and one from the Ilha do Ouro ("Para a Gente Pensar," in *Boletim*, Year III, no. 27, Diocese of Propriá, September 1978).

24 "Colonos Cercam Terras e PM Reprime," *Jornal de Sergipe*, September 20, 1978. Although this article states more than once that the military police were sent to repress and control the invading workers, Frei Enoque is quoted as pointing out that the police treated the people very well and even gave families money to buy food for their children. In spite of the discussion of violence and repression, at this point in the struggle cordiality seems to have coexisted with emotional demands and counter demands, claims and counterclaims. This cordiality waned as the struggle intensified over the coming years and as the Brittos' land changed hands.

25 "Colonos Cercam Terras e PM Reprime," *Jornal de Sergipe*, September 20, 1978.

26 "Religiosos Ameaçados no Baixo São Francisco," *Jornal de Sergipe*, October 19, 1978.

27 In 2000, the pilgrimage was again held on São Pedro Island, with large portraits of Dom José Brandão, who had died earlier that year, and Sister Hermínia, the nun who had spearheaded the Sergipe CPT and who was killed in a bus accident around the same time. During the 2000 pilgrimage, before the Xocó performed their dances, Chief Heleno Bezerra Lima said, "We are Xocó, even if we are not

painted and dressed like Indians." He and two others had headdresses, but as with all the others, they were wearing shorts and t-shirts.

28 "Xokó Resistem Expulsão e Reclamam Criação da Reserve," *Porantim*, December 1979. Over twenty years later, Carlos Ayres Britto attended a memorial event for Dom José Brandão. I approached him there, asking about the 1978 letter. Although a bit flustered, he recounted Dom José's reaction at the time as one of forgiveness, rising above the attack. In this encounter, one can catch a glimpse of the power and finesse of Dom José as a complex actor on the local scene.

29 "Propriá: Prefeito Quer D. Brandão na LSN," *Jornal de Sergipe*, December 5, 1978. For further information on Leandro Maciel's pointing "the red finger" at Dom José Brandão in a letter to President Geisel at the end of 1974, see Gaspari (2003:474).

30 Shaman Júlio of the Kariri-Xocó told me that they invaded Fazenda Modelo because the CODEVASF superintendent, who was a friend of his, told him that they could move in. The government did not object to their claim, and FUNAI finalized the delimitation of the Kariri-Xocó reserve in 1991 (the same year the Brittos' property was added to the Xocó reserve).

31 Hohenthal (1960a:59) did his fieldwork in the early 1950s and reported: "All these surviving have been subject to the acculturated influences of so many generations that, superficially at least, they are culturally indistinct from non-Indian villages of the area. Physically, they show traces of a long and continuous racial mixture with individuals of the primary Negroid and Caucasoid races. No group conserved more than a few words of its original language, and even those words being of doubtful linguistic value."

32 One such voyager was Inocêncio Pires, the identified ancestor later used by the FUNAI anthropologist to trace the origins of the families identified as Xocó.

33 Strikingly similar stories are told in Nicaragua's highlands (Gould 1998:235) and on its Mosquito Coast (Pineda 2001:131), both in relation to indigenous groups gaining land title and then negligently losing it. This theme, which may be a more generalized phenomenon in Latin America, reflects the anger and resignation associated with loss, as well as the willingness to accept some responsibility for the robbing of identity associated with the pillage of land rights.

34 Elsewhere in Brazil, the theme of title given by powerful figures has also survived. For example, the Tupiniquim in Espírito Santo claim their title dates to 1610 when the governor of the captaincy gave them title to part of their territory (S. Williams 1983:152).

35 The Kariri claimed a former settlement of a group they considered their ancestors, the Cariri, whose settlement had been extinguished in 1759 (Arruti 1998b:104).

36 Cícero de Souza Santiago, letter to president of FUNAI, Porto Real de Colégio, Alagoas, May 9, 1979.

37 "Indians Iniciam Encontro na Ilha," *Gazeta de Sergipe*, October 13, 1979. In 1983, anthropologist Clarice Mota (1997:12) witnessed the anxiety of Xocó leadership when she departed to visit the Kariri-Xocó. They worried about the possibility that members of that tribe might attempt to move to the island.

38 Unlike Dom José Brandão, the mayor presented the problem as a personal, political difference between himself and the bishop (but not a disagreement with the Church itself) and distributed his cousin Carlos Ayres Britto's published editorial, "O Coronel e o Bispo," in pamphlet form.

39 Jonathan Warren (2001:101) discusses "how land, and the struggle for it" can have an "Indianizing effect." Although he disavows "racial economism," he recognizes that "land in conjunction with other factors," such as discourse, "can spur Indian resurgence." In the case of the Xocó, it was only when the workers seized the land that they were taken seriously by the government as potential Indians. João Pacheco de Oliveira Filho (1999a) theorizes a process of territorialization that ties identity and land claims to one another.

40 Dom José Brandão de Castro, "Os Indígenas do Nordeste," Propriá: Collection of Dom José Brandão de Castro, (1980), p. 4.

41 In a 1952 Declaration of Archbishops, Bishops, and Prelates of the São Francisco Valley (p. 24), entitled "Da Lei Escrita para a Lei Vivida" (From Written Law to Lived Law), the bishops argued for implementing "colonization" that would give land to the poor and improve the economy, life, health, and technical preparation of the rural population.

42 Article 4 contains three classifications of indigenous communities: isolated, integrating, and integrated, reflecting the assimilationist perspective of the government at the time. The last category would allow FUNAI to "declare an entire community as integrated [into Brazilian society] upon the request of its members" (Singh 2002:60). Notably, this has never been requested by a tribe or initiated by the government.

43 Manuela Carneiro da Cunha (1986:117), who, it may be remembered, was the founder of the Pro-Indian Commission when the Xocó were first petitioning for recognition in 1978, has commented that the development in anthropological theory away from essentialist definitions of ethnicity was influential in the drafting of the new statutory definition of "Indianness." However, in 1987, in her effort to influence the new constitution, she was critical of the 1973 statute (1987:22), focusing on the question of "integration" and "assimilation," the confusion of the two, and their meanings in late twentieth-century Brazil. She pointed out that cultural spaces could vary without affecting the identity of a group and that culture is dynamic and perpetually re-elaborated (1987:25). This is the perspective that has prevailed in relation to northeastern Indians, who would formerly have been considered too acculturated to be classified as "Indians."

44 In the year 2000, the mayoralty of Aracaju was won for the first time by the PT. That year, practically every lawyer and politician I talked to claimed to have helped the Xocó get their land. The younger generation of the Britto family, who sided with the Xocó shortly after recognition, have become identified with the PT, while, ironically, most of the Xocó in 2000 were loyal to local status quo politicians. However, in April 1988, the federal police who were accompanying the FUNAI demarcation team wrote in their report that they had observed a strong influence being exerted by progressive clergy, notably Frei Enoque, who was at the time a parish priest and trying to "transmit PT ideology to the inhabi-

tants—Indians or not." In the 1990s, Frei Enoque defected from the PT and was elected mayor of neighboring Poço Redondo, the poorest county in Brazil, a post to which he was reelected in 2000. After a few years away from county political positions, Enoque was again running for mayor in 2008.

45 Clementino, Girleno, and José Apolônio Xocó, *Nação Xocó da Ilha de São Pedro, Município de Porto da Folha em Sergipe*, letter to FUNAI president, interior minister, and federal judge, June 18, 1989.

46 The judge who granted the injunction, Francisco Melo Novais, was known as a violent man. He had been mayor of Propriá and was a large property owner. People said that he had killed a worker, was responsible for the death of a prosecutor, and had threatened a judge. He was forced to retire by the court in 1997. In May 2002, he was found guilty of murder by a jury and sentenced to eighteen years in prison ("Juiz é Condenado a 18 Anos e Fica em Liberdade," *Correio de Sergipe*, May 4, 2002).

47 "Ocupação Gera Grande Debate Na Assembléia," *Jornal da Manhã*, September 2, 1987.

48 Evaldo Campos's intervention in aid of the Xocó may be considered the first act by the federal attorney's office under the constitutional changes that made that office independent of the three branches of government. Out from under both the executive and judicial branches, the federal attorney began to defend the rights of Indians and minorities, the environment, and the landless.

Chapter 3

1 Transitory Article 68, the quilombo clause, reads: "Aos remanescentes das comunidades dos quilombos que estejam ocupando suas terras é reconhecida a propriedade definitiva, devendo o Estado emitir os títulos respectivos." There is no indication that the clause will be removed or efforts to identify quilombos will wane. Another reason for its inconspicuous placement was the near failure by black-movement representatives to convince the center coalition that a constitutional right to land for rural black communities should be included in the Constitution at all (Leitão 1999:34). Its placement as well as its provision of land only for rural black communities that could prove they were former quilombos were compromises. The text of the quilombo clause uses the expression "remanescentes das comunidades dos quilombos." Various translations of "remanescentes" are used in this context: "remainders" (Arruti 1998a), "survivors" (Linhares 2004), "remnants" (Véran 2002), and "descendants" (French 2002). The term really has no adequate translation. A Mocambo villager defined it as "we don't have the originals anymore."

2 The Palmares Cultural Foundation did not have the power to issue land titles until a presidential decree (Portaria 40 of July 13, 2000). Prior to that, any land titling would have had to be done through INCRA, the land reform agency, although very few were actually accomplished that way. A discussion that has persisted through the years is whether the quilombo issue should be under the jurisdiction of the Ministry of Justice rather than the Ministry of Culture, a route

that, if it had been taken, might have meant resolution of legal issues but, more important, a larger fund with which to work. However, the placement of the matter in the hands of the Ministry of Culture was an ideological statement about the nature of the quilombo question — seen as largely ethnic and cultural, not as a question of land reform or redistributive justice. Beginning in 2003, that changed once again, with INCRA given full jurisdiction over the recognition and titling of quilombo land. The Palmares Foundation is still involved in the early stage of certifying that a particular community considers itself descended from a quilombo.

3 There are no reliable numbers to report, but one study claims that there are almost 3,000 quilombo communities (Araújo dos Anjos 2006), while the number certified by the Palmares Foundation, according to its website, accessed in June 2008, is 1,209, 15 of which are in Sergipe. Fewer than 100 are legally recognized and titled. With the growth of estimated quilombos and the introduction of quotas for Afro-Brazilians in public universities, critics of those measures have become quite vocal.

4 The gradual shift in the political balance in the Brazilian Church came with Pope John Paul II's bishopric appointments and disciplinary actions against radical priests (Löwy 1996:132). In the 1990s, the Vatican nominated a number of Opus Dei priests in Latin America, expelled the Cardenal brothers from their religious order in Nicaragua and Father Aristide from his order in Haiti, and forbade Leonardo Boff in Brazil from teaching, which provoked him to leave the priesthood. Two progressive seminaries in the Northeast were closed in 1989, encouraging the "Charismatic Renewal," which in 1996 had 4 million members in Brazil. But see Burdick (2004) and French (2007) for reconsiderations of the purported death of liberation theology.

5 CPT, "Assembléia Geral da CPT-Sergipe," Seminário São Geraldo, Propriá, December 4–6, 1992. For an alternative analysis of Dom Lessa, see French 2007.

6 As indicated earlier, although I have used them interchangeably, município is different from a U.S. county because Brazilian municípios "possess legal prerogatives not associated with Anglo-American county" and include "both a county seat (sede) and considerable surrounding territory" (Lewin 1987:xxii). Therefore, the prefeito (which I have translated as mayor) of the município of Porto da Folha had to win elections in Mocambo, the polling place for a large area. Each município is composed of an urban area plus the outlying territory. Unlike a county in the United States, a município is not a judicial division.

7 Two years earlier, Mariza had been called upon by Frei Enoque and Padre Isaías to help the Xocó with their land bid, which she said she could not do for lack of legal experience with indigenous law. At that time, she said — and Isaías confirmed — that the scene in Mocambo was depressing, with men sitting in front of their houses drinking, without prospects, dependent on government assistance during election times (Rios interview 2000).

8 Because her mother was a Baptist and her father a follower of Afro-Brazilian religious practices, Mariza's parents were required, after thirty years of civil mar-

riage, to be wed again in a Catholic Church so that she could become a nun (Rios interview 2002).

9   See Harris (1956) for the classic treatment of over 140 different words for specific combinations of skin color, hair texture, shape of nose, in an interior town of Bahia, the neighboring state of Sergipe. Meanings of these words change over time and vary from region to region (Sansone 2003).

10 In December 1992, Dom Lessa expelled Mariza's congregation from the diocese of Propriá as the result of a document criticizing him and the changes in the diocese: priests that only care about politicians and do not understand the reality of the people, a Church with a closed door, priests who arrive in nice cars to perform mass and then leave, priests that act like landowners. The document emerged from a meeting of the CPT with its rural worker constituents (CPT, "Assembléia Geral da CPT-Sergipe," Seminário São Geraldo, Propriá, December 4–6, 1992). In 1995, when Dom Lessa informed the CPT in Sergipe that it had to disband, Inês stayed on with the other CPT cadres (by this time, Mariza had been moved by her congregation to another state), who together formed an NGO, named the Centro Dom José Brandão de Castro by their rural worker constituency.

11 Inês dos Santos Souza, "Relatório da Visita da CPT ao Povoado Mucambo," Propriá: CPT, July 22, 1992.

12 Mariza Rios, "Relatório de Atividades, Povoado Mocambo, Luta Pela Terra," Propriá: CPT, August 6, 1992. Rural trade unions reached their height of effective organizing under the dictatorship, partially due to the laws at their disposal, the role of the Church, and the momentum afforded by the growing rural workers' movement in the Northeast in the early 1960s (B. Maybury-Lewis 1994). When the Xocó struggle began, the Porto da Folha union was strong and active, providing support to the workers. By the time the Mocambo workers began making demands for their rights, the union was losing membership and power (Oliveira and Centro Dom José Brandão de Castro 1999).

13 Otacílio Melo, "Secretário Comprova o Ambiente de Tensão," *Jornal da Cidade*, June 7, 1994.

14 Mariza explained to me that the land question for the CPT and for the MST was "completely different." In MST land struggles, the conflict is provoked by the workers, while the Mocambo struggle and others like it are provoked by the landowner—"the author of the conflict is the landowner." Her purpose in composing her narrative is made explicit: "You can see in my legal briefs that starting the story as I start it is because one day the landowners went there and did this and that and the workers reacted in this way" (Rios interview 2000).

15 Inês dos Santos Souza, "Relatório da Visita da CPT ao Povoado Mucambo," Propriá: CPT, July 22, 1992.

16 João Bosco de Andrade Lima Filho, "Memória de Reunião," Aracaju, Sergipe: Instituto Nacional de Colonização e Reforma Agrária, May 2, 1995. By other accounts, João Cardoso opened the floodgates himself to fish.

17 Paulino, his brother, and the shaman, Raimundo, were listed as witnesses in the 1992 complaint filed with the court. Over the course of the next couple of years,

Xocó Indians were involved in meetings and sometimes went to the courthouse with their relatives from Mocambo and their lawyer and advisors. The last meeting in which the Xocó participated was in September 1993 when the possibility of increasing the Xocó reserve to include the village of Mocambo was explored (CPT, "Relatório da Visita da CPT ao Povoado Mucambo," Propriá: CPT, September 25, 1993). It appears that this was proposed by the Mocambo leaders, although this possible "solution" to their problem with the neighboring landowner was not discussed in later documents, nor did anyone mention it when I asked questions about relations between the two communities. Moreover, since there is no indication as to the identity of the individuals involved in the discussion, it is possible that a momentary alliance between certain people in the two communities was sending up a trial balloon. In a reverse move, in the year 2000 Xocó leaders inquired of FUNAI, in writing, whether they could expand their reserve to include Mocambo. This was taken by the Mocambo families to be a very hostile action, provoked in part by scuffles between quilombo supporters and Xocó living in Mocambo, as well as their allies (Mocambo natives who were against quilombo recognition and the Egídio family).

18 The irony of this sentiment should not go unnoted. Maria José's husband's family had worked for the Brittos and had testified against the Indians in the 1979 lawsuits. Moreover, it was her brother-in-law who had shot Xocó leader Pedrito Santana at a party in Mocambo in retaliation for Gracinha's shooting of their nephew.

19 I found it revealing that Dona Maria began making her annual pilgrimages to Joazeiro (fifteen hours in the back of a truck) to pay homage at the shrine of Padre Cícero during the big year of the Xocó struggle (Maria das Virgens Santos interview 2000). Padre Cícero, a charismatic priest, believed to have performed miracles, was a powerful political figure in the northeastern state of Ceará. He was excommunicated twice by the Holy Roman Inquisition and is still unrecognized by the Church. Nonetheless, he is considered a saint by the common folk in the sertão (Della Cava 1970). People have come from all over the Northeast every year since his death in 1934. Dona Maria does not make the connection herself, but it seemed clear as we talked that the entire circumstance involving Paulino's other wife, his involvement with the struggle, and her son's defiance of her pleas to stay home were very stressful for her, leading her to search for special meaning in her own life, travel to distant places, which provoked jealous reactions from Paulino, and establish her own identity in relation to the folk Catholic faith, which remains at the center of her identity.

20 For a comparison with the United States, it is useful to consider Ariela Gross's (2007) treatment of the Naragansett Indians in the nineteenth century, who attempted to retain both Indian and black identity and were badly treated.

21 Inês dos Santos Souza, "Relatório da Visita da CPT ao Povoado Mucambo," Propriá: CPT, July 22, 1992.

22 As elsewhere in the sertão, the view of judges and courts is encapsulated in this excerpt from a poem written in the 1930s and disseminated as cordel literature (poetry, often set to music, printed on old presses as block prints and sold in

marketplaces all around the northeastern sertão): O que é Democracia? / Nós já cansamos de ver. . . . / Até o ano de trinta / Quem podia se entender? / E no sertão infeliz / O "chefe" era o juiz / E a Justiça—Obedecer. (What is Democracy? / We are already weary of seeing / Until 1930 / Who could understand it? / And in the unhappy sertão / The "boss" was the judge / And to the Court—to Obey) (Lessa 1973).

23 "Está encaminhando junto a justiça competente, seu pedido de reconhecimento de remanescentes de quilombos" (Appeal by Antônio Marques Souza et al. of the Orders issued March 19, 1993, and August 27, 1993, by Judge Antônio Gomes Pascoal, filed October 19, 1993).

24 The executive decree No. 4,887 of November 20, 2003, during the first term of Lula's presidency, came after many years of unsuccessful debate in the House and Senate (NUER 1997). On May 13, 2002, the previous president, Fernando Henrique Cardoso, vetoed the bill, declared it to be unconstitutional, and continued to rely on his own executive decree (No. 3,912 of September 10, 2001) to regulate the quilombo clause (Despacho do Presidente da República No. 370, May 13, 2002). Article 2 of the 2003 decree defines descendants of quilombos to be "ethnoracial groups, according to self-designation, with their own historical trajectory, with specific territorial relations, with presumption of black ancestry related to resistance to oppression historically suffered," and provides that characterization as such a community is "attested to by self-definition." On September 29, 2008, INCRA adopted Normative Instruction No. 49, which lists criteria and specifies procedures for quilombo land grants. The decision to adopt this regulation was, in part, intended to help convince the Supreme Court to rule the 2003 decree to be constitutional. As soon as the regulation was published, national quilombo organizations sent out e-mails denouncing it and submitted a petition to President Lula asking that it be revoked.

25 Observers often mark the massive national strike waves of a million workers, begun by the 1979 São Paulo autoworker strikes, as the earliest move toward the end of military rule. These were led by Luiz Inácio Lula da Silva, founder of the PT that same year. He was elected president of Brazil in 2002 and reelected in 2006.

26 "Uma Nova Palmares, sem Mártires: Os Movimentos Negros se Articulam para Garantir Espaço na Constituinte," O Constituinte, Ano I, No. 1, February 15, 1987, p. 12.

27 In general, in Brazil, there is a preference for "ethnic" over "race" as a defining term of the difference that in the United States would be considered racial. Even the Palmares Foundation and the black consciousness movement have historically avoided the term "race" and, when referring to quilombos, prefer the concept of "ethnicity." For example, in October 2000, the Palmares Foundation distributed a document in preparation for the UN Conference on Racism with the following definition: "Quilombo is a space of freedom, of refuge. It signifies settlement, union, *groups that possess ethnic identity*, common ancestry. Over the course of time there has been a conceptual distortion. Currently, the historiography redefines the concept, not to cling to only the flights and escapes but the

autonomous forms of living, with the pattern and model of common use. The principal historical reference has been the quilombo of Zumbi of Palmares, but should not be the standard model" (my emphasis). The historical explanations for this preference may be traced to the "myth of racial democracy" (the notion that because the fundamental issue in Brazil is class inequality, discrimination based on race is less pronounced).

28 The working group was composed of Ilka Boaventura Leite (Federal University of Santa Catarina), Neusa Gusmão (State University of Sao Pãulo), Lúcia Andrade (Comissão Pro-Índio), Dimas Salustiano da Silva (lawyer, Maranhão human rights organization), João Batista Borges Pereira (Federal University of Sao Pãulo), Eliane Cantarino O'Dwyer (Federal University in Rio de Janeiro [Fluminense]) (treasurer), and João Pacheco de Oliveira (Federal University of Rio de Janeiro) (president).

29 O'Dwyer was quoted in the *Chronicle of Higher Education* a few years later as being "worried that a narrow interpretation could defeat the spirit of the law, excluding other rural groups that need land. But at the same time 'Article 68 has opened a space for negotiation that didn't exist for rural people before. The government is looking at other issues, such as a group's autonomy, and not just its link to slavery'" (Mooney 1998).

30 ABA, "Documento do Grupo de Trabalho sobre Comunidades Negras Rurais," 1994.

31 There is a certain correspondence between the perspective of the Brazilian anthropologists and Pnina Werbner (1997), who analyzed race and ethnicity in England in relation to previously colonial peoples who have settled in their former colonizing countries. Werbner (1997:243, 242) suggests that ethnicity is flexible, negotiated, and situational, providing a "moral and aesthetic community," even a "community of suffering" from which to launch resistance actions, while racism imposes an essentializing discourse that reifies its victims, leaving them without the ability to "find a shared, unitary identity they can all agree upon."

32 The workers met at the parish house and marched to the courthouse with union members from Aracaju, banners, a sound truck, and some Xocó Indians (CPT, "Relatório das Atividades Externas," Propriá: CPT, May 28, 1993), protesting against police violence on May 15 when plaintiffs named in the lawsuit (many of whom were illiterate) were forced to sign a document at gunpoint in their homes in Mocambo without being permitted to talk to a lawyer (Complaint 1993).

33 CPT, "Relatório das Atividades Externas," Propriá: CPT, May 20, 1993.

34 Scholars' lack of interest in separating out black communities from others in the São Francisco valley is reflected in the dearth of information about quilombos in the three-volume ethnographic production of Donald Pierson (1972) used by Dom José Brandão for his research on indigenous peoples there.

35 When the land law of 1850 declared land previously open for indigenous peoples to be available for purchase, the land in Porto da Folha was redistributed to the local elite, who turned it into cattle ranches. The so-called blacks from the foot of the high plateau (*negros-do-pé-da-serra*), ancestors of some of the current

residents of Mocambo, were pushed into three residential centers, including Mocambo, and became day laborers and sharecroppers.

36 This statement by Arruti raises questions of methodology and requires further investigation into the feedback effect ethnographic research can have on those being "studied." As Mocambo's story became one of slavery in response to his questioning, Arruti brought the issue of slavery back into his own narrative as a naturalized reference. In other words, Arruti created the reference to slavery by eliciting it from and writing it down in the presence of the Mocambo residents, and when he wrote his dissertation he cited this reference as evidence that residents talked about (or were conscious of) slavery before they knew of the quilombo clause, leaving subsequent researchers with a quandary.

37 Ironically, seven years later, when Mocambo was issued title by the Palmares Foundation to be held communally by an association, Rio das Rãs was finally granted title through land reform law, with individuals holding title to plots. This followed a decade of court actions and judicial decisions and appeals (Carvalho, Doria, and Oliveira 1996). One reason for this result was the prolonged nature of the lawsuit, filed by the federal attorney against the federal government in 1993, which demanded immediate application of the quilombo clause, raising in the courts for the first time the question of whether enabling legislation was necessary for the constitutional provision. Due to the continuing jurisprudential controversy surrounding the issue, appeals were taken, resulting in delays and reluctance on the part of judges to decide such an important question with such potentially vast repercussions. This is still an issue. The presidential decree of 2003 purporting to legislate enforcement of the quilombo clause has been challenged in court.

38 When Dulce Pereira, then president of the Palmares Foundation, learned that Mariza was working with a community that might be a candidate for recognition, she called Mariza to Brasília to discuss the case (Rios interview 2000).

39 Morro do Chaves was declared a land reform settlement by INCRA in 1991 (Magno da Silva and Lopes 1996). When I visited Morro do Chaves in mid-2000 with Margarette to encourage them to come to the commemoration for Dom José Brandão, her mother came with us to visit her first cousin.

40 There is a rural black community farther downriver, Lagoa Nova, whose members are descended from slaves who worked on a sugar plantation. The slave heritage of the Lagoa Nova community is certain, unlike Mocambo. After the end of slavery, a large company acquired the land. The Lagoa Nova workers, also aided by the CPT, decided to use the agrarian reform path in 1992, believing that the quilombo route would not yield results. During 2000, the Lagoa Nova community was finally granted title by INCRA to the land (after protracted legal wrangling) and had a celebration with INCRA authorities present. A few days later, the company whose land had been expropriated appealed, and as of 2008 the issue still was not resolved.

41 Margarette Lisboa Rocha, "Relatório das Atividades Externas, Mocambo, Luta Pela Terra," Propriá: CPT, August 11, 1993.

42 The appearance of new sandbars made crossing the river treacherous. This problem continues in 2008 and, with the proposed diversion of the river, will likely worsen.

43 Certidão (Certification of Land Transfer), Cartório do Primeiro Ofício e Oficialato do Registro Geral de Imóveis, Comarca de Porto da Folha, December 15, 1993.

44 Deed of Donation (Escritura Pública de Doação), by Flávio Almeida da Silva to Magda Almeida da Silva, March 8, 1994.

Chapter 4

1 CPT, "Relatório da Visita da CPT ao Povoado Mucambo," Propriá: CPT, March 31, 1994.

2 When Mocambo was recognized as a quilombo in 1997, it included Ranchinho, another related village about four miles up the road. A quarter the size of Mocambo, Ranchinho has its own church, and, unlike Mocambo, each of the families owned the small piece of land on which its house sat before title was awarded in 2000.

3 As explained earlier, João de Egídio (nickname for João Batista dos Santos) had been a small landowner and former employee of the Brittos and had testified on behalf of Elizabeth Britto in the lawsuits filed in 1979 against the invading Xocó families. The irony and vicissitudes of political and personal alliances become apparent as this former enemy of the Xocó became one of their most important allies.

4 Brazilian Health Department, <http://portal.saude.gov.br/saude/>, accessed July 11, 2006.

5 His campaign coincided with the formation of the Antônio do Alto Association. When Padre Isaías returned from his six months in Rome in November 1995, he joined the PT, originally to help a group of militant Christians of the local base communities who were not being given space in Dr. Júlio's party, one of the established parties that had been formed in opposition to the party associated with the military dictatorship. Isaías has remained a member of the PT ever since (Nascimento Filho interview 2000).

6 The two had their share of political differences, with Padre Isaías complaining of Frei Enoque's personalistic, "autocratic" manner, although Isaías maintains they coexisted without problems (Nascimento Filho interview 2000). Frei Enoque's ties to the state government are considered instrumental in allowing the MST to succeed in establishing settlements in Poço Redondo. While Padre Isaías was in Rome, Dom Lessa was promoted to archbishop of Aracaju and the diocese of Propriá acquired a new bishop, Dom Mário Rino Sivieri. Dom Mário convinced Isaías that he could continue his work most effectively within the Church, and Isaías agreed to become the parish priest of Poço Redondo when Frei Enoque became mayor.

7 São José's husband is the brother of Neusa Cardoso's maid in Propriá. Whether that connection had anything to do with her decision to side with the contras

is unclear. It is not necessarily a foregone conclusion that connections to land-owners lead to opposition to struggle. For example, another Mocambo resident, Dona Marieta, who considered herself to be white, was the private teacher of the Britto children for many years, and after an initial fear of joining she married a quilombola and became one of the staunchest quilombo supporters.

8 When I visited Mocambo in 2008, São José had joined the quilombo movement, and discussions of who publicly self-identified as black were much diminished.

9 A paper presented at the Sixth Congress of the Association of Latin American Biological Anthropology analyzed genetic material collected in Mocambo in January 1998, reporting that 83 percent of the 300 adults and 200 children resident in Mocambo were born there and that 54 percent were children of parents who were native to the community. Four surnames were shared by 73 percent of the population, and 80 percent of those were children of parents who were native to Mocambo. Using a set of genes, the authors concluded that the population had been assimilated into the overall population of the region and that there was no genetic difference between the Mocambo families and the rest of the population in the region. Faced with the sociolegal "fact" created by the Palmares Foundation through its recognition of Mocambo as a quilombo, the authors felt compelled to address the conundrum created by their results: "Considering also that many old Brazilian quilombos were a point through which flowed not only Africans and African-descended fugitives as indigenous people and whites and that the phenotypical characterization indicated the presence of 8% blacks, 6% whites, and 86% mestiços, this might also suggest that this population is composed of miscegenated individuals probably since its founding" (Oliveira, Novion, Coelho, and Klautau-Guimarães 2000).

10 The exception is that non-Xocó wives of Xocó men may stay. This is the technical rule recited in the Xocó community. However, non-Xocó men have married Xocó women and moved in with their in-laws. The rule is interpreted to mean that men cannot establish homesteads there.

11 A local ranch was condemned under land reform law by INCRA, and plots on that land were offered to the Egídio families in 2002 but were refused by them (João Bosco de Andrade Lima Filho, letter to Procurador Regional da República Paulo Vasconcelos Jacobina, May 7, 2002). These continue, in 2008, to be the subject of negotiation with INCRA, and the Egídio family remains in Mocambo.

12 Maria Aparecida de Oliveira Couto, who claimed to be descended from Antônio do Alto, lived with her husband and nine children in a one-bedroom house with no refrigerator, a common configuration in Mocambo until 2007, when the government built additional houses. Not surprisingly, this created tensions as the families determined whose newly married child would get a house.

13 Based on personal observation, the city of Porto da Folha has a substantial number of very white, blond or red-haired, blue-eyed residents (they are not wealthy and can be seen on the humble streets of the town), who are quite distinctive in the state of Sergipe and different from Aracaju, the capital of the state on the Atlantic coast. The whiteness of these Porto da Folha residents, so distinctive among a largely brown-skinned population, is startling to a visitor from the

United States and provoked me to ask for an explanation. The only explanation given was the Dutch colonization, with some informants adding that the Dutch, unlike the Portuguese, had sent women as well as men to colonize northeastern Brazil, resulting in intact families. The persistence of a noticeably fair-skinned, white population in an area where race mixing is not only common but expected raises questions that deserve further research. If the legend of the persistence of Dutch-descended people in Porto da Folha can be proven, it would be interesting to learn how they maintained their distinctively northern European appearance over a 300-year period in which all the people around them intermarried freely, producing offspring of every shade.

14 Francisco Bezerra Lima, Deposition, Porto da Folha, Sergipe, June 20, 1995; José Inavildo Mouro Souza, Deposition, Porto da Folha, Sergipe, June 20, 1995. One deponent, Francisco Bezerra Lima, was an employee of the man who purchased the property from Neusa. He lived in Mocambo (he called it Mucambo). In response to complaints filed by Mocambo residents, he filed a complaint with the local police in January 1994 that they had invaded the land, wouldn't let him pass, and threatened that they would murder him in his house (Complaint 1/94).

15 Parecer No. 48 of Fundação Cultural Palmares, Ministério da Cultura (Indentificação e Delimitação das Terras ocupadas pela Comunidade Remanescente de Quilombo do Mocambo, Município de Porto da Folha, Estado de Sergipe), published in Diário Oficial, No. 100, May 28, 1997, 1112–14.

16 According to the Antônio do Alto Association bylaws (Article 4), those who are part of the quilombo community are considered members if they were founding members of the association or were in solidarity with the founding of the association. Thereafter, the general assembly (which meets every two years) decides on the admission of new members (Article 5).

17 In 2002, all of the contra and Egídio families made formal demands to the government for indemnification.

18 Departamento de Polícia Federal, Superintendência Regional em Sergipe, Relatório, Aracaju, December 7, 2000.

19 One of the arguments made by lawyers for the Palmares Foundation was that the landowners did not need to be indemnified because quilombo land was held from "time immemorial" and so was deemed never to have been legally held by the landowner. In September 2001, President Fernando Henrique Cardoso issued a decree taking this position, but the new Palmares Foundation president at the time indicated that it was unrealistic to expect landowners to relinquish their property without compensation (Moura interview 2002). In fact, earlier in 2001, Moura had arranged to have Seixas Dória paid for his "cultural patrimony."

20 Letter from Xocó leadership to FUNAI, dated October 4, 1999 (from Chief Damião dos Santos, shaman Raimundo Bezerra Lima, and two councillors, Lindomar Santos Rodrigues and Pedro Rodrigues).

21 One of the explanations given for the conflict had to do with the effects of the decreasing volume of the river and diminishing pasture land for cattle, leading

the Xocó to request that the remanescentes remove their cattle from the Xocó reserve, where they had been allowed to graze since the early 1990s. However, this was secondary to the effects of demarcation of the quilombo territory, which was seen as a threat, so that the call by the Xocó to remove cattle was more likely an effect of the conflict than of environmental changes (Ministério Público Federal, Procuradoria da República no Estado de Sergipe, Minutes from Meeting in Mocambo regarding Inquerito Civil Público, No. 008/99, on December 4, 1999).

22 In 2002, Jacobina won a court decision that declared the land on which Egídio's bar was located to be maritime land owned by the federal government.

23 Portaria No. 006, Initiating Public Civil Investigation (Inquérito Civil Público), Gabinete do Procurador, Procuradoria da República no Estado de Sergipe, November 29, 1999.

24 Departamento de Polícia Federal, Superintendência Regional em Sergipe, Relatório, Aracaju, December 7, 1999; Inês dos Santos Souza, "Relatório de Atividades Externas," Aracaju: Centro Dom José Brandão, August 12, 1999. At this court appearance, it was clarified that any new construction of houses or garages in Mocambo was not advisable, because they would be treated as "bad faith" improvements to the property and would then not be indemnifiable. This assumed that there would be indemnification under land reform rules, which do not permit indemnification for improvements to the land made once notice is given.

25 The Egídio families refused the offer to be relocated to a land reform settlement and agreed to leave Mocambo only upon payment of indemnification. As of 2008, they were still in Mocambo.

26 This argument was necessary from a constitutional perspective. The 1988 Constitution contains a freedom of association clause that the lawyers felt might be violated by requiring that remanescentes join the association in order to exercise rights that were given to them by the quilombo clause. This argument held no water for the quilombo movement and the Centro Dom José Brandão. From a political perspective, it was simply untenable for people who had done everything to oppose and sabotage the movement to now obtain benefits from the struggle in which they had refused to participate.

27 Sandra is the great-niece of Xocó leader Paulino on her mother's side; her father and then-husband are both quilombolas. Her husband at the time was the son of Sr. Antônio, leader of the quilombo movement and coordinator of the Antônio do Alto Association (1998–2000).

28 This lawyer, a black woman, also came in search of indicia of black culture in Mocambo and had to make do with discussions of *rezadeiras* (people who cure with herbs and words) and stories of Lampião. Although she seemed a bit disappointed, nothing at this point could change the status of Mocambo as a quilombo. As with other professionals and academics, images of just what a quilombo community should have been would have to be adjusted to the realities of sertanejo communities now being identified in ethnoracial terms.

29 Marineide Bonfim, "Clima Tenso no Mocambo: Titulação das Terras Não Acabou com Conflito na Área," *Jornal da Manhã*, August 6 and 7, 2000.

30 As the election approached, I often thought of the juxtaposition of the rural setting and the new technology of vòting. Of course, I had no way of knowing that
only one month after the election in Mocambo the "hanging chads" of the ballots
in Florida and the manual recounting of votes would become a source of con-
sternation and teasing. Mocambo residents chided me about the technological
superiority of "backward" Mocambo over the powerful United States. Moreover,
the comparison of family loyalties in the sertão and what people perceived as the
favor that Jeb Bush was doing for his brother to help him become president was
another source of amazement about a First World country that they thought had
left such things "behind."

31 The website is <http://www.tse.gov.br/internet/eleicoes/eleicoes_2000.htm>,
accessed June 30, 2008. Voting has been "mandatory" in Brazil since the 1930s,
although it is possible to submit a blank ballot as a protest against all candidates
or to nullify one's vote by making a mistake. Failure to vote is a minor infraction
that carries a small fine, collected only if the nonvoter wants to obtain certain
government documents. Enforcement is uneven.

Chapter 5

1 The shaman of the Kariri-Xocó is reported to have criticized the election of a
shaman, because the shaman should be chosen through the magic of jurema.
Because Raymundo Bezerra was elected, according to these rivals and cousins
downriver in Alagoas, the Xocó were not authentic (Mota 1997:98).

2 Another dance that marks rural folk Catholicism is the dance of São Gonçalo, descended from a medieval Portuguese religious ceremony and performed within
church walls until outlawed in Portugal in the seventeenth century after it had
already been exported to colonial Brazil (Queiroz 1976). It is still danced in many
villages inside churches and is sometimes associated with annual festivals. For
example, the São Gonçalo dance is performed in Mussuca, a black community
not far from the capital city of Aracaju that claims its origins to be enslaved
Africans who ran away when being transported from the ship to the plantation.
Mussuca has not been recognized as a quilombo, with a variety of explanations
by mediating NGOs, including that it is "not ready" politically for the step and
that it is not truly a "rural" black community.

3 As mentioned in chapter 2, the Kariri-Xocó and Clarice Mota were dubious as
to whether the Xocó, even in 2000, knew how to prepare jurema or understood
just what they were supposed to do in the ouricuri retreat.

4 By the end of the nineteenth century, twenty-seven Indian nations identified
during the eighteenth century were considered extinguished. The Fulni-ô were
recognized in 1926, three more were recognized in the 1930s, and in the 1940s
eight more "surfaced" (including the Kariri-Xocó in 1944). From 1950 until the
mid-1970s, none were recognized. From 1977 to 1979, four new groups "materi-
alized," with fourteen more in the 1980s and ten new groups in the 1990s (eight
of which presented their demands in 1998). By 1998, there were forty indigenous
groups in the Northeast, of which twenty-eight, totaling 48,105 persons distrib-

uted over forty-five areas (247,889 hectares), had been recognized by FUNAI, representing 17 percent of Brazil's indigenous population (Arruti 1998a:97).

5 Known as Sr. Antônio do Ranchinho, he supported the quilombo movement even though he would lose his individual title when the collective title was given to the quilombo association. While I was there, improvements were being made to the house, financed by the son, who worked in a factory in São Paulo. However, unlike accusations against the Egídio families, no one intimated that Sr. Antônio do Ranchinho might be improving his property to benefit from possible government indemnification of landowners on the quilombo land.

6 This may have coincided with the shift in land use to cattle raising, severe drought in the late 1950s, and the government support of cattle raising (Arruti 2002:227).

7 Decree-Law No. 169 of Governor of State of Sergipe, February 22, 1943.

8 The workers would divide their time between working on the inland property of the landowners and working near the river, where they planted and operated as sharecroppers (Arruti 2002:220).

9 George M. Foster's (1965) "Image of Limited Good" is an interesting way to think about the issues raised by an imposed collectivity among peasants under a capitalist system. He proposed that peasants view their environment as one in which all desired things in life (land, wealth, health, friendship, love, manliness, honor, respect, status, power, influence, security) exist in finite quantity and are always in short supply. There is no way directly within the peasant's power to increase the available quantities. "Good" is to be divided but not to be augmented (Foster 1965:296). An apparent relative improvement in someone's position with respect to any "good" is viewed as a threat to the entire community. Since there is often uncertainty as to who is losing, any significant improvement is perceived not as a threat to an individual or family alone but as a threat to all individuals and family (297); thus the reaction is one of extreme individualism (301). When benefits are provided from outside the system, it is seen as luck, and each person looks for ways to maximize that luck (308). Such a view of the social and economic universe might present problems when land is given to these individuals, who must exercise power locally rather than as agents of outside forces.

10 Because of experiences like these, efforts have been made by President Lula's Workers' Party government, elected in 2002 and then again in 2006, to provide assistance specifically to quilombos, and Mocambo is one of the beneficiaries of that policy. In 2007, Mocambo received running water, some irrigation equipment, and eighty new, albeit very small, houses.

11 CPT, "Relatório da Visita da CPT ao Povoado Mucambo," Propriá: CPT, May 17, 1994.

Chapter 6

1 Articles published in the mainstream Brazilian media bore such titles as "Forgotten Africa: Remnants of Ancient Quilombos, 511 Black Communities Live Isolated in the Interior of the Country" (Veja, 1998); and "The Heirs of Chico

Rei" (*Istoé*, 1998). Chico Rei, a slave born in Africa, was reputed to have been a king there and was captured with his entire entourage.

2 Although the constitutional provision does not mention race or color, it has come to be interpreted by activists not only as granting a right to land but also as recognizing quilombo residents as subjects of economic, social, and political rights. They see quilombo recognition as a way to promote full "citizenship." The notion of citizenship in Brazil has come to include all of the rights just listed and is often used to denote going beyond a bare-bones notion of "political citizenship" (see Paoli 1992).

3 The teenagers were encouraged to take charge of the story and the play by the parish priest, Padre Isaías, who continued to advise the quilombo movement. The local Catholic Church was, and continues to be, dedicated to keeping young people within its fold and engaged with the church's projects. Inspiring the teenagers, however, was their interest in the evening soap operas shown on television. Since electricity had come to Mocambo in 1997, they had spent hours watching soap operas, which in Brazil are often historically based. So the possibility of being a "star," even if only for one night, was part of the thrill of preparing for and performing the play. For example, in the version of the play I witnessed, when Antônio do Alto's mother learned of his fate, she cried and railed against the injustice committed against her son. While Antônio's mother, who had been given the name Xica, was wailing, the other participants in the play giggled each time her name was used. I thought this might have been because of a well-known story of a slave woman, Xica da Silva, who was said to have seduced a powerful white colonial official and become his imperious and pampered mistress. The story was the basis for one of the most-watched soap operas. Xica da Silva is an iconic figure in Brazilian popular culture—hence the giggles. The teenagers' decision to insert the reference to another, but opposite, cross-racial seduction as a joke contributed to the frisson of the play.

4 Pilgrimages and pageants are descended from rural folk Catholic practices brought to Brazil from Portugal in the first years of colonization during the sixteenth century (Queiroz 1976). The ludic nature of those practices is the legacy of Portuguese folklore (Marques 1999).

5 Gilberto Freyre, a pioneer in the sociology of the Brazilian Northeast and often considered the originator of the "myth of racial democracy," was born in Recife in 1900, the son of a former slaveholding family. He received a bachelor's degree from Baylor University and a master's degree in 1923 from Columbia University (where he worked with Franz Boas) and is best known for his work on slavery. He taught at Stanford University for a few years in the early 1930s while he finished his research for *The Masters and the Slaves*, first published in 1933. In that book, Freyre reacted against the legal segregation and racism he had seen while going to graduate school in the United States. He differentiated slavery in Brazil from U.S. slavery on the basis of differences between Portuguese and English colonizers (Freyre 1986). His book became a best seller and gave form to a preexisting powerful belief in the difference between the two societies that had circulated for many years. Freyre's iteration became so widespread that Brazil-

ians, on a regular basis, continue to repeat his assertions: that Brazilian slavery was more benign than the U.S. version and that this had led to better relations between black and white people in Brazil by allowing for miscegenation and strong kinship bonds across racial lines ("racial democracy"). On the positive side, Freyre was a vocal opponent of theories of scientific racism and with his book strove to lay to rest the belief that the Brazilian national character had been perverted by "African blood." For Freyre, and for the revised national ideology from the 1930s onward, black people from Africa had, and their descendants continued to have, a positive influence on the country's history, culture, and national identity. "By the 1960s, however, Freyre's arguments were being subjected to criticism. Historians were finding evidence of cruelty to slaves" (Wright and Wolford 2003:118). The legacies of slavery clearly had produced inequality between darker- and lighter-skinned people in Brazil. Even though there is an "ethos of cordiality that floats on the surface" (Wright and Wolford 2003:118) and many white Brazilians (including former president Fernando Henrique Cardoso) insist that everyone is descended from Africans, the discrimination that African-descended Brazilians suffer has been shown to be highly correlated with skin color (Telles 2004).

6 Arruti (2002:219) reports that some people in Mocambo believe that Dom Pedro II assumed that the black people were part of the indigenous mission, not unimaginable given that the inhabitants of both the indigenous reserve and Mocambo are closely related.

7 The "Free Womb" Law of 1871 provided for the registration of all slaves and their children and specified that all children born of slaves after 1871 were to be free.

8 Until abolition in 1888, African-descended Brazilians occupied a variety of status positions in many increments ranging from slave to free. Free people of color were at an advantage legally, with the power to make contracts, dispose of property, defend themselves against their employers, and testify against other freemen. Economic distinctions between free men and slaves were less apparent. Some slaves grew their own food, marketed the surplus, held skilled occupations, could accumulate money to buy freedom, and could work in the cities, living and working on their own and paying a portion of what they earned to their masters. At the same time, some free people suffered discrimination and received little for their labor, such that the distinction between slave and free labor is not very helpful in understanding economic and social relations. "If slaves acted like peasants and peasants were treated like slaves, then the distinctions begin to lose their meaning" (Schwartz 1985:252).

9 Even smallholders who do not technically hold land titles are entitled to indemnification for the improvements they make to land on which they have lived for a significant period if the government expropriates the land for an indigenous reserve or for land reform purposes.

10 Even in such a family, the darker-skinned children are often afforded fewer opportunities in Brazilian society (Telles 2004).

11 The definition of a "cultural performance" has been synopsized by Kirk W. Fuoss and Randall T. G. Hill (2001:111n1) as having six characteristics: (1) it is tempo-

rarily framed; (2) it is spatially framed in a place temporarily marked off; (3) it is programmed; (4) it has an audience; (5) it is scheduled and publicized; and (6) it "heighten[s] occasions involving display."

12 Stuart Alexander Rockefeller discusses the didactic nature of a Bolivian folklore festival drawn from regional patronal fiestas. The festival is transformed into a "spectacle," defined as "a performative event" intended to be "seen by an audience and structured in such a way that the performers and audience are strictly separated, the latter fixed in the role of spectators" (Rockefeller 1998:125).

Conclusion

1 William Loren Katz (1986) reproduces a multitude of photographs as evidence of both the mixed-race heritage of Indians and African Americans and the incorporating of African Americans into Indian communities. The assumption behind this display of images is that it is possible to "tell" who is an "Indian" by looking at them. It is interesting to note that Katz does not mention the Lumbee Indians, referring once to "Croatans," the name once given to the people who lived in southeastern North Carolina, who by the early 1980s had become the "Lumbees." Gerald Sider (1993) traces the names used by the people who now refer to themselves as Lumbee. Although one should not read too much into Katz's omission, it is an indication of the rapid process of identity transformation of the Lumbee Indians since the mid-twentieth century.

2 Practically speaking, there is also a difference between the value of the land claimed by the U.S. tribes and the Xocó territory, although given the ultimate recognition of the Mashpee, I would assert that property and gaming rights do not constitute the primary difference.

3 Although the Branch of Acknowledgment and Research (BAR) of the Bureau of Indian Affairs (BIA) uses a seven-point set of criteria for Indian identity, most of the tribes themselves use blood quantum as a determining factor for admission (Garroutte 2003). The BAR criteria (25 C.F.R. Part 83.7(a)–(g)) are: "(1) the petitioner has been identified as an American Indian entity on a substantially continuous basis since 1900; (2) a predominant portion of the petitioning group comprises a distinct community and has existed as a community from historical times until the present; (3) the petitioner has maintained political influence or authority over its members as an autonomous entity from historical times until the present; (4) it submits to the BAR a copy of the group's present governing document including its membership criteria; (5) the petitioner's membership consists of individuals who descend from a historical Indian tribe or from historical Indian tribes which combined and functioned as a single autonomous political entity. (The petitioner must provide an official membership list certified by the group's governing body. It must also submit a copy of each available former list of members based on the group's own criterion); (6) the membership of the petitioning group is composed principally of persons who are not members of any acknowledged North American Indian tribe; and (7) neither the

petitioner nor its members are the subject of congressional legislation that has expressly terminated or forbidden the federal relationship."

4 In 1956, the U.S. Congress passed an act recognizing that there were Indians living in Robeson County, North Carolina, who shared certain family names (Oxendine, Locklear, Chavis, Lowry) that were found in the roster of earliest English settlements and who "may, with considerable show of reason, trace their origin to an admixture of colonial blood with certain coastal tribes of Indians." The act named them "Lumbee Indians of North Carolina," while at the same time denying them any rights associated with such designation: "Nothing in this Act shall make such Indians eligible for any services performed by the United States for Indians because of their status as Indians, and none of the statutes of the United States which affect Indians because of their status as Indians shall be applicable to the Lumbee Indians" (Berry 1963:159).

5 Brazil has a relatively large population of gypsies (Roma), who began emigrating to Brazil in the sixteenth century as they were expelled from the Iberian peninsula by the Inquisitions.

6 "Territórios da Cidadania destina R$ 232,5 mi para Sergipe," accessed May 20, 2008, at <http://www.incra.gov.br/>.

7 INCRA has arranged for the Egídio family to move to a nearby ranch that is being expropriated under land reform regulations, but the family has so far refused. Also, the process of paying the landowners has dragged on, in large measure due to demands for higher compensation.

8 At the Federal University of Sergipe, for example, which has not instituted quotas, I encountered two students from a newly recognized quilombo, and in the state of Maranhão, with the largest number of recognized quilombos, members of the community have been elected to public office and are attending universities. It should be noted that as this book goes to press the Brazilian Supreme Court is preparing to rule on the constitutionality of the quota system, as well as the quilombo decree issued by President Lula in 2003.

BIBLIOGRAPHY

Abercrombie, Thomas. 1998. *Pathways of Memory and Power: Ethnography and History among an Andean People*. Madison: University of Wisconsin Press.

Agier, Michel. 2002. From Local Legends into Globalized Identities: The Devil, the Priest and the Musician in Tumaco. *Journal of Latin American Anthropology* 7 (2):140–67.

Albó, Xavier. 1994. From Kataristas to MNRistas. In *Indigenous Peoples and Democracy in Latin America*, ed. D. L. Van Cott. New York: St. Martin's Press and Inter-American Dialogue.

Albuquerque, Durval Muniz de, Jr. 1999. *A Invenção do Nordeste e Outras Artes*. Recife, São Paulo: Editora Massangana; Cortez Editora.

Allen, Elizabeth. 1989. Brazil: Indians and the New Constitution. *Third World Quarterly* 10 (4):148–65.

Almeida, Alfredo Wagner Berno de. 1989. Terras de Preta, Terras de Santo, Terras de Índio-Uso Comum e Conflito, Na Trilhados Grandes Projetos. *Cadernos NAEA* 10: 163–96. Belém: Gráfica e Editora Universitária UFPA.

Amantino, Marcia. 2005. A Convivência entre Índios e Negros nas Danças Folclóricas Brasileiras: Uma Análise Histórico-antropológica. In *Dança da Terra: Tradição, História, Linguagem e Teatro*, ed. Z. Ligiero and C. A. d. Santos. Rio de Janeiro: Papel Virtual.

Anderson, Robert N. 1996. The Quilombo of Palmares: A New Overview of a Maroon State in Seventeenth-Century Brazil. *Journal of Latin American Studies* 28:545–66.

Andrade, Lúcia. 1994. O Papel da Perícia Antropológica no Reconhecimento das Terras de Ocupação Tradicional-O Caso das Comunidades Remanescentes de Quilombos do Trombetas (Pará). In *A Perícia Antropológica em Processos Judiciais*, ed. O. S. Silva, L. Luz, and C. M. Helm. Florianópolis: Editora da UFSC.

Antônio Clementino de Melo et al. v. Elizabeth Guimarães Britto. Labor Case. Juizo de Direito da Comarca de Porto da Folha. Filed April 6, 1979 (Judge Antônio Gomes Pascoal; Judge Maria Aparecida Santos Gama da Silva).

Araújo, Alceu Maynard. 1964a. *Folclore Nacional: Danças, Recreação, Música*. Vol. II. São Paulo: Edições Melhoramentos.

———. 1964b. *Folclore Nacional: Festas, Bailados, Mitos e Lendas*. Vol. I. São Paulo: Edições Melhoramentos.

———. 1964c. *Folclore Nacional: Ritos, Sabença, Linguagem, Artes e Técnicas*. Vol. III. São Paulo: Edições Melhoramentos.

Araújo, Telga de. 1999. A Propriedade e sua Função Social. In *Direito Agrário Brasileiro*, ed. R. Laranjeira. São Paulo: Editora Letras.

Araújo dos Anjos, Rafael Sanzio. 2006. *Quilombolas—Tradições e Cultura da Resistência*. São Paulo: AORI Comunicações.

Arkoun, Mohammed, and Joseph Maïla. 2003. *De Manhattan à Bagdad: Au-delà du Bien et du Mal*. Paris: Desclée de Brouwer.

Armony, Ariel C., and Hector E. Schamis. 2005. Babel in Democratization Studies. *Journal of Democracy* 16 (4):113–28.

Arons, Nicholas Gabriel. 2004. *Waiting for Rain: The Politics and Poetry of Drought in Northeast Brazil*. Tucson: University of Arizona Press.

Arruda, João. 1993. *Canudos: Messianismo e Conflito Social, Coleção Teses Cearenses;* 2. Fortaleza: Edições UFC/SECULT.

Arruti, José Maurício Andion. 1995. A Narrativa do Fazimento, ou, Por uma Antropologia Brasileira. *Novos Estudos* 43:235–43.

———. 1997. *Mocambo de Porto da Folha: Paracer Histórico-Antropológico Solicitado pelo Projeto Quilombos—Terras de Preto do Centro de Estudos sobre Território e Populações Tradicionais para o Convênio CETT/Ministério da Cultura (n. E132/96-SE)*.

———. 1998a. From 'Mixed Indians' to 'Indigenous Remainders': Strategies of Ethnocide and Ethnogenesis in Northeastern Brazil. In *The Challenge of Diversity: Indigenous Peoples and Reform of the State in Latin America*, ed. W. Assies, G. v. d. Haar, and A. J. Hoekema. Amsterdam: Thela Thesis.

———. 1998b. Mocambo/Sergipe: Negros e Índios no Artesanato da Memória. *Tempo e Presenço* Suplemento Especial (March/April 1998):26–28.

———. 1999. A Árvore Pankararu: Fluxos e Metáforas da Emergência Étnica no Sertão do São Francisco. In *A Viagem da Volta: Etnicidade, Política e Reelaboração Cultural no Nordeste Indígena*, ed. João Pacheco de Oliveira. Rio de Janeiro: Contra Capa Livraria.

———. 2002. 'Étnias Federais': O Processo de Identificação de 'Remanescentes' Indígenas e Quilombolas no Baixo São Francisco. Ph.D. diss., Museu Nacional, UFRJ, Rio de Janeiro.

———. 2006. *Mocambo: Antropologia e História do Processo de Formação Quilombola*. Bauru, São Paulo: EDUSC.

Ayer de Oliveira, Leinad, ed. 2001. *Quilombos: A Hora e a Vez dos Sobreviventes*. São Paulo: Comissão Pró-Índio.

Ayrosa, Plinio. 1935. Caboclo. *Revista do Arquivo Municipal de São Paulo* 11 (1):67–70.

Baiocchi, Mari de Nasare. 1983. *Negros de Cedro (Estudo Anthropológico de um Bairro Rural de Negros em Goiás)*. São Paulo: Atica.

Balduíno, Tomás. 1992. Fracionalism Indígena e Poder Clerical. In *A Igreja e o Exercício do Poder*, ed. M. H. Arrochellas. Rio de Janeiro: Instituto de Estudos da Religião.

Bandeira, Maria de Lourdes. 1990. Terras Negras: Invisibilidade Expropriadora. In *Textos e Debates: Terras e Territórios de Negros no Brasil*, ed. I. Boaventura. Florianópolis: Núcleo de Estudos sobre Identidade e Relações Interétnicas-UFSC.

Baptista, Karina Cunha. 2003. O Diálogo dos Tempos: História, Memória e

Identidade nos Depoimentos Orais de Descendentes de Escravos Brasileiros. *Primeiros Escritos de Laboritório de História Oral e Imagem (LABHOI)* 11:1–23.

Barreira, César. 1992. *Trilhas e Atalhos do Poder: Conflitos Sociais no Sertão.* Rio de Janeiro: Rio Fundo Editora.

Barreira, Irlys Alencar Firmo. 1998. *Chuvas de Papéis: Ritos e Símobolos de Campanhas Eleitorais no Brasil, Coleção Antropologia da Política.* Rio de Janeiro: Relume Dumará.

Barth, Fredrik. 1969. Introduction. In *Ethnic Groups and Boundaries: The Social Organization of Culture Difference,* ed. F. Barth. Boston: Little, Brown.

Bastide, Roger. 1944. Estudos Afro-Brasileiros. *Revista do Arquivo Municipal (São Paulo)* 10 (September–October):81–103.

Bauman, Richard. 1992. *Folklore, Cultural Performances, and Popular Entertainments: A Communications-Centered Handbook.* New York: Oxford University Press.

Bauman, Richard, and Charles L. Briggs. 1990. Poetics and Performance as Critical Perspectives on Language and Social Life. *Annual Review of Anthropology* 19: 59–88.

Bernardi, Luciano. 1984. Dom José Brandão Bispo de Propriá (Se). *O Mensageiro de Santo Antônio,* April 4, 1984, 10–12.

Berry, Brewton. 1963. *Almost White.* New York: Collier-Macmillan.

Berryman, Phillip. 1987. *Liberation Theology: The Essential Facts about the Revolutionary Movement in Latin America and Beyond.* New York: Pantheon.

Beyers, Christiaan. 2008. The Will-to-Community: Between Loss and Reclamation in Cape Town. In *The Rights and Wrongs of Land Restitution: "Restoring What Was Ours,"* ed. D. Fay and D. James. New York: Routledge.

Bodley, John H. 1999. *Victims of Progress.* 4th ed. Palo Alto, Calif.: Mayfield.

Bomfim, Manoel José do. 1903. *A America Latina, Males de Origem.* Rio de Janeiro: H. Garnier.

Bordewich, Fergus M. 1996. *Killing the White Man's Indian: Reinventing Native Americans at the End of the Twentieth Century.* New York: Doubleday.

Bourdieu, Pierre. 1977. *Outline of a Theory of Practice,* trans. R. Nice. Cambridge: Cambridge University Press.

———. 1984. *Distinction: A Social Critique of the Judgment of Taste.* Cambridge: Harvard University Press.

———. 1987. The Force of Law: Toward a Sociology of the Juridical Field. *Hastings Law Journal* 38 (July 1987):805–53.

Bower, Lisa C., David Theo Goldberg, and Michael C. Musheno. 2001. *Between Law and Culture: Relocating Legal Studies.* Minneapolis: University of Minnesota Press.

Brandão de Castro, Dom José. 1985. Depoimento de D. José Brandão, Bispo de Propriá. In *Igreja e Questão Agrária,* ed. Vanilda Paiva. São Paulo: Edições Loyola.

Brasileiro, Sheila. 1999. O Toré é Coisa só de Índio. In *Brasil: Um País de Negros?,* ed. J. Bacelar and C. Caroso. Rio de Janeiro: Pallas Editora.

Briggs, Charles L. 1996. The Politics of Discursive Authority in Research on the "Invention of Tradition." *Cultural Anthropology* 11 (4):435–69.

Britto, Carlos Ayres. 1978. O Coronel e O Bispo. *Jornal da Cidade*, November 17, 1978, 4.

Britto Aragão, Carlos Roberto. 1997. Propriá e Sua Região: Apogeu, Decadência e Perspectivas. Master's thesis, Universidade Federal de Sergipe, Aracaju.

Brooks, James. 2002. *Confounding the Color Line: The Indian-Black Experience in North America*. Lincoln: University of Nebraska Press.

Brosius, Peter J. 1999. On the Practice of Transnational Cultural Critique. *Identities* 6 (2–3):179–200.

Brubaker, Rogers, and Frederick Cooper. 2000. Beyond "Identity." *Theory and Society* 29:1–47.

Bruneau, Thomas C. 1974. *The Political Transformation of the Brazilian Catholic Church*. Cambridge: Cambridge University Press.

———. 1982. *The Church in Brazil: The Politics of Religion*. Vol. 56 of *Latin American Monographs, Institute of Latin American Studies*. Austin: University of Texas Press.

Brysk, Alison. 2000. *From Tribal Village to Global Village: Indian Rights and International Relations in Latin America*. Stanford, Calif.: Stanford University Press.

Burdick, John. 2004. *Legacies of Liberation: The Progressive Catholic Church in Brazil at the Start of a New Millennium*. Burlington, Vt: Ashgate.

Burns, E. Bradford. 1990. The Destruction of a Folk Past: Euclides da Cunha and Cataclysmic Culture Clash. *Review of Latin American Studies* 3 (1):17–36.

Candido, Antônio. 1964. *Os parceiros do Rio Bonito; Estudo sôbre o Caipira Paulista e a Transformação dos Seus Meios de Vida, Coleção Documentos Brasileiros*, vol. 118. Rio de Janeiro: J. Olympio.

Cardoso de Oliveira, Roberto. 1964. *O Indio e o Mundo dos Brancos*. São Paulo: Difusão Européia do Livro.

Carneiro, Edison, and John Knox. 1963. *Folklore in Brazil*. Rio de Janeiro: Ministry of Education and Culture of Brazil (Companha de Defesa do Folclore Brasileiro).

Carneiro da Cunha, Manuela. 1986. *Antropologia do Brasil: Mito, História, Etnicidade*. São Paulo: Editora Brasiliense.

———. 1987. *Os Direitos do Índio: Ensaios e Documentos*. São Paulo: Editora Brasiliense.

———, ed. 1998. *História dos Índios no Brasil*. 2nd ed. São Paulo: Companhia das Letras.

Carvalho, Georgia O. 2000. The Politics of Indigenous Land Rights in Brazil. *Bulletin of Latin American Research* 19:461–78.

Carvalho, José Jorge de, Siglia Zambrotti Doria, and Adolfo Neves de Oliveira. 1996. *Quilombo do Rio das Rãs: Histórias, Tradições, Lutas*. Salvador: Edufba.

Carvalho Neto, Paulo de. 1994. *Folclore Sergipano*. Aracaju, Sergipe: SESI.

Cascudo, Luís da Câmara. 1962. *Dicionario do Folclore Brasileiro*. 2nd ed. Rio de Janeiro: Instituto Nacional do Livro, Ministerio da Educacao e Cultura.

———. 2000 [1962]. *Vaqueiros e Cantadores: Foclore Poético do Sertão do Ceará, Paraiba, Rio Grande do Norte e Pernambuco*. Rio de Janeiro: Ediouro.

Castro, Josué de. 1966. *Death in the Northeast*. New York: Vintage.

————. 1977. *The Geopolitics of Hunger*. New York: Monthly Review Press.

Chandler, Billy Jaynes. 1978. *The Bandit King: Lampião of Brazil*. College Station: Texas A&M University Press.

Chernela, Janet, and Patricia Pinho. 2004. Constructing a Supernatural Landscape through Talk: Creation and Recreation in the Central Amazon of Brazil. *Journal of Latin American Lore* 22 (1):85–108.

Clifford, James. 1988. Identity in Mashpee. In *The Predicament of Culture: Twentieth Century Ethnography, Literature, and Art*. Cambridge: Harvard University Press.

Cohen, Abner. 1993. *Masquerade Politics: Explorations in the Structure of Urban Cultural Movements*. Berkeley: University of California Press.

Collier, Jane F., Bill Maurer, and Liliana Suárez-Navaz. 1995. Sanctioned Identities: Legal Constructions of Modern Personhood. *Identities: Global Studies in Culture and Power* 2 (1–2):1–27.

Conklin, Beth A. 1997. Body Paint, Feathers, and VCRs: Aesthetics and Authenticity in Amazonian Activism. *American Ethnologist* 24 (4):711–37.

————. 2002. Shamans versus Pirates in the Amazonian Treasure Chest. *American Anthropologist* 104 (4):1050–61.

Conley, John M., and William M. O'Barr. 1990. *Rules versus Relationships: The Ethnography of Legal Discourse*. Chicago: University of Chicago Press.

Connerton, Paul. 1989. *How Societies Remember*. Cambridge: Cambridge University Press.

Conrad, Robert Edgar. 1983. *Children of God's Fire: A Documentary History of Black Slavery in Brazil*. Princeton, N.J.: Princeton University Press.

Costa, J. Roberto, ed. 1926. *Ao Coronel João Fernandes de Britto: Justa Homenagem de Apreço de seus Amigos e Admiradores*. Propriá: n.p.

Coutin, Susan Bibler. 2000. *Legalizing Moves: Salvadoran Immigrants' Struggle for U.S. Residency*. Ann Arbor: University of Michigan Press.

Creed, Gerald W. 2004. Constituted through Conflict: Images of Community (and Nation) in Bulgarian Rural Ritual. *American Anthropologist* 106 (1):56–70.

————. 2006. *The Seductions of Community: Emancipations, Oppressions, Quandaries*. Santa Fe: School of American Research.

Cunha, Euclides da. 1944 (1902). *Rebellion in the Backlands (Os Sertões)*, trans. S. Putnam. Chicago: University of Chicago Press.

D'Acelino, Severo. 1999. *Memorial do Curso: Resgate da Memória Cultural do Mocambo*. Aracaju: Secretaria Estadual da Educação, Desporto e Lazer.

Dallari, Dalmo de Abreu. 1994. Argumento Antropológico e Linguagem Jurídica. In *A Perícia Antropológica em Processos Judiciais*, ed. O. S. Silva, L. Luz, and C. M. Helm. Florianópolis: Editora da UFSC.

Dantas, Beatriz G. 1991. Os Índios em Sergipe. In *Textos para a História de Sergipe*, ed. D. M. d. F. Diniz. Aracaju: UFS/Banese.

Dantas, Beatriz Góis, and Dalmo de Abreu Dallari. 1980. *Terra dos Índios Xocó*. São Paulo: Comissão Pró-Índio.

Dantas, José Ibarê Costa. 1997. *A Tutela Militar em Sergipe, 1964/1984*. Rio de Janeiro: Tempo Brasileiro.

Darian-Smith, Eve. 1999. *Bridging Divides: The Channel Tunnel and English Legal Identity in the New Europe.* Berkeley: University of California Press.

Dassin, Joan, ed. 1986. *Torture in Brazil: A Report by the Archdiocese of São Paulo.* New York: Vintage Books.

De Kadt, Emanuel Jehuda (and Royal Institute of International Affairs). 1970. *Catholic Radicals in Brazil.* New York: Oxford University Press.

Della Cava, Ralph. 1970. *Miracle at Joaseiro.* New York: Columbia University Press.

Domínguez, Virginia R. 1986. *White by Definition.* New Brunswick, N.J.: Rutgers University Press.

Duneier, Mitchell. 2000. Race and Peeing on Sixth Avenue. In *Racing Research, Researching Race: Methodological Dilemmas in Critical Race Studies*, ed. F. W. Twine and J. W. Warren. New York: New York University Press.

Engel, David M., and Frank W. Munger. 1996. Rights, Remembrances, and the Reconciliation of Difference. *Law & Society Review* 30 (1):7–54.

———. 2003. *Rights of Inclusion: Law and Identity in the Life Stories of Americans with Disabilities.* Chicago Series in Law and Society. Chicago: University of Chicago Press.

Fabian, Johannes. 1999. Remembering the Other: Knowledge and Recognition in the Exploration of Central Africa. *Critical Inquiry* 26:49–69.

Faoro, Raimundo. 1993. *Os Donos do Poder: Formação do Patronato Político Brasileiro.* 9th ed. São Paulo: Ed. Globo.

Fentress, James, and Chris Wickham. 1992. *Social Memory.* Oxford: Blackwell.

Ferguson, James, and Akhil Gupta. 2002. Spatializing States: Toward an Ethnography of Neoliberal Governmentality. *American Ethnologist* 29 (4):981–1002.

Fernandes, Bernardo Mançano. 1999. *MST: Formação e Territorialização em São Paulo.* 2nd ed. *Geografia: Teoria e Realidade* 37. São Paulo: Hucitec.

———. 2000. *A Formação do MST no Brasil.* Petrópolis: Vozes.

Fernandes, Floriza Maria Sena. 1997. Catolicismo Popular no Sertão. *Cadernos UFS: História, Canudos 100 Anos* 3 (4):69–78.

Ferreira, Vera, and Antonio Amaury. 1999. *De Virgolino a Lampião.* São Paulo: Ideia Visual.

Field, Les W. 2002. Blood and Traits: Preliminary Observations on the Analysis of Mestizo and Indigenous Identities in Latin America vs. the U.S. *Journal of Latin American Anthropology* 7 (1):2–33.

Fields, Barbara J. 1982. Ideology and Race in American History. In *Region, Race, and Reconstruction*, ed. M. Kousser. New York: Oxford University Press.

Fitzpatrick, Peter. 1997. Distant Relations: The New Constructionism in Critical and Socio-Legal Studies. In *Socio-Legal Studies*, ed. P. A. Thomas. Brookfield, Vt.: Dartmouth.

Forman, Shepard, and Joyce F. Riegelhaupt. 1979. The Political Economy of Patron-Clientship: Brazil and Portugal Compared. In *Brazil: Anthropological Perspectives, Essays in Honor of Charles Wagley*, ed. M. L. Margolis and W. E. Carter. New York: Columbia University Press.

Foster, George M. 1965. Peasant Society and the Image of Limited Good. *American Anthropologist* 67 (2):293–315.

Foucault, Michel. 1991. Governmentality. In *The Foucault Effect: Studies in Governmentality*, ed. G. Burchell. Chicago: University of Chicago Press.

Franco, Maria Sylvia de Carvalho. 1997. *Homens Livres na Ordem Escravocrata*. 4th ed. São Paulo: Editora UNESP.

Frank, Andre Gunder. 1967. *Capitalism and Underdevelopment in Latin America: Historical Studies of Chile and Brazil*. New York: Monthly Review Press.

Fraser, Nancy. 1998. Social Justice in the Age of Identity Politics: Redistribution, Recognition, and Participation. In *The Tanner Lectures on Human Values*, ed. G. B. Peterson. Salt Lake City: University of Utah Press.

———. 2000. Rethinking Recognition. *New Left Review* 3:107–20.

French, Jan Hoffman. 2002. Dancing for Land: Law-Making and Cultural Performance in Northeastern Brazil. *Political and Legal Anthropology Review* 25 (1):19–36.

———. 2004. Mestizaje and Law Making in Indigenous Identity Formation in Northeastern Brazil: "After the Conflict Came the History." *American Anthropologist* 106 (4):663–74.

———. 2007. A Tale of Two Priests and Two Struggles: Liberation Theology from Dictatorship to Democracy in the Brazilian Northeast. *Americas* 63 (3):409–43.

Freyre, Gilberto. 1986. *The Masters and the Slaves: A Study in the Development of Brazilian Civilization*. 2nd English language rev. ed. Berkeley: University of California Press.

Fuoss, Kirk W., and Randall T. G. Hill. 2001. Spectacular Imaginings: Performing Community in Guatemala. In *Global Multiculturalism: Comparative Perspectives on Ethnicity, Race, and Nation*, ed. G. H. Cornwell and E. W. Stoddard. Lanham, Md.: Rowman & Littlefield.

Gadamer, Hans Georg. 1975. *Truth and Method*. New York: Seabury Press.

Garcia, Maria Elena. 2005. *Making Indigenous Citizens: Identities, Education, and Multicultural Development in Peru*. Stanford, Calif.: Stanford University Press.

Gardner, George. 1841. *Viagens no Brasil*. São Paulo: Ed. Nacional.

Garfield, Seth. 2000. Where the Earth Touches the Sky: The Xavante Indians' Struggle for Land in Brazil, 1951–1979. *Hispanic American Historical Review* 80 (3):537–63.

———. 2001. *Indigenous Struggle at the Heart of Brazil: State Policy, Frontier Expansion, and the Xavante Indians, 1937–1988*. Durham: Duke University Press.

Garroutte, Eva Marie. 2003. *Real Indians: Identity and the Survival of Native America*. Berkeley: University of California Press.

Gaspari, Elio. 2003. *A Ditadura Derrotada*. São Paulo: Companhia das Letras.

Geertz, Clifford. 1983. Local Knowledge: Fact and Law in Comparative Perspective. In *Local Knowledge: Further Essays in Interpretive Anthropology*, ed. C. Geertz. New York: Basic Books.

Geipel, John. 1997. Brazil's African Legacy. *History Today* 47 (8):18–24.

Godreau, Isar P. 2002. Changing Space, Making Race: Distance, Nostalgia, and the

Folklorization of Blackness in Puerto Rico. *Identities: Global Studies in Culture and Power* 9:281–304.

Goldberg, David Theo. 2002. *The Racial State*. Malden, Mass.: Blackwell.

Gomes, Mércio Pereira. 2000. *The Indians and Brazil*, trans. J. W. Moon. Gainesville: University Press of Florida. Original ed., 1988, 1991 (in Portuguese).

Gomez, Michael Angelo. 2005. *Reversing Sail: A History of the African Diaspora*. New Approaches to African History. New York: Cambridge University Press.

Gooding-Williams, Robert. 2001. Race, Multiculturalism and Democracy. In *Race*, ed. R. Bernasconi. Malden, Mass.: Blackwell.

Gordon, Colin. 1991. Governmental Rationality: An Introduction. In *The Foucault Effect: Studies in Governmentality*, ed. G. Burchell, C. Gordon, and P. Miller. Chicago: University of Chicago Press.

Gordon, Edmund T., Galio C. Gurdián, and Charles R. Hale. 2003. Rights, Resources, and the Social Memory of Struggle: Reflections on a Study of Indigenous and Black Community Land Rights on Nicaragua's Atlantic Coast. *Human Organization* 62 (4):369–81.

Gould, Jeffrey L. 1998. *To Die in This Way: Nicaraguan Indians and the Myth of Mestizaje, 1880–1965*. Durham, N.C.: Duke University Press.

Graham, Laura R. 2005. Image and Instrumentality in a Xavante Politics of Existential Recognition: The Public Outreach Work of Eténhiritipa Pimentel Barbosa. *American Ethnologist* 32 (4).

Greene, Shane, issue ed. 2007. "Entre 'Lo Indio' y 'Lo Negro': Interrogating the Effects of Latin America's New Afro-Indigenous Multiculturalisms," *Journal of Latin American and Caribbean Anthropology* 12 (2).

Greenhouse, Carol J., and Davydd J. Greenwood. 1998. Introduction: The Ethnography of Democracy and Difference. In *Democracy and Ethnography: Constructing Identities in Multicultural Liberal States*, ed. C. J. Greenhouse. Albany: State University of New York Press.

Greenhouse, Carol J., Barbara Yngvesson, and David M. Engel. 1994. *Law and Community in Three American Towns*. Ithaca: Cornell University Press.

Grinberg, Keila. 1994. *Liberata: A Lei da Ambigüidade*. Rio de Janeiro: Relume Dumará.

Gross, Ariela Julie. 2007. "Of Portuguese Origin": Litigating Identity and Citizenship among the "Little Races" in Nineteenth Century America. *Law and History Review* 25 (3):467–512.

Grünewald, Rodrigo de Azeredo. 2004. As Múltiplas Incertezas do Toré. In *Toré: Regime Encantado dos Índios do Nordeste*, ed. R. d. A. Grünewald. Recife: Fundação Joaquim Nabuco/Editora Massangana.

Gueiros, Optato. 1956. *Lampeão: Memórias de um Oficial Ex-comandante de Forças Volantes*. 4th ed. Salvador, Bahia: Livraria Progresso Editora.

Guimarães, Antônio Sérgio Alfredo. 1999. *Racismo e Anti Racismo no Brasil*. São Paulo: Editora 34.

Guinier, Lani, and Gerald Torres. 2002. *The Miner's Canary: Enlisting Race, Resisting Power, Transforming Democracy*. Cambridge: Harvard University Press.

Gusmão, Neusa Maria Mendes de. 1996. Da Antropologia e do Direito: Impasses da Questão Negra no Campo. *Palmares em Revista* (1):1–13.

Guss, David M. 2000. *The Festive State: Race, Ethnicity, and Nationalism as Cultural Performance*. Berkeley: University of California Press.

Gutierrez, Gustavo. 1975 (1971 in Spanish). *Teologia da Libertação*. Petrópolis: Vozes.

Hale, Charles R. 2002. Does Multiculturalism Menace? Governance, Cultural Rights and the Politics of Identity in Guatemala. *Journal of Latin American Studies* 34:485–524.

———. 2004. Rethinking Indigenous Politics in the Era of the "Indio Permitido." *NACLA Report on the Americas* 38 (2):16–20.

———. 2006. *Más Que Un Indio (More Than an Indian): Racial Ambivalence and the Paradox of Neoliberal Multiculturalism in Guatemala*. Santa Fe: SAR Press.

Hall, Stuart. 1991. Old and New Identities, Old and New Ethnicities. In *Culture, Globalization and the World System: Contemporary Conditions for the Representation of Identity*, ed. A. D. King. New York: Macmillan.

Hanchard, Michael George. 1994. *Orpheus and Power: The Movimento Negro of Rio de Janeiro and São Paulo, Brazil, 1945–1988*. Princeton, N.J.: Princeton University Press.

———. 2000. Racism, Eroticism, and the Paradoxes of a U.S. Black Researcher in Brazil. In *Racing Research, Researching Race: Methodological Dilemmas in Critical Race Studies*, ed. F. W. Twine and J. W. Warren. New York: New York University Press.

Haney-López, Ian. 1996. *White by Law: The Legal Constructions of Race*. New York: New York University Press.

Harris, Marvin. 1956. *Town and Country in Brazil*. New York: Columbia University Press.

Harvey, David. 2000. Cosmopolitanism and the Banality of Geographical Evils. *Public Culture* 12:529–64.

Hemming, John. 2003. *Die If You Must: Brazilian Indians in the Twentieth Century*. London: Macmillan.

Herkenboff, Paulo, ed. 1999. *O Brasil e Os Holandeses*: Sextante Artes.

Hernandez, Tanya Kateri. 2002. Multiracial Matrix: The Role of Race Ideology in the Enforcement of Antidiscrimination Laws, A United States–Latin America Comparison. *Cornell Law Review* 87:1093.

Hill, Jonathan David. 1988. Introduction: Myth and History. In *Rethinking History and Myth: Indigenous South American Perspectives on the Past*, ed. J. D. Hill. Urbana: University of Illinois Press.

Hirschman, Albert O. 1963. *Journeys toward Progress: Studies of Economic Policy-Making in Latin America*. New York: Twentieth Century Fund.

Hobsbawm, E. J. 1969. *Bandits*. New York: Delacorte Press.

Hobsbawm, E. J., and T. O. Ranger, eds. 1983. *The Invention of Tradition*. New York: Cambridge University Press.

Hodgson, Dorothy L. 2002. Introduction: Comparative Perspectives on the Indigenous Rights Movement in Africa and the Americas. *American Anthropologist* 104 (4):1037–49.

Hoffmann, Odile. 2002. Collective Memory and Ethnic Identities in the Colombian Pacific. *Journal of Latin American Anthropology* 7 (2):118–39.

Hohenthal, W. D., Jr. 1960a. As Tribos Indígenas do Média e Baixo São Francisco. *Revista do Museu Paulista*, Nova Série, 12:37–71.

————. 1960b. The General Characteristics of Indian Cultures in the Rio São Francisco Valley. *Revista do Museu Paulista*, Nova Série, 12:73–86.

Hooker, Juliet. 2005. Indigenous Inclusion/Black Exclusion: Race, Ethnicity and Multicultural Citizenship in Latin America. *Journal of Latin American Studies* 37 (2):285–310.

Houtzager, Peter P. 2001. Collective Action and Political Authority: Rural Workers, Church, and State in Brazil. *Theory and Society* 30:1–45.

Hunt, Alan. 1985. The Ideology of Law: Advances and Problems in Recent Applications of the Concept of Ideology to the Analysis of Law. *Law and Society Review* 19 (1):11–37.

Jackson, Jean. 1995. Culture, Genuine and Spurious: The Politics of Indianness in the Vaupés, Colombia. *American Ethnologist* 22:3–27.

Jackson, John L. 2001. *Harlemworld: Doing Race and Class in Contemporary Black America*. Chicago: University of Chicago Press.

Jacob, Cesar Romero, Dora Rodrigues Hees, Philippe Waniez, and Violette Brustlein. 2003. *Atlas da Filiação Religiosa e Indicadores Sociais no Brasil*. São Paulo: Editora PUC.

Johnson, Allen W. 1971. *Sharecroppers of the Sertão: Economics and Dependence on a Brazilian Plantation*. Stanford, Calif.: Stanford University Press.

Johnson, E. Patrick. 2002. Performing Blackness Down Under: The Cafe of the Gate of Salvation. *Text and Performance Quarterly* 22 (2):99–119.

Jolivétte, Andrew J. 2007. *Louisiana Creoles: Cultural Recovery and Mixed-Race Native American Identity*. Lanham, Md.: Rowman and Littlefield.

Joseph, Gilbert M. 1990. On the Trail of Latin American Bandits: A Reexamination of Peasant Resistance. *Latin American Research Review* 25 (3):7–52.

Julião, Francisco. 1972. *Cambao—The Yoke: The Hidden Face of Brazil*. Middlesex, England: Penguin.

Kant de Lima, Roberto. 1995. Bureaucratic Rationality in Brazil and in the United States: Criminal Justice Systems in Comparative Perspective. In *The Brazilian Puzzle*, ed. D. J. Hess and R. A. DaMatta. New York: Columbia University Press.

Katz, William Loren. 1986. *Black Indians: A Hidden Heritage*. New York: Atheneum.

————. 2003. Letter to the Editor. *New York Times*, September 19, 2003, A22.

Kay, Cristóbal. 2002. Agrarian Reform and the Neoliberal Counter-Reform in Latin America. In *The Spaces of Neoliberalism: Land, Place and Family in Latin America*, ed. J. Chase. Bloomfield, Ct.: Kumarian Press.

Kent, R. K. 1965. Palmares: An African State in Brazil. *Journal of Negro History* 6:161–75.

Klein, Herbert. 1986. *African Slavery in Latin America and the Caribbean*. New York: Oxford University Press.

Kuper, Adam. 2005. *The Reinvention of Primitive Society: Transformations of a Myth*. 2nd ed. New York: Routledge.

Laclau, Ernesto. 1996. *Emancipation(s)*. New York: Verso.

Leal, Victor Nunes. 1977. *Coronelismo: The Municipality and Representative Government in Brazil*, trans. J. Henfrey. Cambridge: Cambridge University Press.

Leeds, Anthony. 1964. Brazil and the Myth of Francisco Julião. In *Politics of Change in Latin America*, ed. J. Maier and R. Weatherhead. New York: Praeger.

Leitão, Sérgio. 1999. *Direitos Territoriais das Comunidades Negras Rurais*. São Paulo: Instituto Socioambiental.

Lessa, Orígenes. 1973. *Getúlio Vargas na Literatura de Cordel*. Rio de Janeiro: Editora Documentário.

LeVine, Robert A. 1984. Properties of Culture: An Ethnographic View. In *Culture Theory: Essays on Mind, Self, and Emotion*, ed. R. A. Shweder and R. A. LeVine. New York: Cambridge University Press.

Levine, Robert M. 1992. *Vale of Tears: Revisiting the Canudos Massacre in Northeastern Brazil, 1893–1897*. Berkeley: University of California Press.

Lewin, Linda. 1987. *Politics and Parentela in Paraíba: A Case Study of Family-Based Oligarchy in Brazil*. Princeton, N.J.: Princeton University Press.

———. 1996. Who Was "o Grande Romano?" Genealogical Purity, the Indian "Past," and Whiteness in Brazil's Northeast Backlands, 1750–1900. *Journal of Latin American Lore* 19:129–79.

Li, Tania Murray. 2000. Articulating Indigenous Identity in Indonesia: Resource Politics and the Tribal Slot. *Comparative Studies in Society and History* 42 (1):149–79.

———. 2001. Masyarakat Adat, Difference, and the Limits of Recognition in Indonesia's Forest Zone. *Modern Asian Studies* 35 (2):645–76.

Lima, Antonio Carlos de Souza. 2000. L'Indigènisme au Brèsil Migration et Réappropriations D'un Savoir Adiminstratif. *Revue de Synthèse* 4 (3–4):381–410.

———. 2005. Indigenism in Brazil: The International Migration of State Policies. In *Empires, Nations, and Natives: Anthropology and State-Making*, ed. B. d. L'Estoile, F. G. Neiburg, and L. Sigaud. Durham: Duke University Press.

Lima, Nísia Trindade. 1999. *Um Sertão Chamado Brasil: Intelectuais e Representação Geográfica da Identidade Nacional*. Rio de Janeiro: Editora Revan.

Linhares, Luiz Fernando do Rosário. 2004. Kilombos of Brazil: Identity and Land Entitlement. *Journal of Black Studies* 34 (6):817–37.

Lira, J. G. 1990. *Lampião: Memória de um Soldado de Volante*. Recife: FUNDARPE.

Löwy, Michael. 1996. *The War of Gods: Religion and Politics in Latin America*. Critical Studies in Latin American and Iberian Cultures. New York: Verso.

Magno da Silva, Rosemiro. 1995. *Assentamento de Pequenos Produtores Rurais em Sergipe*. Aracaju: Governo de Sergipe.

———. 2000. *A Luta dos Posseiros de Santana dos Frades*. Aracaju: Editora UFS.

Magno da Silva, Rosemiro, and Eliano Sérgio Azevedo Lopes. 1996. *Conflitos de Terra e Reforma Agrária em Sergipe*. São Cristovão, Sergipe: Editora UFS.

Mainardi, Diogo. 2008. O Quilombo do Mundo. *Veja*, April 23, 2008.

Mainwaring, Scott. 1986. *The Catholic Church and Politics in Brazil, 1916–1985*. Stanford, Calif.: Stanford University Press.

Malkki, Liisa H. 1995. *Purity and Exile: Violence, Memory, and National Cosmology among Hutu Refugees in Tanzania*. Chicago: University of Chicago Press.

Marques, Núbia N. 1999. *O Luso, O Lúdico e o Perene*. Rio de Janeiro: Imago.

Martins, José de Souza. 1985. A Igreja Face à Política Agrária do Estado. In *Igreja e Questão Agrária*, ed. V. Paiva. São Paulo: Edições Loyola.

Mata, Vera Lúcia Calheiros. 1989. A Semente da Terra: Identidade e Conquista Territorial por um Grupo Indígena Integrado. Ph.D. diss., Universidade Federal do Rio de Janeiro.

Maurer, Bill. 1995. Orderly Families for the New Economic Order: Belonging and Citizenship in the British Virgin Islands. *Identities: Global Studies in Culture and Power* 2 (1–2):149–72.

Maybury-Lewis, Biorn. 1994. *The Politics of the Possible: The Brazilian Rural Workers' Trade Union Movement, 1964–1985*. Philadelphia: Temple University Press.

Maybury-Lewis, David. 2002. *Indigenous Peoples, Ethnic Groups, and the State*. 2nd ed. Boston: Allyn and Bacon.

Melatti, Delvair Montagner. 1979. Relatório de Viagem aos Xokós da Ilha de São Pedro. Brasília: FUNAI.

———. 1985. Os Sofridos Xokó da Ilha de São Pedro. Brasília: FUNAI.

Melo, Floro de Araújo. 1982. *O Folclore Nordestino em Suas Mãos (Síntese de Toda Uma Região)*. 1st ed. Rio de Janeiro: n.p.

Mendoza, Zoila S. 2000. *Shaping Society through Dance: Mestizo Ritual Performance in the Peruvian Andes*. Chicago: University of Chicago Press.

Menezes, Octavio. 1952. *Album Fotográfico e Comercial de Propriá*. Propriá: Impressora Guarani.

Merry, Sally Engle. 1990. *Getting Justice and Getting Even: Legal Consciousness among Working-Class Americans*. Chicago: University of Chicago Press.

———. 2000. *Colonizing Hawai'i: The Cultural Power of Law*. Princeton Studies in Culture/Power/History. Princeton, N.J.: Princeton University Press.

Montero, Paula. 1996. *Entre o Mito e a História: O V Centenário do Descobrimento da América*. Petrópolis: Vozes.

Mooney, Carolyn J. 1998. Anthropologists Shed Light on Jungle Communities Founded by Fugitive Slaves. *Chronicle of Higher Education*, May 22, 1998, B2.

Moore, Sally Falk. 1986. *Social Facts and Fabrications: "Customary" Law on Kilimanjaro, 1880–1980*. Cambridge: Cambridge University Press.

Moore, Sally Falk, and Barbara G. Myerhoff. 1977. Introduction. In *Secular Ritual*, ed. S. F. Moore and B. G. Myerhoff. Amsterdam: Van Gorcum.

Mota, Clarice Novaes da. 1997. *Jurema's Children in the Forest of Spirits: Healing and Ritual among two Brazilian Indigenous Groups*. IT Studies in Indigenous Knowledge and Development. London: Intermediate Technology Publications.

Mota, Clarice Novaes da, and Ulysses Paulino de Albuquerque. 2002. *As Muitas Faces da Jurema de Espécie Botânica à Divindade Afro-Indígena*. Recife: Edições Bagaço.

Moura, Clóvis. 1981. *Os Quilombos e a Rebelião Negra*. Vol. 12 of *Tudo é História*. São Paulo: Brasiliense.

Nancy, Jean-Luc. 1991. *The Inoperative Community*. Minneapolis: University of Minnesota Press.

Nascimento, Abdias do. 1980. *O Quilombismo: Documentos de uma Militância Pan-africanista*. Petrópolis: Vozes.

Niezen, Ronald. 2003. *The Origins of Indigenism: Human Rights and the Politics of Identity*. Berkeley: University of California Press.

Nobles, Melissa. 2000. *Shades of Citizenship: Race and the Census in Modern Politics*. Stanford, Calif.: Stanford University Press.

NUER. 1997. *Regulamentação de Terras de Negros no Brasil*, ed. N. d. Estu. 2nd ed. Vol. 1 of *Boletim Informativodos sobre Identidade e REalções Interétnicas/Fundação Cultural Palmares*. Florianópolis: UFSC.

Oakdale, Suzanne. 2004. The Culture-Conscious Brazilian Indian: Representing and Reworking Indianness in Kayabi Political Discourse. *American Ethnologist* 31 (1):60–75.

O'Dwyer, Eliane Cantarino. 1993. Remanescentes de Quilombos na Fronteira Amazônica: A Etnicidade como Instrumento de Luta pela Terra. *Revista da Associação Brasileira de Reforma Agrária (ABRA)* 3 (3):26–38.

Oliveira Filho, João Pacheco de. 1993. *Atlas das Terras Indígenas do Nordeste*. Projeto Estudo sobre Terras Indígenas no Brasil. Rio de Janeiro: Museu Nacional/UFRJ.

————. 1997. Pardos, Mestiços ou Caboclos: Os Índios nos Censos Nacionais (1872–1980). *Horizontes Antropológicos* (UFRGS) 7.

————. 1999a. Uma Etnologia dos "Índios Misturados": Situação Colonial, Territorialização e Fluxos Culturais. In *A Viagem da Volta: Etnicidade, Política e Reelaboração Cultural no Nordeste Indígena*, ed. J. P. d. Oliveira. Rio de Janeiro: Contra Capa Livraria.

————, ed. 1999b. *A Viagem da Volta: Etnicidade, Política e Reelaboração Cultural no Nordeste Indígena*, ed. J. P. d. Oliveira. Rio de Janeiro: Contra Capa Livraria.

————. 2000. Entering and Leaving the "Melting Pot": A History of Brazilian Indians in the National Censuses. *Journal of Latin American Anthropology* 5(1):190–211.

————. 2005. The Anthropologist as Expert: Brazilian Ethnology between Indianism and Indigenism. In *Empires, Nations, and Natives: Anthropology and State-Making*, ed. B. d. L'Estoile, F. G. Neiburg, and L. Sigaud. Durham: Duke University Press.

Oliveira Filho, João Pacheco de, and Alfredo Wagner Berno de Almeida. 1998. *Indigenismo e territorialização: Poderes, rotinas e saberes coloniais no Brasil contemporâneo, Coleção Territórios sociais*. Rio de Janeiro: Contra Capa.

Oliveira, Manoel Rodriguez de. 1979. Fornecimento de Relação de Associados. Porto da Folha, Sergipe, June 25, 1979.

Oliveira, Neilza Barreto de, and Centro Dom José Brandão de Castro. 1999. *Sindicato de Trabalhador Rural: Nosso (Des)Conhecido*. Aracaju: CDJBC.

Oliveira, Silviene, Henry-Philippe de Novion, Elsa Coelho, and Nazaré Klautau-Guimarães. 2000. Análise de Sobrenome e Haplótipo XV-2C/KM-19 em Mocambo (Sergipe-Brasil). Paper read at 6th Congress of Latin American

Association of Biological Anthropology, October 23–27, 2000, Piriápolis, Uruguay.

Page, Joseph A. 1972. *The Revolution That Never Was: Northeast Brazil, 1955–1964*. New York: Grossman.

Pallares, Amalia. 2002. *From Peasant Struggles to Indian Resistance*. Norman: University of Oklahoma Press.

Pang, Eul-Soo. 1974. The Changing Roles of Priests in the Politics of Northeast Brazil, 1889–1964. *Americas* 30 (3):341–72.

Paoli, Maria Celia. 1992. Citizenship, Inequalities, Democracy and Rights: The Making of a Public Space in Brazil. *Social and Legal Studies* 1:143–59.

Pavlich, George. 1996. The Power of Community Mediation: Government and Formation of Self-Identity. *Law & Society Review* 30 (4):707–33.

Pedro II, Dom. 1959. *Diário da viagem ao norte do Brasil*. Salvador: Progresso Editora.

Peixoto, Fernanda Arêas. 2000. *Diálogos Brasileiros: Uma Análise da Obra de Roger Bastide*. São Paulo: Editora da Universidade de São Paulo.

Pereira, Anthony W. 1997. *The End of the Peasantry: The Rural Labor Movement in Northeast Brazil, 1961–1988*. Pitt Latin American Series. Pittsburgh: University of Pittsburgh Press.

Pereira, Edimilson de Almeida, and Steven F. White. 2001. Brazil: Interactions and Conflicts in a Multicultural Society. In *Global Multiculturalism: Comparative Perspectives on Ethnicity, Race, and Nation*, ed. G. H. Cornwell and E. W. Stoddard. Lanham, Md.: Rowman & Littlefield.

Pereira, Edmundo. 2004. Benditos, Toantes e Samba de Coco. In *Toré: Regime Encantado dos Índios do Nordeste*, ed. R. d. A. Grünewald. Recife: Fundação Joaquim Nabuco/Editora Massangana.

Pernambucano de Mello, Frederico. 2001. The Aesthetics of the Cangaço as an Expression of Brazilian Libertarianism. In *Heroes and Artists: Popular Art and the Brazilian Imagination*, ed. T. C. Tribe. Cambridge, England: BrasilConnects and Fitzwilliams Museum.

Perz, Stephen G., Jonathan Warren, and David P. Kennedy. 2008. Contributions of Racial-Ethnic Reclassification and Demographic Processes to Indigenous Population Resurgence: The Case of Brazil. *Latin American Research Review* 43 (2):7–33.

Pierson, Donald. 1972. *O Homem no Vale do São Francisco*. 3 vols. Rio de Janeiro: Ministério do Interior, Superintendência do Vale do São Francisco (SUVALE).

Piletti, Nelson, and Walter Praxedes. 1997. *Dom Hélder Câmara: Entre o Poder e a Profecia*. São Paulo: Editora Ática.

Pineda, Baron L. 2001. Creole Neighborhood or Miskito Community? A Case Study of Identity Politics in a Mosquito Coast Land Dispute. *Journal of Latin American Anthropology* 6 (1):120–55.

Pinto, Clélia Moreira. 2002. A Jurema Sagrada. In *As Muitas Faces da Jurema de Espécie Botânica à Divindade Afro-Indigena*, ed. C. N. d. Mota and U. P. d. Albuquerque. Recife: Edições Bagaço.

Pompa, Cristina. 2003. *Religião como Tradução: Missionários, Tupi e Tapuia no Brasil Colonial*. Bauru, Brazil: EDUSC: ANPOCS.

Postero, N. G., and L. Zamosc, ed. 2004. *The Struggle for Indigenous Rights in Latin America*. Portland, Ore.: Sussex Academic Press.

Queiroz, Maria Isaura Pereira de. 1973. *Bairros Rurais Paulistas: Dinâmica das Relações Bairro Rural-Cidade*. 2nd ed. São Paulo: Livraria Duas Cidades.

———. 1976. *O Campesinato Brasileiro: Ensaios sobre Civilização e Grupos Rústicos no Brasil*. 2nd ed. Petrópolis, Brazil: Editora Vozes Ltda.

Racusen, Seth. 2009 (forthcoming). Identity and Brazilian Affirmative Action. *National Black Law Journal*.

Ramos, Alcida Rita. 1991. A Hall of Mirrors: The Rhetoric of Indigenism in Brazil. *Critique of Anthropology* 11 (2):155–69.

———. 1998. *Indigenism: Ethnic Politics in Brazil*. Madison: University of Wisconsin Press.

———. 2003. Pulp Fictions of Indigenism. In *Race, Nature, and the Politics of Difference*, ed. D. S. Moore, J. Kosek, and A. Pandian. Durham: Duke University Press.

Ramos, Graciliano. 1947. *Vidas Sêcas, Romance*. Rio de Janeiro: J. Olympio.

Ranger, Terence. 1994. The Invention of Tradition Revisited: The Case of Colonial Africa. In *Inventions and Boundaries: Historical and Anthropological Approaches to the Study of Ethnicity and Nationalism*, ed. P. Kaarsholm and J. Hultin. Roskilde, Denmark: Roskilde University.

Reesink, E. B. 1981. *The Peasant in the Sertão: A Short Exploration of His Past and Present*. ICA Publication No. 47. Leiden: Institute of Cultural and Social Studies, Leiden University, Netherlands.

Rick, Hildegart Maria de Castro. 1979. Considerações Antropológicas sobre a Presença Indígena na Ilha de São Pedro-Sergipe. Brasília: FUNAI.

Rivera Ramos, Efrén. 2001. *The Legal Construction of Identity: The Judicial and Social Legacy of American Colonialism in Puerto Rico*. 1st ed. Washington, D.C.: American Psychological Association.

Rockefeller, Stuart Alexander. 1998. "There Is a Culture Here": Spectacle and the Inculcation of Folklore in Highland Bolivia. *Journal of Latin American Anthropology* 3 (2):118–49.

Romero, Sãlvio, and Luís da Câmara Cascudo. 1954. Folclore Brasileiro. *Coleão Documentos Brasileiros*, vol. 75–75B. Rio de Janeiro: Olympio.

Rose, Nikolas, Pat O'Malley, and Mariana Valverde. 2006. Governmentality. *Annual Review of Law and Social Science* 2:83–104.

Sá, Antônio Fernando de Araújo. 1997. Canudos Plural: Memórias em Confronto nas Comemorações dos Centenários de Canudos (1993–1997). Paper read at Seminário Nacional "O Sertão Vai Virar Praia: Revisão Historiográfica do Centenário de Canudos," June 5–6, 1997, Universidade de Brasília.

Safa, Helen. 2005. Challenging Mestizaje: A Gender Perspective on Indigenous and Afrodescendant Movements in Latin America. *Critique of Anthropology* 25 (3):307–30.

Sahlins, Marshall. 1999. Two or Three Things That I Know about Culture. *Journal of the Royal Anthropological Institute* 5 (3):399–421.

Saillant, Francine, and Louis Forline. 2001. Memória Fugitiva, Identidade Flexível: Caboclos na Amazônia. In *Devorando o Tempo: Brasil, o País sem Memória*, ed. A. Leibing and S. Benninghoff-Lühl. São Paulo: Editora Mandarim.

Sampaio Silva, Orlando, Lídia Luz, and Cecília Maria Helm, eds. 1994. *A Perícia Antropológica em Processos Judiciais*. Florianópolis, Brazil: Editora da UFSC.

Sansone, Livio. 2003. *Blackness without Ethnicity: Constructing Race in Brazil*. New York: Palgrave Macmillan.

Santner, Eric L. 2001. *On the Psychotheology of Everyday Life: Reflections on Freud and Rosenzweig*. Chicago: University of Chicago Press.

Sarat, Austin. 1990. "The Law Is All Over": Power, Resistance and the Legal Consciousness of the Welfare Poor. *Yale Journal of Law & the Humanities* 2:343–79.

Sarat, Austin, and Thomas R. Kearns. 1993. Beyond the Great Divide: Forms of Legal Scholarship and Everyday Life. In *Law in Everyday Life*, ed. A. Sarat and T. R. Kearns. Ann Arbor: University of Michigan Press.

Schechner, Richard. 1988. *Performance Theory*. New York: Routledge.

Schwartz, Stuart B. 1985. *Sugar Plantations in the Formation of Brazilian Society: Bahia, 1550–1835*. Cambridge: Cambridge University Press.

———. 1992. *Slaves, Peasants, and Rebels: Reconsidering Brazilian Slavery*. Urbana: University of Illinois Press.

Schwartzman, Stephan, Ana Valéria Araújo, and Paulo Pankararú. 1996. Brazil: The Legal Battle Over Indigenous Rights. *NACLA Report on the Americas* 29 (5):36–43.

Scott, James C. 1985. *Weapons of the Weak: Everyday Forms of Peasant Resistance*. New Haven: Yale University Press.

Segato, Rita L. 1998. The Color-Blind Subject of Myth; Or, Where to Find Africa in the Nation. *Annual Review of Anthropology* 27:129–51.

Seixas Dória, João. 1965. *Eu, Réu Sem Crime*. Rio de Janeiro: Editora Codecri.

Serbin, Kenneth. 1992. Os Seminários, Crise, Experiências e Síntese. In *Catolicismo: Modernidade e Tradição*, ed. P. Sanchis. São Paulo: Loyola/ISER.

———. 2000. *Secret Dialogues: Church-State Relations, Torture, and Social Justice in Authoritarian Brazil*. Pittsburgh: University of Pittsburgh Press.

Sheriff, Robin E. 2001. *Dreaming Equality: Color, Race, and Racism in Urban Brazil*. New Brunswick, N.J.: Rutgers University Press.

Shirley, Robert W. 1979. Law in Rural Brazil. In *Brazil: Anthropological Perspectives, Essays in Honor of Charles Wagley*, ed. M. L. Margolis and W. E. Carter. New York: Columbia University Press.

Sider, Gerald M. 1993. *Lumbee Indian Histories: Race, Ethnicity and Indian Identity in the Southern United States*. New York: Cambridge University Press.

Silbey, Susan. 1985. Ideals and Practices in the Study of Law. *Legal Studies Forum* 9:7–22.

Silva, Ligia Maria Osório. 1996. *Terras Devolutas e Latifúndio: Efeitos da Lei de 1850*. Coleção Repertórios. Campinas, Brazil: Editora da Unicamp.

————. 1997. Terra, Direito e Poder: O Latifúndio Improdutivo na Legislação Agrária Brasileira. *Boletim da ABA* 27.

Silverstein, Michael, and Greg Urban. 1996. *Natural Histories of Discourse*. Chicago: University of Chicago Press.

Singh, Priti. 2002. *Governance of Indigenous People in Latin America*. Delhi, India: Authorspress.

Skidmore, Thomas E., and Peter H. Smith. 1992. *Modern Latin America*. 3rd ed. New York: Oxford University Press.

Slater, Candace. 1982. *Stories on a String: The Brazilian Literatura de Cordel*. Berkeley: University of California Press.

Sommer, Doris. 2006. *Cultural Agency in the Americas*. Durham: Duke University Press.

Souto Maior, Laércio. 1985. *São os Nordestinos uma Minoria Racial?* Londrina, Brazil: Livraria Arles Editora.

Souza, Ilda (Sila) Ribeiro de. 1997. *Angicos: Eu Sobrevivi*. São Paulo: Oficina Cultural Monica Buonfiglio.

Souza Lima, Antônio Carlos. 2005. Indigenism in Brazil: The International Migration of State Policies. In *Empires, Nations, and Natives: Anthropology and State-Making*, ed. B. L'Estoile, F. Neiburg, and L. Sigaud. Durham, N.C.: Duke University Press.

Speed, Shannon. 2008. *Rights in Rebellion: Indigenous Struggle and Human Rights in Chiapas*. Stanford, Calif.: Stanford University Press.

Speed, Shannon, and Alvaro Reyes. 2001. "In Our Own Defense": Rights and Resistance in Chiapas. *Political and Legal Anthropology Review* 25 (1):69–89.

Spivak, Gayatri Chakravorty. 1988. Can the Subaltern Speak? In *Marxism and the Interpretation of Culture*, ed. C. Nelson and L. Grossberg. Urbana: University of Illinois Press.

Staples, Brent. 2003. When Racial Discrimination Is Not Just Black and White. *New York Times*, September 12, 2003, A26.

Starr, June, and Jane F. Collier, eds. 1989. *History and Power in the Study of Law: New Directions in Legal Anthropology*. Ithaca: Cornell University Press.

Steil, Carlos Alberto. 1996. *O Sertão das Romarias: Um Estudo Antropológico sobre o Santuário de Bom Jesus da Lapa-Bahia*. Petrópolis, Brazil: Vozes.

————. 1998. Rio das Rãs/Bahia: A Etnicização da Política. *Tempo e Presenço*, Suplemento Especial (March/April 1998):21–23.

Stolzenberg, Nomi Maya. 2000. The Culture of Property. *Daedalus* 129 (4): 169–92.

Strong, Pauline Turner, and Barrik Van Winkle. 1996. "Indian Blood": Reflections on the Reckoning and Refiguring of Native North American Identity. *Cultural Anthropology* 11 (4):547–76.

Sturm, Circe. 2002. *Blood Politics: Race, Culture, and Identity in the Cherokee Nation of Oklahoma*. Berkeley: University of California Press.

Suess, Paulo. 1980. *Em Defesa dos Povos Indígenas: Documentação e Legislação*. São Paulo: Edições Loyola.

Sylvain, Renée. 2005. Disorderly Development: Globalization and the Idea of "Culture" in the Kalahari. *American Ethnologist* 32 (3):354–70.

Taylor, Charles. 1992. The Politics of Recognition. In *Multiculturalism and "The Politics of Recognition": An Essay,* ed. C. Taylor. Princeton, N.J.: Princeton University Press.

Teixeira da Silva, Francisco Carlos. 1999. Conflito de Terras numa Fronteira Antiga: O Sertão do Sao Francisco no Seculo XIX. *Tempo (Revista do Departamento de Historia da Universidade Fluminense)* (7):9–28.

Telles, Edward Eric. 2004. *Race in Another America: The Significance of Skin Color in Brazil.* Princeton, N.J.: Princeton University Press.

Thompson, E. P. 1975. *Whigs and Hunters: The Origin of the Black Act.* New York: Pantheon.

Tribe, Tania Costa. 2001. Popular Culture and the Arts of Twentieth-Century Brazil. In *Heroes and Artists: Popular Art and the Brazilian Imagination,* ed. T. C. Tribe. Cambridge, England: BrasilConnects and Fitzwilliams Museum.

Turner, Terence. 1991. Representing, Resisting, Rethinking: Historical Transformations of Kayapo Culture and Anthropological Consciousness. In *Colonial Situations: Essays on the Contextualization of Ethnographic Knowledge,* ed. G. W. Stocking Jr. Madison: University of Wisconsin Press.

Turner, Victor Witter. 1986. *The Anthropology of Performance.* New York: Performing Arts Journal.

Urban, Greg. 1991. *A Discourse-Centered Approach to Culture: Native South American Myths and Rituals.* 1st ed. Texas Linguistics Series. Austin: University of Texas Press.

———. 2001. *Metaculture: How Culture Moves through the World.* Public Worlds, vol. 8. Minneapolis: University of Minnesota Press.

Valadares, P. 1978. Xokós: Fome e a Morte. *Desacato,* September 1978, 6–7.

Valverde, Mariana. 2003. *Law's Dream of a Common Knowledge.* Cultural Lives of Law. Princeton, N.J.: Princeton University Press.

Van Cott, Donna Lee. 2000. *The Friendly Liquidation of the Past: The Politics of Diversity in Latin America.* Pitt Latin American Series. Pittsburgh: University of Pittsburgh Press.

———. 2005. *From Movements to Parties in Latin America: The Evolution of Ethnic Politics.* New York: Cambridge University Press.

Vargas-Cetina, Gabriela. 2003. Representations of Indigenousness. *Anthropology News* 9.

Véran, Jean-François. 2002. Quilombos and Land Rights in Contemporary Brazil. *Cultural Survival Quarterly* 25 (4):20.

———. 2003. *L'esclavage en Héritage (Brésil): Le Droit à la Terre des Descendants de Marrons.* Paris: Karthala.

Viotti Da Costa, Emília. 2000. *The Brazilian Empire: Myths and Histories.* Rev. ed. Chicago: University of Chicago Press.

Viveiros de Castro, Eduardo. 1999. Etonologia Brasileira. In *O Que Ler na Ciência Social Brasileira (1970–1995): Antropologia,* vol. 1, ed. S. Miceli. São Paulo: Editora Sumaré.

Vlastos, Stephen. 1998. *Mirror of Modernity: Invented Traditions of Modern Japan.* Berkeley: University of California Press.

Vogt, Carlos, and Peter Fry. 1996. *Cafundó: A África no Brasil*. São Paulo: Ed. da Unicamp, Companhia das Letras.

Wade, Peter. 1997. *Race and Ethnicity in Latin America*, ed. J. Pearce. Critical Studies on Latin America. London: Pluto Press.

———. 2002. *Race, Nature and Culture: An Anthropological Perspective*. Anthropology, Culture, and Society. London: Pluto Press.

Warren, Jonathan W. 2001. *Racial Revolutions: Antiracism and Indian Resurgence in Brazil*. Durham: Duke University Press.

———. 2004. Socialist Saudades: Lula's Victory, Indigenous Movements, and the Latin American Left. In *The Struggle for Indigenous Rights in Latin America*, ed. N. G. Postero and L. Zamosc. Portland, Ore.: Sussex Academic Press.

Warren, Kay. 1992. Transforming Memories and Histories: The Meanings of Ethnic Resurgence for Mayan Indians. In *Americas: New Interpretive Essays*, ed. A. Stepan. New York: Oxford University Press.

Werbner, Pnina. 1997. Essentialising Essentialism, Essentialising Silence: Ambivalence and Multiplicity in the Constructions of Racism and Ethnicity. In *Debating Cultural Hybridity: Multi-Cultural Identities and the Politics of Anti-Racism*, ed. P. Werbner and T. Modood. London: Zed Books.

Weston, Nancy A. 1997. The Fate, Violence, and Rhetoric of Contemporary Legal Thought: Reflections on the Amherst Series, the Loss of Truth, and Law. *Law and Social Inquiry* 22:733.

Whitten, Norman E., Jr., and Rachel Corr. 1999. Imagery of "Blackness" in Indigenous Myth, Discourse, and Ritual. In *Representations of Blackness and the Performance of Identities*, ed. J. Rahier. Westport, Conn.: Bergin & Garvey.

Williams, Brackette F. 1989. A Class Act: Anthropology and the Race to Nation across Ethnic Terrain. *Annual Review of Anthropology* 18:401–44.

Williams, Raymond. 1977. *Marxism and Literature*. Oxford: Oxford University Press.

Williams, Robert A., Jr. 1990. Encounters on the Frontiers of International Human Rights Law: Redefining the Terms of Indigenous Peoples' Survival in the World. *Duke Law Journal* 660.

Williams, Suzanne. 1983. Land Rights and the Manipulation of Identity: Official Indian Policy in Brazil. *Journal of Latin American Studies* 15 (1):137–61.

Wilson, Richard. 1993. Anchored Communities: Identity and History of the Maya-Q'eqchi'. *Man*, New Series 28 (1):121–38.

———. 1995. *Maya Resurgence in Guatemala: Qeqchi Experiences*. Norman: University of Oklahoma Press.

Wilson, Terry P. 1992. Blood Quantums: Native America Mixed Bloods. In *Racially Mixed People in America*, ed. M. P. P. Root. Newbury Park, Calif.: Sage Publications.

Wolford, Wendy Wei-Chen. 2001. This Land Is Ours Now: Social Movement Formation and the Struggle for Agrarian Reform in Brazil. Ph.D. diss., University of California, Berkeley.

Wright, Angus, and Wendy Wolford. 2003. *To Inherit the Earth: The Landless Movement and the Struggle for a New Brazil*. Oakland, Calif.: Food First Books.

Xokó, Apolônio. 1985. Comunicação dos Fatos que Estão Acontecendo com a Tribo Xokó. Aldeia Xokó, Ilha de São Pedro, June 3, 1985.

Yngvesson, Barbara. 1993. *Virtuous Citizens, Disruptive Subjects: Order and Complaint in a New England Court.* New York: Routledge.

Zanetti, Edmilson. 1985. Reduzidos a 200, Ameaçados de Extinção. *O São Paulo,* December 6–12, 1985.

Interviews by Author

Acácio dos Santos, Maripaulo. Aracaju, Sergipe, July 25–27, December 20, 2000.

Apolônio, José. Aracaju, Sergipe, May 26, 1998, February 8, 2000.

Britto, Carlos Ayres. Aracaju, Sergipe, September 12, 2000.

Campos, Evaldo. Aracaju, Sergipe, February 11, 2000.

Cardoso, Neusa and João. Propriá, Sergipe, August 23, 2000.

Couto, Maria Aparecida de Oliveira. Mocambo, Sergipe, April 14, 2000.

D'Acelino, Severo (Professor Severo). Aracaju, Sergipe, April 3, 2000.

Dantas, Beatriz Góis. Aracaju, Sergipe, May 26, 1998.

Jacobina, Paulo Vasconcelos. Aracaju, Sergipe, February 9, December 20, 2000, June 18–19, 2002; Brasília, May 22, 2008.

Lino da Silva, Antônio. Mocambo, Sergipe, April 7, April 13, October 1, 2000; Mocambo, Sergipe, June 21, 2002.

Melo, Frei Enoque Salvador de. Aracaju, Sergipe, May 22, 1998; interview by Maria Neide Sobral da Silva, Poço Redondo, Sergipe, 1997.

Melo, Neuza de Souza. Mocambo, Sergipe, April 13, 2000.

Melo, Paulameire Acácio dos Santos. Mocambo, Sergipe, April 10, 2000.

Moura, Carlos Alves. Atlanta, Ga., April 6, 2002.

Nascimento Filho, Isaías Carlos. Propriá, Sergipe, August 4, 2000.

Rios, Mariza. Colatina, Espírito Santo, May 20, 2000; Rio de Janeiro, July 2, 2002; Belo Horizonte, Minas Gerais, May 13, 2008.

Rocha, Margarette Lisboa. Aracaju, Sergipe, May 1998; Aracaju, Sergipe, January–December 2000.

Santos, Deildes dos. Aracaju, Sergipe, February 7, 2000.

Santos, Maria das Virgens. Mocambo, Sergipe, July 25–27, September 21, October 1, 2000.

Santos, Maria José Bezerra dos. Mocambo, Sergipe, August 10, 2000.

Santos Filho, José Alvino. Aracaju, Sergipe, September 19, 2000.

Seixas Dória, João de. Aracaju, Sergipe, May 26, 1998, May 16, 2000.

Souza, Antônio Marques de. Mocambo, Sergipe, June 14, 2000.

Souza, Inês dos Santos. Aracaju, Sergipe, May 1998, January–December 2000.

Travasso, Maria José Rodrigues. Mocambo, Sergipe, August 10, 2000.

INDEX